"This book fills a gap in the leadership literature for both scholars and for leaders. Well-documented with practical and realistic advice – not a cookie-cutter, one-size-fits-all approach."

— **Barry Z. Posner,** *Accolti Professor of Leadership, Leavey School of Business, Santa Clara University*

"Finally, there is a serious treatment of how leaders and organizations should respond during unfortunate but inevitable circumstances in the personal lives of those we entrust with responsibility. Hickman and Knouse's work is a sensitive, careful, and original study of a neglected but important topic in leadership studies."

— **Kenneth P. Ruscio,** *Senior Distinguished Lecturer, Jepson School of Leadership Studies, University of Richmond and President Emeritus, Washington and Lee University*

WHEN LEADERS FACE PERSONAL CRISIS

This book examines a relatively unexplored area of leadership research – personal aspects of leadership – by considering the impact of leaders navigating their own personal crises on their relationships with teams, peers, and supervisors. Through original research as well as an integrative review of the literature, Hickman and Knouse focus on the "leader-as-person in crisis," including the real-life personal crises and experiences of leaders. This important volume offers a detailed and thoughtful description of intersecting factors that contribute to the ways in which leaders experience and cope with personal crises to spur additional research attention to this neglected area. This book also offers current and prospective leaders advice and direction on effectively navigating personal crises.

Gill Robinson Hickman is Professor of Leadership Studies Emerita in the Jepson School of Leadership Studies at the University of Richmond.

Laura E. Knouse is Associate Professor of Psychology at the University of Richmond and a licensed clinical psychologist.

Leadership: Research and Practice

A James MacGregor Burns Academy of Leadership Collaboration

Series Editors

Georgia Sorenson, *Ph.D, Møller Leadership Scholar and Møller By-Fellow, Churchill College, University of Cambridge, Founder of the James MacGregor Academy of Leadership at the University of Maryland, and co-founder of the International Leadership Association*

Ronald E. Riggio, *Ph.D, Henry R. Kravis Professor of Leadership and Organizational Psychology and former Director of the Kravis Leadership Institute at Claremont McKenna College*

For more information about this series, please visit: www.routledge.com/psychology/series/LEADERSHIP

WHEN LEADERS FACE PERSONAL CRISIS

The Human Side of Leadership

Gill Robinson Hickman and Laura E. Knouse

To Bob and Alice —
Thank you for all your
caring support over the
years. We were able to truly
thrive and make lasting
contributions to leadership
studies because of you!
Hope you enjoy the book!
Warmest wishes,
Gill

Routledge
Taylor & Francis Group

LONDON AND NEW YORK

First published 2020
by Routledge
2 Park Square, Milton Park, Abingdon, Oxon, OX14 4RN

and by Routledge
52 Vanderbilt Avenue, New York, NY 10017

Routledge is an imprint of the Taylor & Francis Group, an informa business

Library of Congress Cataloging-in-Publication Data
A catalog record for this book has been requested

ISBN: 978-0-367-34564-8 (hbk)
ISBN: 978-0-367-34565-5 (pbk)
ISBN: 978-0-429-32657-8 (ebk)

Typeset in Bembo
by Apex CoVantage, LLC

To my talented, intelligent, funny, and loving daughter, Kimberly Crago, who inspired this book.

And, in loving memory of my dear friends Arlane O. Robinson and Ruben Scott.

To my father, William E. Knouse, who modeled persistence; and to my mother, Faye M. Knouse, who taught me resilience.

BRIEF CONTENTS

CONTENTS

SERIES FOREWORD

Finally, a book that understands that leadership and followership are more than roles in a group.

Imagine this: A small group of six people in an executive session are developing a strategic vision for their organization. The usual back and forth, challenging, and grandstanding is going on as well as productive work.

But behind each person in our imaginary group sits a shadowy, invisible person – the so-called "private person." In our imaginary group, one person is going through a painful divorce, another has a severely disabled child, and another is caregiving for an aged parent. The mother of an opioid addicted teen, someone confronting bankruptcy, and a person moonlighting on a graduate degree round out the group. In short, a cauldron of unseen and unspoken dynamics.

These private persons may be known or unknown to the others but the point is, the whole person is always part of the equation, not some disembodied "rational" actor, as most leadership research would contend.

Leadership scholar Gill Hickman and clinical psychologist Laura Knouse explore what happens when a leader or CEO confronts a personal crisis at the workplace. For the purposes of this research, the authors focus on four leader crisis types – the leader's own physical or psychological illness or injury, physical or psychological illness or injury of a family member, death of a family member (the most frequent personal crisis), and divorce or a relationship breakup.

This book is very helpful to anyone in a leadership position but it is not a self-help book in the usual sense. It is carefully researched, and its findings are embedded in theory (notably Conservation of Resources Theory, Communication Privacy Management theory, status distance theory, social processing theory, and other established psychological work) as well as the authors' own research.

Cultural expectations of leaders and organizational norms of leadership sometimes collide with personal and professional need for support. Leadership traits and values reinforced by organizational culture in a Western cultural context – independence, competence, certainty – may seem to be contradicted by a leader's disclosure of a personal crisis. The book is enhanced by wonderful quotes from the authors' own research studies of participants who take a wide variety of approaches to how they navigate a personal crisis at work.

To tell or not to tell? Spoiler alert: in the workplace most CEOs do selectively confide their difficulties to at least some workplace colleagues. Some do not and for good reasons. Perceived ideas about organizational safety, resource scarcity or abundance, social constraints and stigmas (cancer, divorce, suicide), power dynamics, and leader trait variances all play a part in how that decision plays out, for the leader and for the organization.

The last chapters on how to create organizations of reciprocal care and six proposals to consider for research and practice round out this extraordinary book.

Georgia Sorenson
Møller Institute, University of Cambridge

Ronald E. Riggio
Claremont McKenna College

PREFACE

This book represents our attempt to begin to address one personal aspect of leadership – how leaders can best cope with personal crises. Personal crises happen to most people in their lifetime, and they happen to leaders. This is an area of study that is greatly needed and ready for exploration. On a personal note, like most people, both of us have experienced personal crisis – one of us while in a major leadership role. (In fact, we jokingly told our editor that we could have titled this book, "Writing a Book About Personal Crisis During Personal Crisis!"). In addition, when we have spoken about our research to scholarly and professional audiences and leaders who have experienced their own crises, we are met with interest, enthusiasm, curiosity, and sometimes deeply personal responses. These responses have signaled to us that we have been on the "right track" to pursue the scholarship described in this book.

Recent quotations below from *The Leadership Quarterly* and the *Journal of Occupational Health Psychology* illustrate another key source of motivation for the research presented in this book – the puzzling neglect of the personal aspects of leadership in the leadership studies literature (emphasis added).

> And yet at the same time, major reviews of the leadership literature have *largely ignored the subject of stress*. [These reviews] have all *failed to address leader stress* as a potential antecedent of leader behaviors or follower stress as potential consequence.
>
> *(Harms, Credé, Tynan, Leon, & Jeung, 2017, p. 178)*

> The consistency across researchers, continents, and decades with which *leaders' mental health has been ignored*, both as a topic in itself and in comparison to the interest in employees' mental health, is so stark that it raises the question of why this neglect has occurred.
>
> *(Barling & Cloutier, 2016, p. 395)*

There has been limited parallel research interest in leaders' well-being more generally, or leaders' well-being as an antecedent of leaders' behaviors. This imbalance is so stark, one could argue that the *lack of interest in leaders' well-being* derives from several assumptions: That (1) all leaders enjoy a positive state of psychological health, as a result of which research is not needed, (2) research findings on employee well-being and distress generalize fully to the nature and effects of leaders' psychological functioning, and/or (3) even if all leaders are not psychologically healthy, psychological distress has no negative consequences for leaders, their employees, or their organizations. We question the legitimacy of all these assumptions.

(Byrne et al., 2014, p. 345)

In leadership studies, we research many characteristics of leaders and leadership, but rarely do we study aspects of the leader as a human being beyond personality factors or traits. Nearly two decades ago, the first author observed a striking absence of research on personal aspects of leadership in the scholarly literature, making the case for "research that focus(es) on individuals in the leadership process as people, who must live, learn, experience, and cope with all of the issues of life, while fulfilling their roles as effective leaders and followers" (Hickman & Creighton-Zollar, 2000, p. 59). In the years since, there continues to be a lack of research attention to leaders' well-being and to the ways in which personal aspects of their lives interact with their leadership roles. This research gap is not only problematic from an ethical and humanistic standpoint – after all, we demand much from our leaders and should be concerned with their well-being – but, as Byrne et al. (2014) observed, the notion that leader well-being and psychological health have no impact on their team or on their organizations seems far-fetched on its face and is not supported by existing research. Furthermore, as both researchers and practitioners, we recognize the pressing need for thoughtful, evidence-based recommendations for leaders struggling to balance personal and professional concerns.

We sincerely hope that our work not only will inspire additional interest in the topic of leadership in personal crisis but also that it will draw greater scholarly attention to the personal aspects of leadership more generally. We are eager to see where the next two decades of work take this important area of inquiry.

References

Barling, J., & Cloutier, A. (2016). Leaders' mental health at work: Empirical, methodological, and policy directions. *Journal of Occupational Health Psychology, 22*(3), 394. https://doi.org/10.1037/ocp0000055

Byrne, A., Dionisi, A. M., Barling, J., Akers, A., Robertson, J., Lys, R., . . . Dupré, K. (2014). The depleted leader: The influence of leaders' diminished psychological resources on leadership behaviors. *The Leadership Quarterly, 25*(2), 344–357. https://doi.org/10.1016/j.leaqua.2013.09.003

Harms, P. D., Credé, M., Tynan, M., Leon, M., & Jeung, W. (2017). Leadership and stress: A meta-analytic review. *The Leadership Quarterly, 28*(1), 178–194. https://doi.org/10.1016/j.leaqua.2016.10.006

Hickman, G. R., & Creighton-Zollar, A. (2000). Leadership during personal crisis. In B. Kellerman & L. R. Matusak (Eds.), *Cutting edge: Leadership* (pp. 59–64). Retrieved from https://scholarship.richmond.edu/jepson-faculty-publications/50/

ACKNOWLEDGEMENTS

Our deepest gratitude goes to the first group of interviewees in our preliminary study who willingly bared their souls to tell their stories. Although you must remain anonymous, we thank you from the depths of our hearts. To our initial interviewers during the preliminary stage, Zuri Walker, Lisa Mirabelli, Albert H. Fein, and Nancy S. Isaacson, your diligence and dedication were invaluable to this project.

To Ann Creighton-Zollar, there are no words of appreciation that can adequately express Gill's gratitude for coauthoring the first published article on "leadership during personal crisis" with you.

We wish to thank our dear friend and colleague, Crystal Hoyt, for bringing us together as coauthors. It was a perfect match that only you could have made. Thank you.

Many people helped us get our survey into the hands of leaders from corporations, nonprofit organizations, universities, and school districts throughout the country. For their assistance in distributing our survey, we are forever grateful to: Ray Robinson, Ronald Crutcher, Thad Williamson, Randy Raggio, Charles Grant, Jamelle Wilson, Greta Harris, Barbara Sipe, and Craig Kocher.

We sincerely thank the wonderful undergraduate research assistants who helped with this project: Lauren Oddo, Elizabeth Bodalski, and Olivia Harding. The opportunity to work with students like you is why we chose the University of Richmond.

Laura:
I wish to express gratitude to the School of Arts and Sciences at the University of Richmond for summer research fellowship support for this work. My sincere thanks to Angie Hilliker and Kristin Bezio for being the paragons of workplace friendship, to my colleagues in the Department of Psychology at the University of Richmond who supported this cross-disciplinary adventure, and to my Jepson School colleagues who have welcomed me always. Deep gratitude to Russell A. Barkley for

confidence in me that often exceeded my own, and thanks to my parents for the innumerable gifts they gave to allow me to do this meaningful work. Finally, deepest thanks to my husband, Steve Barkley, for his patience, steadfast support, and gifts of food.

Gill:
To my dear husband, G. Michael Hickman, who is my rock, my cheerleader, my proofreader, commentator, and the love of my life, I appreciate all you do during my writing projects and every day. Thank you.

INTRODUCTION

JULIA'S STORY[1]

I found a solemn and grieving woman as I entered the CEO's office. Julia had lost her son, her best friend, several months earlier in a sudden fluke accident. She was despondent and teary throughout the interview. I asked if she wanted to stop, but she insisted that we continue the interview. She wanted to add her story to the research in honor of her son.

Julia was acutely aware of the enormity of her leadership role as CEO and wanted to make sure that she didn't make unwise decisions or let anything fall through the cracks while she was still reeling from the death of her son. She asked her vice president and closest friend in the company to listen carefully to her discussions in meetings and let her know immediately, with complete candor, if she was off base in her decision-making. This second check on her actions would assure that the company did not suffer when she was distracted or unhappy.

Julia said that before experiencing the loss of her son, she would give all the expected condolences and take all the expected actions that a company executive takes when one of her employees loses a loved one. Now she takes time to be caring, attentive, and accommodating because she fully understands how they feel. Important aspects of Julia's leadership practice were transformed through navigating a personal crisis, and she believes that she is more effective as a leader now that she is attentive to the impact of personal crises on her staff.

---

1 Stories throughout the book are actual accounts based on the information provided by participants. However, all names and some other identifying information about respondents have been changed to protect the identities of participants.

Leaders in personal crisis

Julia's story provides insight into the personal side of leaders' experiences during personal crises. Like many scholarly endeavors, our interest in the study of leaders in personal crisis grew out of our personal experiences and generated research into a topic that is not often discussed and seldom examined in leadership studies. We define a "personal" crisis as a disruptive event or emergency that affects the leader in a private or intimate area of his or her life. The research primarily focuses on leaders who occupy an appointed upper management or executive level position in a business, nonprofit, governmental, or community organization, or an elected official.

How do individuals handle their leadership responsibilities with their team and colleagues when they experience the death of a spouse, child, or parent; suffer a life-threatening illness; care for a physically or mentally ill child; go through a divorce; or care for a parent with Alzheimer's? How do they handle their own needs during the crisis? And which leadership practices during a personal crisis are associated with the highest level of leader effectiveness and satisfaction? An initial exploratory study by the first author entailed extensive interviews or written responses from 15 individuals who had experienced a personal crisis while serving in a leadership role. Later, the second author, a psychology researcher and licensed clinical psychologist, joined the investigation as coauthor and research colleague. The results of the initial interviews provided a base for the development of a qualitative survey-based research project, which then informed the development of a descriptive model and quantitative follow-up survey that more deeply examined important factors associated with effective leadership during a personal crisis. The results of these projects, along with an integrative review of the literature, form the basis of this book.

Presidential candidate Barack Obama lost his maternal grandmother during the 2008 campaign. His grandmother, who helped raise him, was a vital person in his life. Yet, the public only saw him shed a few tears as he talked about her during a rally. As a candidate and subsequently the president, how did the loss of his grandmother affect his leadership, his interaction with staff, his actions, and decision making? What did he do to handle his own needs, his grief, and his health and welfare? How would he advise others in leadership positions to handle a personal crisis? Several U.S. presidents similarly experienced personal crises while in office – Abraham Lincoln lost a child; Woodrow Wilson's first wife died while he was in office; and Franklin Roosevelt and John Kennedy battled chronic health problems.[2] Beyond presidents, personal crises are prevalent among leaders in all segments of society. In one of our surveys, we found that 73% of leaders indicated that they had experienced a personal crisis, by our definition, while in their leadership role. Clearly, the subject matter of this book is not only significant but is also prevalent – the rule rather than the exception.

---

2 For more information about U.S. presidents who experienced personal crises, see Engle, J. A. & Knock, T. J. (2017). *When life strikes the president: Scandal, death, and illness in the White House.* New York, NY: Oxford University Press.

There is a growing awareness in popular business literature about the impact of personal crises on executives – but where are the scholarly studies? Several Kellogg leadership fellows and scholars have noted that studies involving "personal aspects" of leadership were noticeably absent from leadership research (Hickman & Creighton-Zollar, 2000). Participants at this session indicated "they wanted research that focused on individuals and groups in the leadership process as 'people,' who must live, learn, experience, and cope with all of the issues of life while fulfilling their roles as effective leaders and followers" (p. 59). This book is, in many ways, a response to that call to action because, unfortunately, scholarship on the personal aspects of leadership continues to be perplexingly absent from the field of leadership studies.

The studies

The first exploratory study involved interviews with ten potentially "information-rich" participants who experienced a personal crisis while serving in a leadership role. An additional five participants provided written responses to our open-ended questions (see Appendix A). We used the results to increase our understanding of this phenomenon, and the study yielded insights that informed future research.

After reviewing the information gleaned from these interviews, we developed an exploratory survey study (referred to here as Study 1) to begin to address several research questions and to gain information from open-ended responses toward a follow-up survey. The study used mixed methods, meaning that both qualitative (open-ended; descriptive) and quantitative (closed-ended) survey items were used (see Appendix B). Research aims for Study 1 included learning how leaders experience and react to a personal crisis; how they handled the crisis, personally and professionally; and what they recommend to other leaders in similar situations. We also explored which personal, strategic, and organizational factors might have the strongest relationship to leaders' positive perceived handling of the crisis – in other words, what seemed to work best for them in what kinds of situations. The sample was recruited from an online survey pool and consisted of 49 leaders (20 women, 29 men) who had experienced a personal crisis. We presented the results of this exploratory study at the 2016 conference of the International Leadership Association and subsequently used the information we gleaned from it to design a second survey study.

The purpose of the second study (referred to here as Study 2) was to see whether the patterns we observed in Study 1 were consistent in a new sample of participants and to measure additional factors that the information obtained from Study 1 suggested were important to a full understanding of leadership in a personal crisis. To design Study 2, we used responses obtained in Study 1 to construct checklists of possible responses to some questions and consulted the scholarly literature in psychology and management to identify concepts and established surveys that we could use to capture important traits and situational factors (see Appendix C). As such, Study 2 contained more closed-ended, quantitative questions than did Study 1, and we obtained responses from a larger online sample: 167 executive leaders and middle managers who had experienced a personal crisis at least one year in the past. Throughout the book, we identify instances where the responses of executive leaders differed from those of middle managers. Additional information about participants in Study 2 and the survey methods are presented in Appendix C. Additional supplemental materials, including all survey items, are available online via Open Science Framework (https://osf.io/tdbzs/?view_only=2ebd6bb1faf14f9eb 17b8defb368f25b), and qualified researchers who would like access to our data may contact Dr. Knouse directly (lknouse@richmond.edu).

Using these data, data from the previous studies, and information about personal crises and coping from the scholarly literature in clinical and social psychology, management and leadership studies, we coauthored this book to summarize our findings and outline new directions in research and practice.

Framework of the book

We organized the book around a descriptive framework that guides the chapters and content. The framework in Figure 0.1 begins with the type of crisis leaders experience – the leaders' own physical or psychological illness or injury; physical or psychological illness or injury of a family member; death of a family member, and divorce or a relationship breakup. Once a crisis occurs, leaders make a disclosure decision – that is, deciding whether to tell staff, peers, and supervisors or keep the crisis private, and whether to seek help to get through the crisis. Leaders use coping strategies in their personal lives to sustain their well-being and employ strategies and approaches in the workplace to handle their leadership responsibilities. The organization's interpersonal environment influences their decision to disclose, seek help,

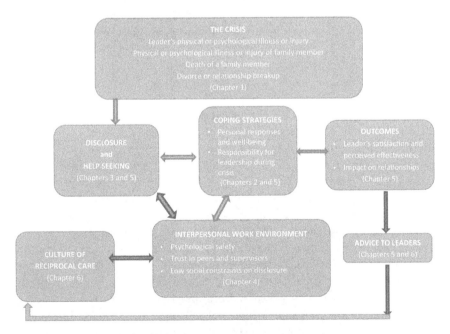

FIGURE 0.1 Framework for the book

and use coping strategies. These factors are associated with leaders' satisfaction with and perceived effectiveness outcomes in handling the crisis. Over time, they are able to reflect on the crisis experience and provide advice to current and prospective leaders about handling personal crises. Finally, we propose a culture of reciprocal care based on outcomes and advice from the leaders in our survey and information from studies in the literature.

We open each chapter in the book with a short vignette or set of quotations about the personal crisis of a leader in our study. Each chapter details the findings from our study participants and provides information from relevant research in the field. Chapter 1, "Personal Crisis as a Stressful Life Event," identifies the four types of crises in our study and situates the leader as a person-in-crisis. We present research from a wide variety of disciplines that define the nature of the crisis (such as bereavement and grief; heart attack, stroke, or mood disorders; and informal care-giving for a sick family member) and examine what an individual might experience as a person going through a specific type of crisis. Chapter 2, "Coping with Crisis," focuses on various coping strategies to adapt to the demands of a crisis. It explains the Conservation of Resources Theory to help us understand the effects of a personal crisis on leaders, presents data on coping approaches used by our survey participants, and provides conclusions about effective coping strategies from relevant literature. In Chapter 3, "Deciding to Disclose, Asking for Help," we examine the costs and benefits of disclosure and help-seeking for leaders, assess our participants' responses about their disclosure decisions, and suggest an approach to decision-making around these important coping strategies. In Chapter 4, "The Organization's Interpersonal Environment," we focus on how influences in the interpersonal work environment contribute to the leader's handling of his or her crisis, including psychological safety, trust in peers and supervisors, and social constraints on disclosure. In other words, we examine whether leaders believe it is "safe" to be vulnerable and reach out to others when coping with the crisis and whether they generally trust the intentions of others in the organization and how this influences responses to crisis. Chapter 5, "Responsibility for Leadership: Adaptive Approaches," examines the approaches leaders use to carry out essential leadership responsibilities while experiencing a personal crisis and the advice that they give other leaders about handling work responsibilities. We also examine the role of workplace relationships and friend-ships as social support for leaders in crisis and highlight our finding of a potential "relationship growth benefit" associated with disclosure of a personal crisis at work. In Chapter 6, "Toward a Culture of Reciprocal Care: Advice and Recommenda-tions," we provide insight from our research, advice from leaders in our study, and information from the literature on how organizations might create environments where psychological safety and mutual trust permeate the organization. And leaders of these organizations create, model, and participate in reciprocal care through the supporting culture they generate, policies and programs they establish, and prac-tices they validate. Chapter 7, "Leaders in Personal Crisis: Proposals for Practice and Research," concludes the book with several proposals that emerge from our research and the extant literature. They serve as a compilation of what we learned about personal crises during our study and a starting point for future research and practice on personal aspects of leadership.

Throughout the book, we consider the impact of leaders navigating their own personal crises on their relationships with teams, peers, and supervisors. We believe that understanding the impact of leaders' personal crises must take into account the effect of the crisis on the quality of these relationships. Crises present the leader with the opportunity to reach out to trusted others for organizational and emotional support and even to strengthen existing relationships, but these potential benefits are tempered by the risks associated with showing one's vulnerability to others. Leaders must make an informed decision about how to navigate a personal crisis within each relationship in a way that ultimately helps them and the people around them in the organization cope and even thrive. Taking a thoughtful, pragmatic stance toward such decisions can seem impossible when one is in the midst of a crisis, and so preparing leaders to anticipate and respond to crises in their own lives and the lives of others in their organization can increase the likelihood of positive outcomes for all. We hope that the "leader-as-person-in-crisis" perspective we advocate in this book can prepare leaders to think broadly and deeply about the factors to consider when a personal crisis impacts their role.

Our aim is both academic and practical. The book examines a relatively unexplored area of leadership research (with the exception of personality factors) – personal aspects of leadership – through a study of leadership during a personal crisis. We aim to offer a detailed and thoughtful description of intersecting factors that contribute to the ways in which leaders experience and cope with personal crises that may spur additional research attention to this important yet neglected area. In the same way, we hope to affect leadership practice by offering advice and direction to current and prospective leaders on effectively navigating a personal crisis.

Reference

Hickman, G. R., & Creighton-Zollar, A. (2000). Leadership during personal crisis. In B. Kellerman & L. R. Matusak (Eds.), *Cutting edge: Leadership* (pp. 59–64). Retrieved from https://scholarship.richmond.edu/jepson-faculty-publications/50/

1

PERSONAL CRISIS AS A STRESSFUL LIFE EVENT

STEVEN'S STORY

Two years ago, my wife was diagnosed with breast cancer. This was extremely traumatic for the both of us. It really affected me and her as well.

Of course, we managed the crisis by going to her doctor's visits to have the cancer treated. It was a life event that neither of us could have foreseen; so, there is no one to blame and no reason to feel ashamed or embarrassed about it.

I tried my best not to let the crisis affect my work. I tried not to take out any anger on my employees or get too sad to lead. I decided to tell most of my staff about the crisis just to let them know what was going on. I also shared it with a few of my colleagues and supervisors. I was very open to talking about the crisis with basically anyone. I am satisfied with my decisions about who to talk to at work concerning my personal crisis. I don't regret anything. For people I didn't tell about the crisis, I don't know if they could tell something was wrong.

It felt very safe in my company to share information about the crisis. My organization is a very supportive place for employees to share a personal crisis and handle the impact of it. I am satisfied with the way I handled the crisis in my leadership role and I am happy to say there was no impact on my relationships with my staff and coworkers or supervisors.

On a personal basis, I naturally discussed the crisis with my family members. I just tried my very best to think positively. I also prayed a lot. I found prayer was an effective way for me to cope with the crisis but trying to think positively was less effective.

This crisis really made me think about how precious life is. I was able to remain hopeful during the crisis. I just prayed a lot and stayed as positive as I can. But, I do not consider this personal crisis a turning point event. It was big, but not turning-point big.

My advice to others who face a personal crisis while in a leadership role is to share it with your coworkers. It helps workers to understand you more as a person. I would also advise them to talk it out with whoever they feel comfortable with at work or at home so that they can cope with it. Talking always helps.

I have never really received any training on what I should do during a personal crisis. I just did what I thought was right. I think that there should be classes to help people like me.

EMILY'S STORY

I experienced a very messy divorce from the father of my first child. The first few months were difficult while I tried to handle the crisis, manage 60 employees, and raise my son. I do not blame myself for the crisis though I am a little embarrassed about the situation.

I tried to do everything alone. I didn't take care of myself. I was really hurt and lost self-confidence. I decided to go to therapy for professional help and turned to my mom for personal support.

I didn't tell my staff or supervisor and didn't talk to anyone about my personal life. I tried to leave my personal problems at home and just soldier through at work taking one day at a time. If I needed a minute to cry, I would go in my office and cry. One day, however, a colleague saw me crying. I needed someone to talk to so I told the colleague about my crisis.

I was satisfied with my decision not to share my crisis with most people at work. I don't like airing my dirty laundry. I was concerned that people would look at me differently after I told them what happened. I don't know whether my staff and supervisors could tell something was wrong since I didn't really talk about it. My work environment is not really psychologically unsafe but it is slightly unsupportive. Business comes first. Though, I must say that the few colleagues I told were supportive.

I was able to remain hopeful during the crisis. I just thought about my son and his future. I wanted the best for him. The crisis was a turning point event for me. I regained my self-confidence and my life improved a great deal after everything was over.

I would advise other leaders not to share their personal crisis at work. I think it changes the work dynamic and people lose a little respect for you. If it is affecting your work, talk to your supervisor. Otherwise keep it to yourself. Talk to a therapist instead of sharing the crisis at work. You need it even if you don't think you do. Talk to friends and family. They can be a good support system.

My training on handling personal crisis came from my employees. I learned how to treat them when they experienced adversity in their personal lives. Based on these experiences, I think organizations should have counseling services available to support employees even if it is just over the phone.

How to use this chapter: We hope that readers will use this chapter in a manner that is most relevant for them. Leaders who recently or previously experienced a specific personal crisis may prefer to read about their specific crisis type, while academic readers may want to explore all crisis types and examine the cited research studies in more depth.

In our first survey study, we found that the majority of leaders experienced a personal crisis at some point during their tenure in leadership roles. Steven and Emily's stories are examples of the range of crises – a spouse's illness and a divorce – that leaders in our studies experienced; and they exemplify two different approaches to disclosure of the crisis at work which we examine in Chapters 3 and 5. Participants consistently identified four types of crises – death of a family member, the leader's own physical or psychological illness or injury, physical or psychological illness or injury of a family member, and divorce or a relationship breakup. We recognize that there are other types of crises that affect leaders; however, in this text we focus only on the crises that the leaders in our survey identified most frequently.

In Study 2, the most frequent personal crisis was the death of a family member followed by the leader's own illness or injury, physical or psychological illness or injury of a family member, and a divorce or relationship breakup, as illustrated in Figure 1.1.

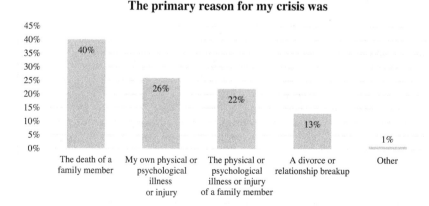

The primary reason for my crisis was

FIGURE 1.1 Reason for Personal Crisis

Note: Totals may not equal 100% due to rounding.

The leader as person-in-crisis

Leaders are quite used to handling organizational crises. There are workshops, courses, articles, and books dedicated to equipping them to respond to crises in the workplace. A crisis that affects leaders personally is a different matter. Leaders may not be accustomed to handling their own vulnerability, and they may not be prepared for the duration of a personal crisis. As one popular journal contributor commented:

> Entrepreneurs [and other executive leaders] aren't used to asking for help. Many are accustomed to being the hero, solving everyone else's problem and excellent in responding to an outside crisis. Yet some business leaders are not so great at caring for themselves and attending to their own needs.
>
> *(Huhman, 2014)*

Participants in Study 2 reported that their crisis lasted an average of 23 months, with 34% reporting that the duration of their crisis was one to three years (see Figure 1.2). The longer the crisis lasted the less effective leaders felt they were in handling the crisis in their leadership role. However, the duration of the crisis was not related to overall satisfaction in handling the crisis.[1]

Leaders experience fully human responses to a personal crisis. At their core, personal crisis events threaten the things that people hold most dear – their health, family, relationships, social standing, sense of self, and sense of meaning. Responses to crises, whether they are actions or emotions, can be understood as responses to the threat, harm, or loss caused or represented by the crisis event. Many of these

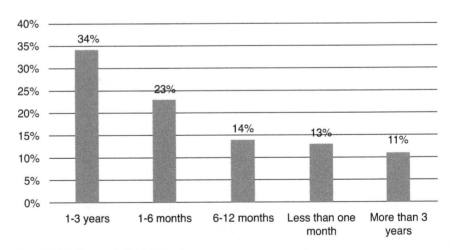

FIGURE 1.2 Personal Crisis Duration

Note: Five percent did not answer.

1 Correlation (Pearson's *r*) between duration and perceived effectiveness was −.14 (*p* = .04). Correlation with satisfaction was .04 (*p* = .31).

responses are involuntary or "hard wired" components of humans' evolved responses to threat or loss events (Lazarus, 2006). For example, a current or imminent threat to one's well-being triggers fear and anxiety, irrevocable losses generate sadness, and harm to those we love and what we value and provokes frustration and anger (Lazarus, 2006). Importantly, these emotional responses have behavioral or action components that, in our evolutionary past, served to increase the likelihood of successfully managing these threats. Fear and anxiety are accompanied by escape, avoidance, or shoring up resources for the future. Sadness motivates pulling back during a time of vulnerability and signals to others the need for care and resources. Anger and frustration activate efforts to push through barriers or neutralize a source of harm. In sum, although crisis situations themselves may fall outside of a person's typical life circumstances, emotional and behavioral responses to a crisis are often not unexpected, given our evolutionary history and the degree of threat, harm, or loss that such crises represent. They affect a person's sense of well-being and stability.

Leaders in our study experienced a wide range of physical, emotional, and psychological responses across all four crises types. The majority experienced feeling depressed (71%), sadness (65%), loss of sleep (62%), and stress/worry (50%) (see Figure 1.3). Executive leaders and middle managers differ slightly on their experiences of depression and sadness. More middle managers (78%) reported feeling depressed during a personal crisis than executive leaders (62%); similarly, more managers (74%) than leaders (54%) reported feeling sad. We are uncertain whether these differences are due to more experience with personal crises among executive leaders than middle managers or other reasons. More research is needed on personal crises among leaders and middle managers to explain these differences where they exist.

Several leaders in our survey reported positive effects during the crisis, such as, I remained positive/positive thinking (37%), realized my strength (37%), developed a philosophical perspective (31%), took better care of myself (23%), and took control (17%).

In the remaining sections, we look at how the four crises types identified by participants in our survey affect the "leader-as-person" in crisis. We provide our participants' responses in Figure 1.3 along with research studies on how a person in crisis experiences these various situations.

Effects of different crisis types

The leader as bereaved person – death of a family member

> My dad passed away from ALS. He was my hero. It was hard to explain to coworkers how sad it made me.
>
> *Survey participant*

> My husband was diagnosed with cancer in October [date deleted]. Despite surgery, radiation and chemo therapy, he died in April [date deleted]. I took him to every doctor's appointment and treatment and stayed with him in the hospital after two surgeries. I was absent from work for blocks of time.
>
> *Survey participant*

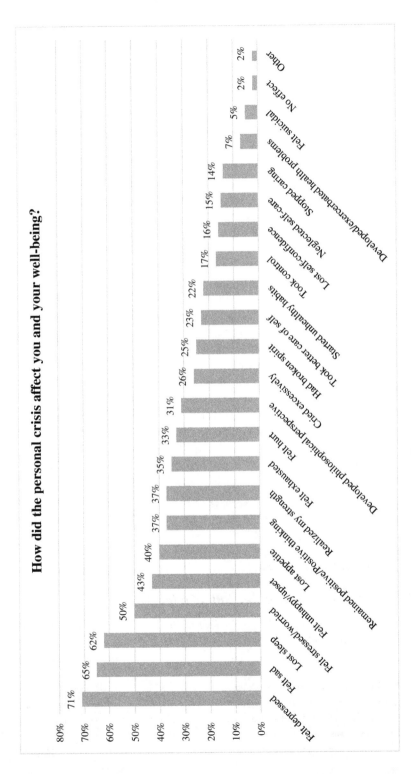

FIGURE 1.3 Effect of Personal Crisis on Leaders – Across All Crisis Types

I had a personal crisis which was the passing of my mother from pancreatic cancer, 2 years ago. She was diagnosed and passed away 4 months later. She was in an incredible amount of pain, and I was torn with having to be at work and be by her side. I felt distracted a lot at work and often became agitated at employees. There were times I was unable to handle my emotions even though I was as neutral on my job as I could be.

Survey participant

My sibling passed away unexpectedly in a high-speed auto collision. I felt like my world stopped and things that were previously considered important seemed trivial in comparison. It was difficult for me to continue in my leadership, but people were understanding and supportive and I was able to remain in my role.

Survey participant

Forty percent of the individuals in our study reported experiencing the death of a family member while serving in a leadership role (Figure 1.1). Experts refer to the recent loss of a significant person through death as "bereavement" and the emotional response to bereavement as "grief" (Stroebe, Schut, & Stroebe, 2007). Grief is expressed through psychological and physical reactions that are typical of those identified by leaders experiencing loss in our survey – depressed feelings (80%), sadness (73%), loss of sleep (67%), and unhappy/upset (50%), as detailed in Table 1.1.

Even though leaders in our study indicated feelings of depression as a response to all four crisis types, 80% of those who lost a loved one reported that they felt depressed. Depression is such a common response to loss of a significant person that people who are bereaved for fewer than two months were, for many years, excluded from the diagnosis of major depressive disorder (Stroebe et al., 2007).

Reactions to bereavement vary for each individual, and there is not one response that fits everyone. Still, most people progress favorably through the grieving

TABLE 1.1 Effect on Well-being – By Each Crisis Type

Crisis type	Death of a family member	Illness/injury of self/leader	Illness/injury of family member	Divorce/relationship breakup
Highest responses	80% – Felt depressed	65% – Felt depressed	64% – Felt depressed	76% – Felt sad
	73% – Felt sad	61% – Felt sad	64% Felt stressed/worried	67% – Felt depressed
	67% – Lost sleep	58% – Felt stressed/worried	58% – Lost sleep	67% – Lost sleep
	50% – Felt unhappy/upset	58% – Lost sleep	50% – Felt sad	57% – Lost appetite
			50% – Remained positive/positive thinking	52% – Felt hurt

process, which means that over time they can think of "the deceased without pain, despite some sadness remaining, recover an interest in life, feel more hopeful, experience gratification again and adapt to new roles" (Fernández-Alcántara, Pérez-Marfil, Catena-Martínez, & Cruz-Quintana, 2017, p. 563). However, there are certain situations where loss of a family member may involve more complex grief processes.

Loss of a spouse

Stroebe et al. (2007) reviewed 16 studies on the relationship between bereavement and physical and mental health. They found that spousal bereavement may have a substantial effect on the well-being of a surviving spouse, and in a low percentage of people it carries an early risk of mortality (commonly known as dying of a broken heart). There are also gender and racial differences in responses to spousal death. Researchers report a higher rate of bereavement-related deaths in white vs. black surviving spouses and greater increases in risk of mortality in younger than older bereaved spouses. With regard to sex differences, Stroebe et al. (2007) cite their earlier findings that widowers are more at risk for death than widows – 5% of widowers 55 years and older die in the first six months after losing a spouse. Mortality was "very high for accidental and violent causes [such as suicide] and alcohol-related diseases, moderate for chronic ischemic heart disease and lung cancer, and small for other causes of death" (Stroebe et al., 2007, p. 1962). Mortality risks are typically greater in the earlier months of grieving and decrease in later months.

Unsurprisingly, many people who have experienced death of a spouse experience both physical and psychological health problems in the early stages of bereavement. Several studies reported physical symptoms ranging from minor ailments (headaches, dizziness, indigestion, and chest pain) to high rates of disability and illness to greater use of medical services and drug use (Stroebe et al., 2007). Common psychological symptoms in bereaved individuals at six months' duration range from suicidal ideation to depression, anxiety, distress, somatic (relating to the body) symptoms, insomnia, and social dysfunction.

Loss of a child

Loss of a child has been recognized as among the most stressful negative life events one can experience (Dohrenwend, Askenasy, Krasnoff, & Dohrenwend, 1978). Research studies identified sex differences in bereavement of parents who have lost a child. In general, mothers have greater difficulty than fathers. Both parents have an increased risk of death from unnatural causes in the early stages of bereavement, especially after the death of a younger child. However, mothers have a greater risk of mortality from natural and unnatural causes after the death of a child that can extend up to 18 years, whereas fathers have a greater risk of death from unnatural causes early on in their bereavement (Stroebe et al., 2007).

Bereavement over time

The effects of bereavement in most people change over time. Fernández-Alcántara et al. (2017) report that the "task model," sometimes used in counseling and therapy, describes four tasks in the grieving process:

> (a) cognitively and emotionally accept the reality of loss; (b) openly express emotions and registered pain; (c) adapt to the new reality in which the loved one is no longer present; and (d) emotionally relocate the deceased person and continue living.
>
> *(p. 1562)*

Support during the grieving process ranges from finding comfort in the care of friends and family to seeking interventions from professional therapists. Most bereaved people grieve and find support within the confines of their friends and family. Researchers point out that "for social support to be effective, a need must be recognized, the potential supporter must be capable and willing, and the gesture must be perceived as helpful by the receiver" (Logan, Thornton, & Breen, 2018, p. 104).

The leader as patient – the leader's own physical or psychological illness or injury

> I was diagnosed with breast cancer at the age of 47. My mom had died of breast cancer when I was 16. I had young children. I was convinced that I was going to die and leave my children like my mother had left my sisters and me. I had to focus on myself and my treatment, leaving others to fend for themselves.
>
> *Survey participant*

> [I] was blindsided by a car and all air bags opened. I could not get out of my car and [I was transported] to the hospital.
>
> *Survey participant*

> I have been very depressed throughout the past few months. I was diagnosed with major depression and have been taking medication for about a year but it's been getting worse lately. I've almost been unable to get out of bed in the morning or at all. It's been hard to bring my attention to my job.
>
> *Survey participant*

Survey participants reported their own illness or injury as the second most frequent crisis type (26%) (see Figure 1.1). Their own illness or injury left them feeling depressed (65%), sad (61%), stressed or worried (58%), and experiencing sleep loss (58%) (see Table 1.1). This crisis type is one of the areas where executives and middle managers in our study differ – 18% of executives vs. 31% of managers identified their own illness as the source of their personal crisis. It is difficult to determine why this difference exists. One possible reason for this disparity may be that senior leaders have possibly reached a stage in life where they are experiencing an increasing number of close family member losses as their most distressing personal crisis. It is also important to note that the difference was not large (13%), and so future studies will need to examine whether this difference is reliable.

Health challenges and daily living

Executive leaders face two kinds of health challenges while they are ill – their own personal health and the health of their organizations (Chapters 2 and 6 discuss the impact on organizations). In this section, we will examine aspects of serious illness, such as cancer, heart disease, stroke, mental illness, and injury to the "leader-as-person" in crisis.

Cancer

Leaders with a diagnosis of cancer face treatment options that include chemotherapy, radiation therapy, and surgery, which typically require time lost from work and daily management of subsequent symptoms (e.g., fatigue, hair loss, nausea and vomiting, appetite change, weight loss, and pain, among others) (Devlin, Denson, & Whitford, 2017). Cancer treatment may frequently result in changes in brain and cognitive functioning, sometimes referred to as "chemobrain" or "chemofog." "Cognitive deficits [including declines in retention, processing speed, verbal memory, and executive function] can significantly impair activities of daily living, employment, social relationships, recreation, and active participation in the community" (Li & Caeyenberghs, 2018, pp. 305, 314).

The encouraging news is that more people with cancer are surviving for longer periods of time. Still, some patients may experience late effects of cancer even after treatment has ended, according to the Mayo Clinic (2019). Late effects of chemotherapy and radiation therapy may result in dental problems, early menopause, heart problems, increased risk of other cancers, infertility, lung disease, and osteoporosis; surgery may bring about lymphedema; hormone therapy may result in blood clots, hot flashes, and sexual side effects; and late effects are unknown for immunotherapy and targeted therapy (Mayo Clinic, 2019). These medical conditions may affect leaders' ability to return to work or impact absenteeism and presenteeism.

Another challenge to everyday living is that cancer survivors may not have certain needs and concerns met after treatment by their cancer specialists. Researchers in one study asked cancer survivors to identify both met and unmet needs resulting from a range of cancer types, including breast, prostate, melanoma, uterine, colon or rectal, lymphoma and leukemia, lung, multiple cancers, and others (Geller, Vacek, Flynn, Lord, & Cranmer, 2014). While many of their needs were met (e.g., information about their cancer diagnosis, access to high-quality care, and access to screening for recurrence or other cancers), there were several prominent areas where survivors indicated that they needed further support:

- Help reducing stress in their life;
- Help finding ways to reduce their worrying;

- Help managing their concerns about the cancer coming back;
- Help dealing with the impact that cancer has on their relationship with their partner;
- Help to address problems with their sex life; and
- More information about possible side effects of their treatment.

(Geller et al., 2014, p. E14)

Notably, many of these concerns are psychological or social in nature rather than medical, reflecting impacts of the crisis that may be particularly disruptive to leaders who are trying to function in or return to their leadership role.

Stroke

In addition to cancer, millions of Americans live with the after effects of strokes. Ashley, Lee, and Heaton (2019) report that in 2017, almost 800,000 people experienced new or recurring strokes annually, and African Americans below age 65 were two to five times more likely to experience strokes at younger ages than Caucasians. Strokes, like cancer, may leave individuals with physical, emotional, and cognitive losses, despite continuing improvements in treatment; and strokes are the leading cause of long-term disabilities in the U.S. (Ashley et al., 2019). According to the National Stroke Association (n.d.), post-stroke conditions can be numerous and varied:

- Physical – paralysis (loss of muscles in a part of the body); fatigue (lack of energy and need for frequent breaks); dysphagia (difficulty swallowing); foot drop (difficulty picking up the front part of a foot); hemiparesis (muscle weakness on one side of the body depending on which side of the brain is damaged); incontinence (loss of bladder or bowel control); seizures and epilepsy (spasms or convulsions); sleep problems; pain (local pain such as joint pain, or central pain because the brain does not understand messages from the body); spasticity (limited coordination, muscle movement, and painful muscle spasms); and vision loss or perception problems.
- Emotional – depression (feelings of anger, frustration, anxiety, sadness, fear, and hopelessness); and Pseudobulbar affect (outburst of uncontrollable crying or laughing).
- Cognition – the process of thinking, remembering, and recognizing things.

Most patients face some type of after-stroke care based on the nature and variety of possible effects of strokes. Patients who are discharged from the hospital risk the possibility of readmission within 30 days (Bishop & Bushnell, 2017). To reduce the chances of readmission, patients may need help with medication management for secondary stroke prevention (long-term antithrombotic therapy to reduce the formation of blood clots), lifestyle modification (physical activity, weight reduction, dietary change, smoking cessation, early diagnosis and treatment of depression), rehabilitation and recovery (telemedicine, and physical and occupational therapy) (Bishop & Bushnell, 2017). The after effects of chronic stroke require rehabilitation along with substantive changes to one's life style and medication.

Heart attack

Myocardial infarction (MI), known as heart attack, is a leading cause of disability and death in the United States. Complications that result from heart attacks include heart failure, angina, arrhythmias, stroke, or death. However, preventive therapies and reperfusion (restoring blood flow to an organ or tissue) have decreased short-term mortality following MI (Mollon & Bhattacharjee, 2017).

With more people surviving heart attacks, the critical matter for survivors is quality of life. Mollon and Bhattacharjee (2017) conducted a survey in which they matched 16,729 individuals who experienced heart attacks with 50,187 non-MI individuals to determine quality of life outcomes for survivors of MI. They found that heart attack survivors experienced lower quality of life in areas of general health, physical health, and mental health compared to the general population (the comparison group). The researchers recommended clinical intervention that focuses on physical functioning, activities of daily living, and improving access to mental health services, especially since depression is a prevalent condition among MI survivors.

Even patients who experience a minor heart attack report being shaken by the disease and being thrown into a demanding journey of life. Simonÿ, Dreyer, Pedersen, and Birkelund (2017) conducted a qualitative study to determine how patients in Denmark who experienced a minor heart attack and participated in cardiac rehabilitation experienced their life situation. Three themes emerged from their analysis.

- Difficulty accepting the disease. Patients initially reacted by downplaying the disease and tried to avoid facing reality because they were afraid. During the acute phase, they felt vulnerable, helpless and anxious that there was no guarantee of their survival.
- Understanding that life has become frail. Patients began to realize that they were suffering from a chronic and potentially fatal condition and they were fearful of what might happen in the future. They were frightened that the disease was worsening when they felt symptoms and that they were in danger of dying. They began to realize that their lives were fragile and forever changed.
- An altered life. Patients experienced physical deterioration due to fatigue and insufficient energy to pursue the activities in life they previously enjoyed. They were concerned about resuming basic activities such as driving, taking care of their homes and gardens, traveling, and engagement in social activities. With less strength and energy, some altered work schedules, took sick leave, and even considered retiring.

(Simonÿ et al., 2017, pp. 235–236)

The researchers emphasize that being afflicted by a minor heart attack is not a minor thing. Participation in cardiac rehabilitation and being together with other patients and health professionals during the process helps to facilitate the transitions that cardiac patients undergo – initial fear of death; feelings of helplessness and vulnerability; and learning to live with a new reality where achieving joy and meaningfulness are challenged and changed (Simonÿ et al., 2017).

Leaders in our survey who experience physical illnesses, including cancer, stroke, or heart attack, relied on support from family and friends, among other sources, to cope with their crises (see Chapter 2). Yet, there are considerable resources that organizations can provide to support leaders in a personal crisis and simultaneously strengthen their companies, nonprofits, institutions of higher education, and school systems. Chapter 6 provides a framework for encompassing these potential resources within the organization's culture, policies, and programs.

Mental illness

The World Health Organization estimates that 1 in 17 adults experience serious mental illness in the United States each year, and 44 million adults, including individuals in the workforce, are affected by mental illness annually (Follmer & Jones, 2018). Kessler et al. (2005) estimated that 46.6% of Americans experienced a mental disorder at some point in their lifetime, meaning that mental disorders, taken together, are not uncommon experiences. These statistics imply that many leaders may also experience mental illness due to the prevalence of this condition in our society. Mental illness includes more than 200 classified mental health disorders that are "characterized by dysregulation of mood, thought, and/or behavior" (Follmer & Jones, 2018, p. 325) that can range from depression and anxiety to bipolar disorder and schizophrenia. People in the workforce, like others with mental illness, must contend with an array of symptoms that involve – physical (symptoms that affect the body, such as loss of appetite, sleep disturbance, and muscle aches); emotional (symptoms that affect an individual's mood); cognitive (symptoms that interfere with perception, acquisition, and comprehension of information); and behavioral (symptoms that involve marked changes in one's actions) (Follmer & Jones, 2018, p. 329). These symptoms can impact a person's functioning at work and contribute to absenteeism or time away from work due to illness.

Although describing the full array of mental disorders in this section is beyond the scope of this book, we will describe three types – mood disorders (depression and bipolar disorder), anxiety disorders, and attention-deficit/hyperactivity disorder (ADHD) – that have relatively high prevalence rates in the population and that were identified by our participants in the interview phase and Study 1 of our data collection.

Mood disorders: depression

Kessler et al. (2005) estimated that 16.6% of Americans experience major depressive disorder at some point in their lifetime. The key feature of major depressive disorder is pervasive depressed mood and/or loss of interest or pleasure that causes significant impairment (American Psychiatric Association, 2013). How do individuals experience depression? Kelly et al. (2011) examined whether individuals' experiences of depression (ranging from mild to severe) overlap with clinical assessment of the condition. They found that the experiences described by people in the study overlapped with diagnostic criteria in the vast majority (93%) of conceptual categories (Kelly et al., 2011). The highest number of participant experiences in each subdomain include: mood (sadness/depressed affect, lowered threshold for negative affect, irritability, crying,); cognition (interpersonal alienation and sensitivity, loneliness/decreased sense of closeness and support, helplessness/loss of mastery and self-efficacy, hopelessness); behavior (interpersonal conflict/impairment, social withdrawal/isolation; impaired functioning); somatic complaints (change in weight, increased pain, poor/perceived health/general somatic concerns, general sleep difficulties); and suicidality (thoughts of death or self-injury, thoughts that life is not worth living) (Kelly et al., 2011). Overall, the categories that were most frequently identified by participants entailed sadness/depressed affect, interpersonal alienation or sensitivity, interpersonal conflict, and social withdrawal (Kelly et al., 2011). Study participants identified nine concepts that were not a part of the list of diagnostic criteria, including increased anger and anxiety.

Fortunately, major depression is treatable. Treatments found to be effective include specific psychotherapies such as cognitive-behavioral therapy (CBT) and interpersonal therapy (IPT) as well as anti-depressant medications and other treatments (National Institute of Mental Health, 2015).

Taken together, the effects of depression clearly have the potential to impact the functioning of the leader – in both his or her personal and professional capacities. Furthermore, due to persistent stigma around mental illness (Follmer & Jones, 2018), leaders may be less likely to disclose or seek help related to mental illnesses than physical illnesses. Issues surrounding leaders' disclosure will be examined in Chapter 3.

Mood disorders: bipolar disorder

Bipolar disorder (BD) is a mood disorder characterized by both periods of depressed mood and periods of abnormally elevated mood, which are associated with other impairing symptoms. Kessler et al. (2005) estimated that 3.9% of Americans experience bipolar disorders at some point in their lifetime. While there have been many quantitative studies on bipolar disorder, several researchers conducted interviews from the perspective of individual patients, their caregivers, and their spouses.

Michalak, Yatham, Kolesar, and Lam (2006) researched patients' experiences of how bipolar disorder affects their quality of life. They categorized the data into six themes: routine (daily structure); independence (from family, financial independence, and autonomy from the health care system); stigma and disclosure (marginalization or stereotyping); identity (a person's subjective feelings about themselves); social support (social relationships); and spirituality (religious or spiritual experience). In concurrence with quantitative studies, the researchers found that most individuals in their study experienced a profound effect on their quality of life as a result of bipolar disorder, "often having serious and enduring effects on their ability to have a good education, a meaningful vocation, financial independence, and healthy social and intimate relationships" (Michalak et al., 2006, p. 34).

They asked participants to rank categories that were most important in determining a good quality of life. Their top priorities included several factors that overlap with more than one category: (1) social support (needing friendships or intimate relationships where people do not try to fix or judge them and just accept them), (2) physical and mental health, (3) financial health and independence; and (4) basic needs and vocation. The study provided insight into several areas that quantitative studies frequently do not examine – for example, stigma and disclosure in the workplace, which participants believed often result in dismissal, demotion, and other negative effects on their career; loss of identity and self-esteem, which can occur during mania or depression when individuals may lose perspective on who they are, or they may let the diagnosis define them; the effect of routine on well-being where some individuals recognize that having an established routine is important to maintaining quality of life, while others view routine as confining and need more flexibility in their schedule to function effectively.

Like major depressive disorder, bipolar disorders are also treatable. The primary treatment for BD is certain mood-stabilizing medications (National Institute of Mental Health, 2018). Certain psychotherapies, such as cognitive therapy (CT) and family-focused therapy (FFT), may also be helpful in combination with medication (National Institute of Mental Health, 2018; Society of Clinical Psychology, 2016b).

Anxiety disorders

Taken as a group, anxiety disorders are the most commonly experienced mental disorders, affecting an estimated 28.8% of Americans at some point in their lifetime, referred to as the "lifetime prevalence rate" (Kessler et al., 2005). Anxiety disorders include specific phobias (impairing fears of specific objects or situations; 12.5% lifetime prevalence), social phobia (impairing fears of social situations; 12.1% lifetime prevalence), posttraumatic stress disorder (PTSD; impairing symptoms of re-experiencing, physical arousal, and avoidance following a traumatic event; 6.8% lifetime prevalence), generalized anxiety disorder (GAD; characterized by impairing and uncontrollable worry about a variety of things; 5.7% lifetime prevalence), panic disorder (experience of multiple unexpected panic attacks and fear and avoidance related to future attacks; 4.7% lifetime prevalence), and obsessive-compulsive disorder (OCD; impairing and distressing intrusive thoughts and compulsive actions intended to reduce those thoughts; 1.6% lifetime prevalence). As is evident from the prevalence rates of these disorders, the anxiety disorders often overlap and co-occur within the same person, and they can also frequently co-occur with other mental disorders (Bandelow & Michaelis, 2015).

While anxiety disorders differ in their specific features, they share some common underlying processes (Barlow et al., 2010). Anxiety disorders are associated with unpleasant and distressing physical symptoms of anxiety and cognitive symptoms (e.g., worry, intrusive thoughts). Anxiety disorders also share the process of avoidance whereby people (understandably) distance themselves physically or mentally from the source of the anxiety. While avoidance can help to reduce anxiety in the short term, avoidance can maintain or even increase the experience of anxiety over the long term. In addition, avoidance can prevent people from doing things in their life that are important and meaningful to them. Finally, anxiety disorders often involve certain patterns of thinking about the feared object or situation – for example, over-estimating the threat posed by the situation or the consequences of the feared event and under-estimating one's ability to cope with the situation or event (Barlow et al., 2010).

While we are unaware of specific studies examining the prevalence of anxiety disorders in leaders, it is not difficult to imagine how the symptoms of an anxiety disorder would have a negative effect on the personal well-being and, potentially, the professional functioning of a leader. Fortunately, like other mental disorders, anxiety disorders are treatable. Effective treatments include different forms of cognitive-behavioral therapy (CBT) and other specific psychotherapies (Society of Clinical Psychology, 2016a). Certain medications can also be helpful in the treatment of anxiety disorders (Anxiety and Depression Association of America, 2019).

Attention-deficit/hyperactivity disorder (ADHD)

ADHD is a developmental disorder characterized by age-inappropriate and impairing inattention and/or hyperactivity and impulsivity (American Psychiatric Association, 2013). Once conceptualized as a childhood-only disorder, studies indicate that about one-third of cases persist into adulthood and another one-third of people diagnosed earlier in life will continue to experience substantial impairment related to symptoms (Barkley, Murphy, & Fischer, 2008). ADHD in adults is associated with significant functional impairment in a range of domains, including work, education, relationships, managing daily responsibilities, managing finances, health maintenance behaviors, and driving (Barkley et al., 2008). We were only able to locate one published study reporting the estimated prevalence of ADHD in leaders. Carleton and Barling (2018) found that 5% of their sample of 98 senior managers was classified as "high risk" for ADHD based on a short screening questionnaire – a rate that is comparable to the estimated prevalence of ADHD for adults in general (4.4%; Kessler et al., 2006). These researchers also found that ADHD symptoms in leaders were associated with more frequent passive leadership (i.e., less frequently giving employees feedback, rewards, and sanctions) as rated by followers – an effect that seemed to be related to increased daytime sleepiness. When thinking more broadly about all of the responsibilities and skills required in a leadership role, it is not difficult to imagine how problems with attention, task completion, and impulsive behavior might contribute to impairment.

Because ADHD is, by definition, a disorder that is first experienced in child-hood or adolescence (American Psychiatric Association, 2013), leaders are unlikely to experience a new onset of ADHD as a personal crisis. Yet leaders with ADHD who have coped adequately with their symptoms over time or who have relied on other strengths and supports to succeed may experience increased impairment from their ADHD when job demands change, when other stressful events occur, or when previously available sources of support are disrupted. For leaders who have not been previously diagnosed with ADHD, receiving a new diagnosis may bring a sense of relief and validation but also negative emotions such as frustration and regret when thinking about the past (Young, Bramham, Gray, & Rose, 2008). The most important factor in a positive outcome for leaders experiencing ADHD is probably finding an effective treatment. Fortunately, ADHD in adults is a treatable condition with specific medications, such as stimulants and atomoxetine, as effective evidence-based treatments (Prince, Wilens, Spencer, & Biederman, 2006), and specific skills-based psychotherapies such as cognitive-behavioral therapy (CBT) showing promise alone or in combination with medications (Knouse, Teller, & Brooks, 2017).

Mental illness in organizations

The organizational scholarship on employees with mental illness and leaders specifi-cally remains somewhat limited. Follmer and Jones (2018) determined that most of the research on mental illnesses is conducted in clinical psychology, psychiatry, and rehabilitation services, outside the fields of industrial psychology and man-agement. The researchers conducted an interdisciplinary review of 117 articles to synthesize what is known about employees with mental illness. They acknowledge that individuals in the workforce may show signs of mental illness, although others may not recognize the disorder; that is, these employees conceal their social identity. The researchers found three different perspectives represented in the literature – the perspectives of individuals with mental illness; perceptions of other coworkers and managers; and views of the employers who hire people with mental illness.

First, from an individual perspective, employees with mental illness cope with:

- Impairment (e.g., problems involving communicating with others, ability to engage in decision making, workplace accidents, concentration, and restrictions on social interactions);
- Task performance and at-work productivity (e.g., loss of work productivity, difficulty controlling anxiety and emotions at work, withdrawal and sickness absences, discrepancies between desired and actual performance);
- Barrier perceptions (e.g., gaps in employment history, displays of symptoms, low mood, low confidence, poor communication skills);
- Job type (e.g., individuals in executive, professional, administrative support, and household services positions had higher lifetime risk of developing major depression versus a lower lifetime risk of developing depression among laborers, people in protective services, and transportation);

- Job and career attitudes (e.g., people with depression are more likely to report lower job satisfaction, and people with ADHD are predicted to encounter commitment anxiety, external conflict and dysfunctional career thoughts.

(Follmer & Jones, 2018, pp. 333–335)

Second, the researchers found that perceptions and attitudes of other coworkers and managers can be negative due to stereotyping and discrimination. Mental illness is highly stigmatizing due to stereotypes that the employee's mental illness will disrupt workers' productivity, and employees with certain illnesses (bipolar disorder or depression) were perceived as having low competence and warmth. Several studies in Follmer and Jones' (2018) review of research showed that employees with mental illness received both overt and subtle discrimination despite legal protections against bias in the Americans with Disabilities Act (ADA).

Third, the researchers found that organizations generally view the hiring of people with mental illness from a cost perspective, that is, the costs organizations will incur as a result of reduced productivity, absenteeism, and health care.

Mental health challenges specifically among leaders may be associated with "resource depletion." Leaders need a variety of personal resources to function effectively, including "cognitive (i.e., self-control, emotional intelligence), attitudinal (i.e., self-confidence, sense of mastery), and affective (i.e., optimism, hope) personal characteristics" (Byrne et al., 2014, p. 345). Studies on negative effects of mental health challenges show that even subclinical levels of depressive symptoms can "manifest in difficulties in concentration and decision-making; feelings of sadness, pessimism, and worthlessness; and problems with sleeping," which can deplete resources that leaders need for transformational leadership (Barling & Cloutier, 2016, p. 396). Other studies reveal that leaders' high levels of anxiety were associated with low levels of transformational leadership (Byrne et al., 2014, p. 353), higher levels of abusive supervision, and unethical behavior (Barling & Cloutier, 2016). These studies support the perception that mental health challenges such as anxiety and depression are associated with resource depletion and may impact the quality and effectiveness of leadership in organizations. The topic of leader resources is explored further in Chapter 2.

Ellison, Russinova, MacDonald-Wilson, and Lyass (2003) conducted one of the few studies on workplace disclosure of psychiatric conditions among 495 professionals and managers. They were surprised to find that 80.9% (of a subset of business, educational, and technical services workers)[2] disclosed their mental illness at work – half disclosed under at least one unfavorable circumstance (experiencing symptoms and needing to explain them, hospitalization while employed, or upon diagnosis of mental illness), while one-third disclosed when they felt comfortable (feeling that employment was secure, disclosure would not lead to negative consequences, feeling appreciated by their boss, feeling respected by colleagues, and having a supportive environment) (Ellison et al., 2003).

Forty-seven non-disclosers (of a 209-participant subset) reported that they did not plan to disclose under any circumstances, had a general concern that disclosure

---

2 Mental health workers (140) were excluded from this sample because they were employed as peer support specialists where their mental illness status was known and was a requirement for the position.

would create problems for them, felt they could keep their jobs without disclosing, wanted to be perceived like everyone else, felt disclosure would lead to biased work evaluations, thought disclosure would negatively impact future promotions, feared coworkers would gossip about them or start to avoid them, or received advice from their therapist not to disclose (Ellison et al., 2003).

Ellison et al. (2003) concluded that several meaningful factors converged across the reasons for disclosure in their study, including "confidence in the job, capacity to regulate one's condition on the job, having learned how to manage one's illness, knowledge of ADA, and feeling socially connected" (p. 12).

It is understandable why many employees, including CEOs and senior executives, might remain reluctant to disclose their mental illness. Executive-level employees may fear the repercussions to themselves and the potential repercussions to their organizations. Perryman, Butler, Martin, and Ferris (2010) note that even though CEOs have the right to medical privacy under the Health Insurance Portability and Accountability Act of 1996 (HIPAA), "not all employees are created equal" (p. 23). CEOs are the public face of organizations and inherently undergo higher public scrutiny than other employees. Yet, some executives choose to disclose their mental health conditions publicly to remove the stigma of mental illness. A more in-depth discussion of crisis-related disclosure is presented in Chapter 3.

Factors that facilitate employment and thriving for workers with mental disorders include: individual factors (treatment of specific diagnosed illnesses, supported employment programs, and skill training); organizational factors (accommodations for the employee such as modified work schedules and time, developing a supportive organizational climate, establishing EAP programs, and stigma reduction workshops for coworkers and managers); and effects on organizational outcomes (providing resources such as prevention programs focused on mental health) (Follmer & Jones, 2018, pp. 3338–3342). These approaches help shift the perspectives of organizations from an emphasis on costs to an emphasis on contributions that employees with mental illness can make to the organization and society (see also Chapter 6 concerning organizational support for leaders and members affected by mental illness).

Injury

The top sources of injuries for adults ages 18–64 involve falls from heights and from same level, motor vehicle (MV) accidents, overexertion of back or spine, upper extremity, lower extremity, and other, struck by falling object or person and caught in between objects (Smith, Sorock, Wellman, Courtney, & Pransky, 2006). We will examine the impact of two of the most prevalent injuries to individuals – motor vehicle accidents and falls.

Motor vehicle accidents

Alghnam and colleagues (2015) conducted a study to provide the patients' perspective concerning long-term implications of vehicle crashes on health-related quality of life (HRQOL) of survivors. They examined self-care, depression, mobility, pain, and usual activity quality of life domains. The 590 adult participants who sustained injuries from MV accidents reported higher incidents of lasting disabilities – depression, mobility, and pain – beyond the first year than participants who were not exposed to MV injuries (Alghnam, Wegener, Bhalla, Colantuoni, & Castillo, 2015). The areas of self-care and usual activities demonstrated the most improvement after one year. However, quality of life indicators in the other domains improved slightly for MV survivors but remained lower than the general population.

Many people sustain musculoskeletal injuries that affect joints, bones, muscles, and the spine as a result of motor vehicle accidents; and these injuries have a long-term impact on one's ability to work (Gane, Brakenridge, Smits, & Johnston, 2018). Bortsov et al. (2014) found that patients in their study who were involved in MV accidents most often reported pain in the axial region of the body (neck, shoulders, and back). The axial region is essential because movement of the neck and back are necessary for most life functions. Pain in this region is associated with the worst physical and mental health in the general population. Among the 859 participants in the study, axial pain had the greatest impact on several life functions (general activity, enjoyment of life, mood, normal relations with other people, and sleep) after assessments at six weeks, six months, and one year. The researchers report that widespread musculoskeletal pain often affects a person's working ability, life satisfaction, and general health.

Wiseman, Foster, and Curtis (2016) focused on the emotional well-being of patients with physical injuries and the lack of attention from clinicians to the emotional impact of the injury. They highlight the strong link between ongoing physical pain from injury and the person's emotional well-being. Common emotions expressed by participants in the study were primarily negative, including fear, anger, frustration, guilt, despondency, stress, anxiety, feeling down, and suicidality. The researchers conclude that, prior to release from the hospital, patients and their family members should be informed about potential emotional responses following injury and provided with information about resources for mental health services if they experience these emotional responses (Wiseman et al., 2016).

Falls

Falls account for a considerable number of accidents each year. M. C. Young, Radtka, Frankel, Arabian, and Rabinovici (2014) conducted a comparative study using data from two trauma centers in Massachusetts and Pennsylvania of fall from standing (FFS) versus fall from a height (FFH) to examine the intuitive notion that low-impact injuries are rarely life-threatening injuries. Falls from standing are often undertriaged due to this popular misconception. Surprisingly, the study revealed that "patients admitted to a trauma center sustained significant injuries with identical severity and almost a similar pattern observed in FFH patients" (M. C. Young et al., 2014, p. 211). Several significant findings include:

- Fall from standing patients were older, had more comorbidities (two chronic diseases or conditions), and were taking more medication.

- FFS patients had more ICU admissions and complications as well as prolonged length of stay in the hospital.
- Fall from standing patients sustained more frequent traumatic brain injury (TBI) than fall from a height.
- More FFS patients were sent to nursing homes versus more FFH patients who were discharged home.
- Discharge to rehabilitation and mortality were similar in both groups.
- Patients with both types of falls had almost an identical pattern of injuries. FFS patients had higher rates of traumatic brain injury while FFS had more chest and spine injuries.

(M. C. Young et al., 2014)

The leader as caregiver – physical or psychological illness or injury of a family member

> My wife was diagnosed with breast cancer. Obviously, it was unexpected and it came at a very stressful time for me. We had two small children, and both of us worked in jobs where the market was uncertain. I tried not to let it affect me at work.
>
> *Survey participant*

> My husband was diagnosed with cancer. I experienced fear and depression, but at the same time I had to stay strong for both my husband and my daughter.
>
> *Survey participant*

> My wife went into early labor with our daughter three months early. She [our daughter] had to be put on a ventilator. [She] couldn't breathe on her own. She couldn't eat. She only weighed 3 lbs. 3 oz. . . . . She was in the hospital for 6 weeks.
>
> *Survey participant*

> My daughter was having mental health issues that were causing and could potentially cause harm to herself. She is my adult child and I was trying to help her to get the help she needed.
>
> *Survey participant*

Among the participants in our survey, 22% identified their personal crisis as illness or injury of a family member (see Figure 1.1). They reported feeling depressed (64%) and equally stressed or worried (64%). Many lost sleep (58%) and felt sad (50%), while others were also able to remain positive or engage in positive thinking (50%) (see Table 1.1). Wittenberg, Saada, and Prosser (2013) report similar emotional health effects on family members across family illness type (arthritis, cancer, Alzheimer's disease/dementia, depression, and cerebral palsy) and family relationship type (spouse, child, or parent). Family members reported experiencing sadness, depression, worry, fear, stress, and anxiety as well as limitations on social activities in response to a family member's illness (Wittenberg et al., 2013).

Caregiving

Leaders may assume partial or total caregiver roles for family members who are sick or injured. Caregiving specifically refers to care provided by family members or friends rather than a professional who is paid for services (Schulz & Sherwood, 2008). Ågård, Egerod, Tønnesen, and Lomborg (2015) found that assuming the caregiving role entailed a shift in responsibilities, beginning with committing to caregiving, acquiring caregiving skills, negotiating the level of caregiving based on the patient's capabilities, and gradually leaving the caregiving role. Caregiving for a spouse who has experienced a critical illness typically entails observing the spouse's condition on an ongoing basis, assisting in the patient's recovery, and taking on household and childcare activities, coaching the patient's continuing progress, advocating for the patient with health professionals throughout the process, and managing medical and social activities (Ågård et al., 2015).

Researchers report that caregiving has the features of a chronic stress experience. It creates physical and psychological strain over extended periods of time, is accompanied by high levels of unpredictability and uncontrollability, has the capacity to create secondary stress in multiple life domains such as work and family relationships, and frequently requires high levels of vigilance (Schulz & Sherwood, 2008). These chronic stress factors can lead to poor physical health and self-care, psychological health, and even the death of caregivers. Schulz and Sherwood (2008) report that older caregivers, people in lower socioeconomic levels, and people with fewer social support resources are most at risk.

Family members in PICU/ICU

Post-intensive care responsibilities for children and adults typically involve stressful caregiving responsibilities. Families who experience having a critically ill or injured child in the pediatric intensive care unit (PICU) indicate that their most severe stressor is "role alteration," which entails a sense of helplessness that parents experience when they lose their customary control over providing safety and advocacy for their child (Shudy et al., 2006). The effects on parents post-discharge include psychological impacts (psychiatric and/or posttraumatic stress disorder especially among mothers), physical health impacts (numbness, malaise, fatigue, headaches, irritability, and disruption in sleep and meal patterns) and social impacts (economics, family roles, function, cohesion and interpersonal relations such as marital conflict and divorce) (Shudy et al., 2006).

Researchers now refer to the cluster of psychological complications (acute stress disorder, PTSD, depression, and complicated grief) as "postintensive care syndrome-family" (PICS-F), which family members may experience after their child or adult loved one leaves critical care (Davidson, Jones, & Bienvenu, 2012). Davidson et al. (2012) reported that PTSD symptoms may be higher in adult relatives of patients than in parents of children; and certain risk factors may increase the likelihood of PICS-F including "family members whose loved ones died or who were believed to be at high risk for death in the ICU . . . whose loved ones became ill unexpectedly . . . or who were ill <5 years . . . and who experienced additional stressors . . . including additional hospitalization" (p. 619). The researchers suggest educating ICU staff on assessing family needs to reduce family stress, frequent updates by the team to family in language they can understand and in varied formats (verbal, written, and video), helping families make sense of what has happened, encouraging family to participate in care as appropriate, inclusion in medical decision-making, physicians who are comforting, supportive nurses, family debriefing, and follow-up after discharge from the ICU may function to promote adaptive coping and mitigate effects of adverse psychological outcomes (Davidson et al., 2012).

Family members with chronic illness

Leaders may also need to provide care for family members with chronic illnesses such as diabetes, heart failure, chronic lung disease, and arthritis. Cost-saving considerations in health care, including shortened hospital stays, mean more people with chronic illnesses receive care at home. Lim and Zebrack (2004) report that even the use of complex sophisticated equipment to treat chronically ill patients is being carried out by inexperienced family caregivers who lack training, support, information, and other resources. These demands can often affect the caregiver's quality of life and leave them feeling exhausted, alone, and overwhelmed. Caregivers who are employed struggle with challenges such as missing work, taking days off, retiring early, and even resigning in order to take care of chronically ill family members (Lim & Zebrack, 2004).

Family members with dementia

Several negative effects of caring for a relative with dementia are similar to chronic stress factors, but there are factors involved in care for dementia patients that create different demands on caregivers. One in five caregivers of relatives with dementia become depressed, and these caregivers display poorer physical health than non-caregivers or caregivers for family members with other health issues (Pini et al., 2018). Researchers contend that caregiving for relatives with dementia creates more challenging conditions than caring for a person with physical disabilities alone. Dementia patients "typically require more supervision, are less likely to express gratitude for the help they receive, and are more likely to be depressed" (Schulz & Sherwood, 2008, p. 108).

Providing care for relatives with dementia often affects the caregivers' ability to fulfill their own needs. Their relative's dementia impacts the caregivers':

> ability to continue to feel close to their relative, even though they wished to do so; the ability to feel in control of day-to-day life and the future; their ability to fulfill their needs to have time and space for relaxation or spontaneity; and their need to feel connected to others.
>
> (Pini et al., 2018, p. e75)

Additionally, the complex and challenging emotion work of caring for a relative with dementia is often unnoticed or undervalued by family members, friends, and support service professionals. Emotion work involves managing the feelings of others while managing or changing your own feelings "through cognitive, bodily, and expressive techniques such as changing one's ideas or thoughts, bodily response (e.g., breathing), and expressive gestures (e.g., smiling or crying)" (Herron, Funk, & Spencer, 2019, p. 2). Caregivers struggle to manage their feelings of anger, irritation, and annoyance toward the family member with dementia; to manage their fear and experiences with verbal abuse and physical aggression; to handle their expectations and those of others to prioritize the needs of the person with dementia and not complain, and to manage their expectations to avoid conflict and be a good caregiver (Herron et al., 2019). The responsibility of emotion work can be harmful to the well-being of the caregiver. Researchers urge support for caregivers through better, more nuanced education materials that address emotion work, information on self-care, practical support such as assistance with household chores, and help with determining when and how to exit the caring role.

Family members with serious mental illness

Several leaders in our study reported having family members with serious mental illness (SMI). SMIs may include "major depression, schizophrenia, bipolar disorder, obsessive compulsive disorder [OCD], panic disorder, posttraumatic stress disorder [PTSD], and borderline personality disorder" (Crowe & Brinkley, 2015, p. 286) and chronic and severe substance abuse problems. Family members provide much of the caregiving for people with SMI like caregiving for other chronic illnesses.

The number of hours spent caregiving, the relationship of the caregiver to the family member with SMI, the behavior of the family member, and perceived satisfaction with treatment contribute to the overall functioning and quality of life of caregivers. Crowe and Brinkley (2015) found in their study of 169 caregivers of family members with SMI that most participants felt that they gave lots of time and lots of energy to caregiving regardless of the actual time spent. The ones who spent 20 hours or less as caregivers reported significantly less depression than those who spent more than 20 hours per week. Family members who cared for their own children spent more time caring for them but described feeling less depressed than caregivers for other relatives.

Difficult behaviors and symptoms by the family member with SMI increased the distress of the caregiver and discord in the family. However, almost all participants in the study reported that their family member was receiving treatment, and most were satisfied with the treatment that their relative received. The study emphasized the role of family counselors to provide more support to caregivers by exploring ways to reduce caregiving time through seeking outside supports, screening caregivers for depression, and identifying and decreasing difficult behaviors as a goal of treatment for the relative with SMI. Other studies suggest the use of individual and family therapy, education, and problem-solving programs for caregivers (Lim & Zebrack, 2004).

The caregiving literature notes several positive outcomes of caregiving – increased resilience, family adaptation, and coping, sensitivity to others with disabilities, and a sense of family inner strength (Pickett-Schenk et al., as cited in Crowe & Brinkley, 2015). Schulz and Sherwood (2008) reported that a study by Tarlow et al. found caregiving made the caregivers feel needed and good about themselves, gave meaning to their lives, helped them develop new skills and strengthened relationships.

The leader as newly single – divorce or a relationship breakup

> After 20 years of marriage and recent purchase of a large home, my husband decided he didn't want to be married. I was devastated.
>
> *Survey participant*

> Divorce is an emotional roller coaster. It can make you feel crazy, frightened, depressed and giddy. You suddenly have to navigate legal, financial, parenting, and relationship issues that you probably never expected to confront.
>
> *Survey participant*

> I went through a separation and then subsequently a divorce while having a very young child. During this time, I was starting my [type of firm deleted] firm and had to maintain focus on my work while at the same time dealing with the personal pressures of figuring out how to organize my life.
>
> *Survey participant*

Divorce

We found no evidence to substantiate that CEOs or senior leaders experience higher divorce rates than the general population, as espoused in popular media; but we do know that many senior leaders work exceptionally long hours, travel frequently, and have family time disrupted by work matters. These work-life disruptions may place a strain on marriages or couple relations. Thirteen percent of participants in Study 2 identified divorce or a relationship breakup as the primary reason for their personal crisis (see Figure 1.1). They reported feeling sad (76%) and depressed (67%), experiencing loss of sleep (67%), appetite loss (57%), and feeling hurt (52%) as a result of ending a marriage or relationship (see Table 1.1).

Several researchers investigated characteristics of divorce and the factors that facilitate well-being post-divorce. Symoens, Bastaits, Mortelmans, and Bracke (2013) emphasize that divorce is a "process" rather than a discrete event – divorce is "a tumultuous period in which people must rearrange many affairs and might have to rebuild their identity" (p. 179). They emphasize that conflict during a divorce is a key stressor along with moving and disrupting social networks, enduring an often-lengthy divorce process, dealing with legal proceedings, and interacting with an ex-spouse. Several of our participants in Study 1 commented on the stress of moving and their grief and pain during the divorce process.

Symoens et al. (2013) examined gender differences and characteristics of divorce in relation to well-being – that is, who initiated the divorce, perception of having been treated fairly, moving at separation, level of conflict, and duration of the divorce process. They found both predictable and surprising results.

- More women than men initiated divorce on their own.
- Almost as many men as women indicated they shared initiation of the divorce process (i.e., the partners jointly initiated the divorce).
- Women reported more feelings of depression than men.
- Half the respondents thought the division of goods was fair to both parties while 33% of men and 39% of women felt they were disadvantaged.
- About half the respondents moved at the time of separation; somewhat more men (54%) than women (47%).
- The average divorce process took 12–13 months.
- Women reported slightly more conflict than men.
- Sixty-five percent of divorcees have minor children from the former marriage.
- More women than men finished higher academic or nonacademic education but more women were at risk for poverty.
- Forty-four percent of divorced men and 34% of divorced women live with new partners.

(Symoens et al., 2013)

With regard to well-being:

- Sole and joint initiators of divorce report more positive adjustment after divorce than non-initiators; and they demonstrate greater resilience (also noted in Frisby, Booth-Butterfield, Dillow, Martin, & Weber, 2012).
- Initiation of divorce benefits both men and women equally.
- Men and women are depressed when they feel goods are divided to their disadvantage.
- Surprisingly, longer divorce processes do not equate to lower levels of satisfaction or more depression. Quality rather than speed is most important to well-being.
- Among participants, neither moving at separation nor conflict show lower levels of satisfaction or more depression.
- Prolonged conflict after divorce does have a negative effect on the well-being of men and women.
- Positive conflict in which both partners can give voice to their grievances and find a solution (negotiation) might be healthier for divorced partners (see also Frisby et al., 2012).
- Having a new partner seems to enhance mental health after divorce (Symoens et al., 2013).

Relationship breakup

> I went through an end of an 11-year relationship. We were about to get married [when the other person] called it off. At the time I just thought we were taking a break, as we had done several times before. But apparently, [the other person] had other plans and I wasn't included in them. I was the assistant vice president for a company and had a lot of duties and responsibilities. Going through the demise of this relationship affected the way I functioned daily and my job. It was a very hard time in my life.
>
> *Survey participant*

Two studies of unmarried couples provide insight into the experience of relationship breakups. Rhoades, Kamp Dush, Atkins, Stanley, and Markman (2011) tested whether dissolving an unmarried relationship resulted in increases in psychological distress and decreases in life satisfaction. Among the 1295 individuals in their study before and after a breakup, their findings suggest that the breakup of a romantic relationship is associated with stressors such as psychological distress and decrease in satisfaction with life. There were several characteristics related to declines after a breakup – more investments of resources (e.g., self-disclosures, mutual friends, shared possessions, longer time in the relationship, cohabiting/living together, and plans to marry) were associated with greater individual decline; and more contact with ex-partners led to greater decline in life satisfaction (Rhoades et al., 2011). Conversely, dating someone new, like the findings about divorced couples, and having higher relationship quality prior to the breakup resulted in smaller declines in life satisfaction after dissolution.

Le, Dove, Agnew, Korn, and Mutso (2010) analyzed 137 studies to examine the extent to which "individual factors" (e.g., such as self-esteem or attachment), "characteristics of relationships" (e.g., commitment, satisfaction, and love), and "external factors" (e.g., social network support) were associated with breakups among nonmarried couples. They found that individual factors had small to nonsignificant effects on breakups, relationship factors were better predictors of breakup than individual factors, and the external factor of network support was a moderate predictor of breakups. Additionally, lower commitment and higher dependence, along with other relationship factors such as diminished love, trust, inclusion of self in other (IOS), and self-disclosure are strong predictors of dissolution. Factors such as self-disclosure and closeness were strong predictors of dissolution in samples with more females, while satisfaction and adjustment were strong predictors in samples with more males.

Impact of the leader's divorce on the organization

Dionisi and Barling (2019) contend that work and family are "intertwined." In their study of 123 paired leaders and their team members, the researchers found that romantic relationship conflicts (marital discord) were significantly associated with leaders' depressive symptoms (which deplete leaders' resources at work) and may ultimately contribute to negative leadership behaviors (e.g., verbal and nonverbal hostility) (Dionisi & Barling, 2019). If leaders wonder whether marital conflict such as divorce might impact their work, these researchers would most likely answer affirmatively.

Divorce or relationship breakup can also have a harmful effect on CEO productivity. A study of the impact of CEO divorce on shareholders reports that "divorce can affect the productivity, concentration, and energy levels of the CEO" (Larcker, McCall, & Tayan, 2013, p. 1). Based on previous studies, the researchers contend that divorce can negatively impact a company's productivity and in extreme cases may cause some CEOs to step down or retire. Larcker et al. (2013) report that "among 24 CEOs who got divorced between 2009 and 2012, seven (29 percent) stepped down within two years of the settlement" even though most had seven to 12 years of tenure and were just hitting their stride (p. 2). In an interview with the lead author of the study, David Larcker conveyed that data concerning the CEOs who left office within a year or two after divorce,

> Caused us to think boards had a responsibility to have a grasp on the married lives of their CEOs and possibly other senior executives . . . finding a trusted board member who is close to the CEO and who can check in from time to time on "how is your home life going?" is a start [on how a board should become involved], I would think.
>
> *(Cunningham, 2014, p. 59)*

Conclusion

The experiences of our participants, as illustrated by their poignant quotations at the beginning of each section and survey results, exemplify the disruptive effects, pain, and complexity that accompany a personal crisis. Information from research studies throughout the chapter expand our understanding of the human experiences involved in our four crisis types – the leader's own physical or psychological illness or injury, physical or psychological illness or injury of a family member, death of a family member, and divorce or a relationship breakup. Taken together, personal experiences, survey data, and research studies provide a rare window into the experiences of the "leader-as-person" in crisis. In subsequent chapters, we examine in more depth aspects of the leader as a unique position, including the impact of disclosure of a personal crisis on their company's performance and reputation.

References

Ågård, A. S., Egerod, I., Tønnesen, E., & Lomborg, K. (2015). From spouse to caregiver and back: A grounded theory study of post-intensive care unit spousal caregiving. *Journal of Advanced Nursing, 71*(8), 1892–1903. https://doi.org/10.1111/jan.12657

Alghnam, S., Wegener, S. T., Bhalla, K., Colantuoni, E., & Castillo, R. (2015). Long-term outcomes of individuals injured in motor vehicle crashes: A population-based study. *Injury, 46*(8), 1503–1508. https://doi.org/10.1016/j.injury.2015.06.004

American Psychiatric Association. (2013). *Diagnostic and statistical manual of mental disorders* (5th ed.). Washington, DC: American Psychiatry Publishing.

Anxiety and Depression Association of America. (2019). *Medication treatment for anxiety disorders*. Retrieved August 18, 2019 from https://adaa.org/finding-help/treatment/medication

Ashley, K. D., Lee, L. T., & Heaton, K. (2019). Return to work among stroke survivors. *Workplace Health & Safety, 67*(2), 87–94. https://doi.org/10.1177/2165079918812483

Bandelow, B., & Michaelis, S. (2015). Epidemiology of anxiety disorders in the 21st century. *Dialogues in Clinical Neuroscience, 17*(3), 327–335.

Barkley, R. A., Murphy, K. R., & Fischer, M. (2008). *ADHD in adults: What the science says.* New York: Guilford Press.

Barling, J., & Cloutier, A. (2016). Leaders' mental health at work: Empirical, methodological, and policy directions. *Journal of Occupational Health Psychology, 22*(3), 394. https://doi.org/10.1037/ocp0000055

Barlow, D. H., Ellard, K. K., Fairholme, C. P., Farchione, T. J., Boisseau, C. L., Allen, L. B., & Ehrenreich-May, J. T. (2010). *Unified protocol for transdiagnostic treatment of emotional disorders: Workbook.* Retrieved from www.oxfordclinicalpsych.com/view/10.1093/med:psych/9780199772674.001.0001/med-9780199772674

Bishop, L., & Bushnell, C. (2017). Post hospital discharge care for complex chronic conditions: The unique challenges facing stroke patients in their homes. *Current Cardiovascular Risk Reports, 11*(12), 36. https://doi.org/10.1007/s12170-017-0560-7

Bortsov, A. V., Platts-Mills, T. F., Peak, D. A., Jones, J. S., Swor, R. A., Domeier, R. M., . . . McLean, S. A. (2014). Effect of pain location and duration on life function in the year after motor vehicle collision. *Pain, 155*(9), 1836–1845. https://doi.org/10.1016/j.pain.2014.06.013

Byrne, A., Dionisi, A. M., Barling, J., Akers, A., Robertson, J., Lys, R., . . . Dupré, K. (2014). The depleted leader: The influence of leaders' diminished psychological resources on leadership behaviors. *The Leadership Quarterly, 25*(2), 344–357. https://doi.org/10.1016/j.leaqua.2013.09.003

Carleton, E. L., & Barling, J. (2018). Adult attention deficit hyperactivity disorder symptoms and passive leadership: The mediating role of daytime sleepiness. *Stress and Health, 34*(5), 663–673. https://doi.org/10.1002/smi.2833

Crowe, A., & Brinkley, J. (2015). Distress in caregivers of a family member with serious mental illness. *The Family Journal, 23*(3), 286–294. https://doi.org/10.1177/1066480715572967

Cunningham, J. M. (2014). CEO divorce and the board. *Directorship; Boston,* 59–60.

Davidson, J. E., Jones, C., & Bienvenu, O. J. (2012). Family response to critical illness: Postintensive care syndrome – Family. *Critical Care Medicine, 40*(2), 618. https://doi.org/10.1097/CCM.0b013e318236ebf9

Devlin, E. J., Denson, L. A., & Whitford, H. S. (2017). Cancer treatment side effects: A meta-analysis of the relationship between response expectancies and experience. *Journal of Pain and Symptom Management, 54*(2), 245–258.e2. https://doi.org/10.1016/j.jpainsymman.2017.03.017

Dionisi, A. M., & Barling, J. (2019). What happens at home does not stay at home: The role of family and romantic partner conflict in destructive leadership. *Stress and Health, 35*(3), 304–317. https://doi.org/10.1002/smi.2858

Dohrenwend, B. S., Askenasy, A. R., Krasnoff, L., & Dohrenwend, B. P. (1978). Exemplification of a method for scaling life events: The PERI Life Events Scale. *Journal of Health and Social Behavior, 19*(2), 205–229. https://doi.org/10.2307/2136536

Ellison, M. L., Russinova, Z., MacDonald-Wilson, K. L., & Lyass, A. (2003). Patterns and correlates of workplace disclosure among professionals and managers with psychiatric conditions. *Journal of Vocational Rehabilitation, 18*(1), 3–13.

Fernández-Alcántara, M., Pérez-Marfil, M. N., Catena-Martínez, A., & Cruz-Quintana, F. (2017). Grieving and loss processes: Latest findings and complexities. *Estudios de Psicología, 38*(3), 561–581. https://doi.org/10.1080/02109395.2017.1328210

Follmer, K. B., & Jones, K. S. (2018). Mental illness in the workplace: An interdisciplinary review and organizational research agenda. *Journal of Management, 44*(1), 325–351. https://doi.org/10.1177/0149206317741194

Frisby, B. N., Booth-Butterfield, M., Dillow, M. R., Martin, M. M., & Weber, K. D. (2012). Face and resilience in divorce: The impact on emotions, stress, and post-divorce relationships. *Journal of Social and Personal Relationships, 29*(6), 715–735. https://doi.org/10.1177/0265407512443452

Gane, E. M., Brakenridge, C. L., Smits, E. J., & Johnston, V. (2018). The impact of musculoskeletal injuries sustained in road traffic crashes on work-related outcomes: A protocol for a systematic review. *Systematic Reviews, 7*(1), 202. https://doi.org/10.1186/s13643-018-0869-4

Geller, B. M., Vacek, P. M., Flynn, B. S., Lord, K., & Cranmer, D. (2014). What are cancer survivors' needs and how well are they being met? *The Journal of Family Practice, 63*(10), E7–E16.

Herron, R. V., Funk, L. M., & Spencer, D. (2019). Responding the "wrong way": The emotion work of caring for a family member with dementia. *The Gerontologist, 59*(5), e470–e478. https://doi.org/10.1093/geront/gnz047

Huhman, H. R. (2014, November 5). Running a business while dealing with a personal loss. *Entrepreneur.* Retrieved August 1, 2019 from www.entrepreneur.com/article/239231

Kelly, M. A. R., Morse, J. Q., Stover, A., Hofkens, T., Huisman, E., Shulman, S., . . . Pilkonis, P. A. (2011). Describing depression: Congruence between patient experiences and clinical assessments. *British Journal of Clinical Psychology, 50*(1), 46–66. https://doi.org/10.1348/014466510X493926

Kessler, R. C., Adler, L., Barkley, R. A., Biederman, J., Conners, C. K., Demler, O., . . . Zaslavsky, A. M. (2006). The prevalence and correlates of adult ADHD in the United States: Results from the National Comorbidity Survey Replication. *American Journal of Psychiatry, 163*(4), 716–723. https://doi.org/10.1176/appi.ajp.163.4.716

Kessler, R. C., Berglund, P., Demler, O., Jin, R., Merikangas, K. R., & Walters, E. E. (2005). Lifetime prevalence and age-of-onset distributions of DSM-IV disorders in the National Comorbidity Survey Replication. *Archives of General Psychiatry, 62*(6), 593–602. https://doi.org/10.1001/archpsyc.62.6.593

Knouse, L. E., Teller, J., & Brooks, M. A. (2017). Meta-analysis of cognitive – Behavioral treatments for adult ADHD. *Journal of Consulting and Clinical Psychology, 85*(7), 737–750. https://doi.org/10.1037/ccp0000216

Larcker, D. F., McCall, A. L., & Tayan, B. (2013). *Separation anxiety: The impact of CEO divorce on shareholders* (SSRN Scholarly Paper No. ID 2331605). Retrieved from Social Science Research Network website: https://papers.ssrn.com/abstract=2331605

Lazarus, R. S. (2006). Emotions and interpersonal relationships: Toward a person-centered conceptualization of emotions and coping. *Journal of Personality, 74*(1), 9–46. https://doi.org/10.1111/j.1467-6494.2005.00368.x

Le, B., Dove, N. L., Agnew, C. R., Korn, M. S., & Mutso, A. A. (2010). Predicting nonmarital romantic relationship dissolution: A meta-analytic synthesis. *Personal Relationships*, *17*(3), 377–390. https://doi.org/10.1111/j.1475-6811.2010.01285.x

Li, M., & Caeyenberghs, K. (2018). Longitudinal assessment of chemotherapy-induced changes in brain and cognitive functioning: A systematic review. *Neuroscience & Biobehavioral Reviews*, *92*, 304–317. https://doi.org/10.1016/j.neubiorev.2018.05.019

Lim, J., & Zebrack, B. (2004). Caring for family members with chronic physical illness: A critical review of caregiver literature. *Health and Quality of Life Outcomes*, *2*(1), 50. https://doi.org/10.1186/1477-7525-2-50

Logan, E. L., Thornton, J. A., & Breen, L. J. (2018). What determines supportive behaviours following bereavement? A systematic review and call to action. *Death Studies*, *42*(2), 104–114. https://doi.org/10.1080/07481187.2017.1329760

Mayo Clinic. (2019, February 19). Managing the lingering side effects of cancer treatment. *Mayo Clinic*. Retrieved August 12, 2019 from www.mayoclinic.org/diseases-conditions/cancer/in-depth/cancer-survivor/art-20045524

Michalak, E. E., Yatham, L. N., Kolesar, S., & Lam, R. W. (2006). Bipolar disorder and quality of life: A patient-centered perspective. *Quality of Life Research*, *15*(1), 25–37. https://doi.org/10.1007/s11136-005-0376-7

Mollon, L., & Bhattacharjee, S. (2017). Health related quality of life among myocardial infarction survivors in the United States: A propensity score matched analysis. *Health and Quality of Life Outcomes*, *15*(1), 235. https://doi.org/10.1186/s12955-017-0809-3

National Institute of Mental Health. (2015). *Depression: What you need to know* (No. 15–3561). National Institute of Mental Health. Retrieved from www.nimh.nih.gov/health/publications/depression-what-you-need-to-know/index.shtml#pub4

National Institute of Mental Health. (2018). *Bipolar disorder*. Retrieved August 18, 2019 from www.nimh.nih.gov/health/publications/bipolar-disorder/index.shtml#pub5

National Stroke Association. (n.d.). *Post-stroke conditions – National stroke association*. Retrieved August 1, 2019 from www.stroke.org/we-can-help/survivors/stroke-recovery/post-stroke-conditions/

Perryman, A. A., Butler, F. C., Martin, J. A., & Ferris, G. R. (2010). When the CEO is ill: Keeping quiet or going public? *Business Horizons*, *53*(1), 21–29. https://doi.org/10.1016/j.bushor.2009.08.006

Pini, S., Ingleson, E., Megson, M., Clare, L., Wright, P., & Oyebode, J. R. (2018). A needs-led framework for understanding the impact of caring for a family member with dementia. *The Gerontologist*, *58*(2), e68–e77. https://doi.org/10.1093/geront/gnx148

Prince, J., Wilens, T., Spencer, T., & Biederman, J. (2006). Pharmacotherapy of ADHD in adults. In R. A. Barkley (Ed.), *Attention-deficit hyperactivity disorder: A handbook for diagnosis and treatment* (3rd ed., pp. 704–736). New York: Guilford.

Rhoades, G. K., Kamp Dush, C. M., Atkins, D. C., Stanley, S. M., & Markman, H. J. (2011). Breaking up is hard to do: The impact of unmarried relationship dissolution on mental health and life satisfaction. *Journal of Family Psychology*, *25*(3), 366. https://doi.org/10.1037/a0023627

Schulz, R., & Sherwood, P. R. (2008). Physical and mental health effects of family caregiving. *The American Journal of Nursing*, *108*(9 Suppl), 23–27. https://doi.org/10.1097/01.NAJ.0000336406.45248.4c

Shudy, M., Almeida, M. L. de, Ly, S., Landon, C., Groft, S., Jenkins, T. L., & Nicholson, C. E. (2006). Impact of pediatric critical illness and injury on families: A systematic literature review. *Pediatrics*, *118*(Suppl 3), S203–S218. https://doi.org/10.1542/peds.2006-0951B

Simonÿ, C. P., Dreyer, P., Pedersen, B. D., & Birkelund, R. (2017). It is not just a minor thing – A phenomenological-hermeneutic study of patients' experiences when afflicted by a minor heart attack and participating in cardiac rehabilitation. *Scandinavian Journal of Caring Sciences*, *31*(2), 232–240. https://doi.org/10.1111/scs.12334

Smith, G. S., Sorock, G. S., Wellman, H. M., Courtney, T. K., & Pransky, G. S. (2006). Blurring the distinctions between on and off the job injuries: Similarities and differences in circumstances. *Injury Prevention*, *12*(4), 236–241. https://doi.org/10.1136/ip.2006.011676

Society of Clinical Psychology. (2016a). *Research supported psychological treatments*. Retrieved August 18, 2019 from www.div12.org/psychological-treatments/

Society of Clinical Psychology. (2016b). *Research supported psychological treatments: Bipolar disorder*. Retrieved August 18, 2019 from www.div12.org/diagnosis/bipolar-disorder/

Stroebe, M., Schut, H., & Stroebe, W. (2007). Health outcomes of bereavement. *The Lancet*, *370*(9603), 1960–1973. https://doi.org/10.1016/S0140-6736(07)61816-9

Symoens, S., Bastaits, K., Mortelmans, D., & Bracke, P. (2013). Breaking up, breaking hearts? Characteristics of the divorce process and well-being after divorce. *Journal of Divorce & Remarriage*, *54*(3), 177–196. https://doi.org/10.1080/10502556.2013.773792

Wiseman, T., Foster, K., & Curtis, K. (2016). The experience of emotional wellbeing for patients with physical injury: A qualitative follow-up study. *Injury*, *47*(9), 1983–1989. https://doi.org/10.1016/j.injury.2016.03.021

Wittenberg, E., Saada, A., & Prosser, L. A. (2013). How illness affects family members: A qualitative interview survey. *Patient*, *6*(4), 257–268. https://doi.org/10.1007/s40271-013-0030-3

Young, M. C., Radtka, J., Frankel, H., Arabian, S., & Rabinovici, R. (2014). Fall from standing induces significant injuries. *The American Surgeon; Atlanta*, *80*(2), 210–212.

Young, S., Bramham, J., Gray, K., & Rose, E. (2008). The experience of receiving a diagnosis and treatment of ADHD in adulthood: A qualitative study of clinically referred patients using interpretative phenomenological analysis. *Journal of Attention Disorders*, *11*(4), 493–503.

2

COPING WITH CRISIS

> I always felt it helped me to talk about it. I think that people who are on the outside looking in think, "Gosh, you couldn't want to talk about that, it's too painful," but I guess I always felt like it was helpful for me to talk to my friends and close associates about that; it just helps you relieve the stress, and if you've got good friends, they help you carry that burden, so I guess that was a pretty important part of it also.
>
> – *Survey participant*

Defining coping and resilience

Responses to crisis can be understood as responses to the threat, harm, or loss caused or represented by the crisis event. Some responses to crisis can be characterized as "coping responses," which are "efforts to prevent or diminish threat, harm, and loss, or to reduce associated distress" (Carver & Connor-Smith, 2010, p. 685). Coping can also be conceptualized as an effort to adapt to the demands, both practical and emotional, presented by the crisis (Lazarus, 2006). Coping responses may be very deliberate and planful, or they may occur on the "spur of the moment," or even, at times, occur outside of awareness (for example, "getting lost" in one's work, which may serve to keep one's mind off of the emotionally distressing aspects of the crisis). Like other behavior, coping efforts can change from moment to moment, and different types of coping responses may arise at different points in the sequence of coping with personal crisis. As the demands of the situation change, people may employ different strategies to try to reduce harm and distress. Thus, it is important to recognize that coping is not one single act or simple solution to the complexities of a personal crisis (Skinner & Zimmer-Gembeck, 2016). These features of coping have made it a difficult topic to study scientifically, yet the coping literature in psychology has yielded some consistent general conclusions about more and less effective coping, which will be reviewed later in this chapter. Even in the context of these general conclusions, however, it is important to recognize that each set of personal circumstances, each organization, and each leader is unique. Successfully coping with a personal crisis will require each leader to thoughtfully consider his or her circumstances and to be willing to flexibly employ different types of coping strategies across the sequence of events that constitutes a personal crisis.

In many stressful circumstances, humans find ways to persist, thrive, and even grow. The outcome of successful coping efforts is often described as "resilience." Resilience is defined by the American Psychological Association (2019) as "the process of adapting well in the face of adversity, trauma, tragedy, threats or significant sources of stress." Personal and professional resilience is clearly a desirable outcome for the leader in crisis and for the organization that supports that leader. This chapter provides an inventory of the coping strategies that leaders in our studies employed and found helpful followed by a description of patterns of coping that have been associated with resilience in the broader psychology literature.

We begin by describing the coping responses of leaders who participated in our studies. Next, we consider how an influential theory of coping with stressful events, the Conservation of Resources Theory (COR), helps us understand the effects of personal crises on leaders and consider their patterns of coping responses. Then, we provide an overview of key concepts in the academic coping literature and connect these concepts to responses given by our participants. We conclude the chapter with an overview of the research on effective coping and provide summary thoughts for leaders in crisis.

Coping responses in our studies of leaders

What information about coping emerged from our studies of leaders who had experienced personal crises? In Study 2, we asked participants to think about and report on what strategies they believed had been the "most effective" in managing the crisis with respect to their own well-being. We formulated the options given to participants based on Study 1 participants' responses to open-ended questions about coping. Study 2 participants were able to select as many strategies as they felt were effective for them. We also asked participants to tell us which people in their personal life they had discussed the crisis with. Finally, we examined responses from Study 1 participants to identify coping strategies that had ultimately been less helpful.

Effective strategies for personal well-being

Table 2.1 displays the percentage of participants, in descending order, endorsing each coping strategy as having a positive impact on their personal well-being. Consistent with the well-known role of social support in effective coping (Taylor, 2011), the most frequently endorsed coping strategies were seeking support from family and friends – the only coping strategies endorsed by a majority of participants. In contrast, only 12% of participants reported that handling the crisis on their own had been an effective coping strategy. Social support from a spouse or partner was less frequently reported, perhaps due to the fact that not all participants had a partner (24% did not) and that a portion of participants (13%) reported that their primary crisis involved divorce or relationship breakup. Slightly more middle managers (48%) endorsed seeking support from a spouse or partner than executive leaders (32%), $p = .04$. Overall, 89% of participants reported that seeking support from at least one informal source (family, spouse, friends) had been effective in managing the impact of the crisis on their well-being.

Next, nearly half of participants reported that staying busy with life ("business as usual") and focusing on work had been an effective coping strategy for them, and another third endorsed engagement with hobbies as an effective strategy, with 70% of participants in the sample endorsing at least one of these strategies as effective. Thus, it appears that engaging in non-crisis-related activities was an important element of coping for many leaders in our sample. About one-third of participants reported that some kind of short-term respite (spending time alone, taking a few days off) had been helpful in their personal coping, while fewer participants (22%)

TABLE 2.1 Percentage of participants in Study 2 endorsing each coping strategy in response to: "Which of these approaches was most effective in helping to manage the impact of the crisis on your own well-being? Check all that apply."

Coping response	Percent endorsing
Support from family	71%
Support from friends	62%
Stayed busy with daily life (business as usual)	47%
Focused on work	41%
Support from spouse/partner	41%
Spent time alone	37%
Focus on my child/children	36%
Took time off (e.g., a long weekend, one or two days off)	35%
Engaged in physical exercise	35%
Psychological counseling/therapy	34%
Stayed in the present/mindfulness	31%
Remained positive/engaged in positive thinking	29%
Engaged in hobbies/activities	29%
Thought about positive memories of loved ones/friends	28%
Remembered my own self-worth	27%
Remained calm	27%
Thought about what makes me feel better	26%
Engaged in healthy eating	26%
Maintained work-life balance	25%
Medical care from physicians/specialists	25%
Relied on religious/spiritual beliefs or practices (e.g., praying, attending religious services, meditation)	25%
Got sufficient sleep/rest	22%
Took a leave of absence from work	22%
Took medication as prescribed	18%
Took a vacation	17%
Maintained my personal happiness	16%
Obtained personal services (e.g., hair care, massages, nail care)	13%
Handled the crisis on my own	12%
Physical therapy	11%
Other: volunteering, reading books	1%

Note: Responses ordered by percentage of participants reporting in descending frequency.

had found a more formal leave of absence from work helpful in their coping. Taken together, however, 71% of participants endorsed some kind of short- or longer-term respite as helpful for their well-being during the crisis.

Some participants endorsed what psychologists would call "cognitive strategies," or changing the way that they thought about the crisis in an effort to change its emotional impact – for example, positive thinking, bringing to mind positive memories, reflecting on one's own self-worth, and staying attentive to the present through mindfulness. Slightly more middle managers (34%) endorsed thinking about positive memories of loved ones than executive leaders (20%), $p = .04$. Overall, 71% of participants endorsed at least one cognitive strategy as effective. Activities that could be characterized as "self-care" also appeared, with any one strategy endorsed by one-third of participants or less (physical exercise, healthy eating, ensuring good sleep) but, overall, 61% of participants endorsed at least one self-care strategy. As appropriate to certain crises, participants also endorsed use of medical services as helpful (39% endorsed at least one), and 34% of the sample reported that participating in psychological counseling or therapy had been helpful. In this sample, only 25% of leaders reported that religious or spiritual practices had helped to manage the impact of the crisis on their well-being.

Less effective strategies: evidence from Study 1

Due to time and space constraints, in Study 2, we did not ask participants about approaches to the crisis that they perceived to have been less effective. However, we did obtain more detailed free responses from our Study 1 participants ($n = 49$) regarding which strategies they perceived to be less effective for handling the problem, for their own well-being, and for managing the crisis in terms of their leadership role.

When reporting less effective efforts to resolve the crisis, participants most frequently described some form of avoidance regarding thinking, talking, disclosing, or acting with respect to the crisis (14% of participants). Sample responses in this category included "Trying to do everything alone," "Put(ting) a smile on my face and pretending that everything was okay," and "being lazy and avoiding the problem." The second most prevalent less helpful strategy was instances of unhelpful social support (12% of participants). Apparent reasons for the ineffectiveness of support were diverse and included the unreliability of others ("When I had to rely on others, I often had to compensate for their failing to follow through on professional and personal requests.") and the specific nature of support provoking negative thoughts and emotions ("Hanging out with friends was the least effective, as I didn't want to see happy couples!").

When reporting on less effective strategies for managing the impact of the crisis on personal well-being, unhelpful social support was again mentioned by 12% of participants (e.g., "Spending time with family was somewhat hard; my parents specifically seemed to dwell on the situation very much," and, "Friendships, because repeating yourself to different people all the time gets kind of old."). The same number of participants mentioned not engaging in help-seeking or self-care as a less effective move for their own well-being (e.g., "I really didn't do too much to manage the impact of the crisis on my own well-being. I should have been more proactive on trying to find ways to maintain my physical and mental health."). Finally, 8% of participants mentioned that substance use had been an unhelpful coping strategy for their well-being.

Finally, when reporting on less effective strategies for managing the crisis with respect to their leadership roles, 14% of participants mentioned unsuccessful attempts to suppress thoughts and emotions about the crisis while at work (e.g., "Putting on a brave face," "Burying myself in paperwork," "Trying to separate my work and personal life during the work day. Sometimes it is just impossible."). Ten percent of participants also mentioned avoiding disclosure about the crisis at work as a less helpful strategy (e.g., "Maybe not sharing with anyone at work, since it's difficult to keep it in all the time."). It is important to note, however, that a few other participants (6%) mentioned instances of disclosure as unhelpful in managing their leadership role (e.g., "I think letting them know what was going on made me appear a bit weak.). Finally, some participants described instances of delegation (6%) and modifying work arrangements (8%) that turned out to be less helpful in managing their leadership role (e.g., "Working weekends and from home, this led the company in expecting [me] to keep doing this after the crisis was over.").

Focus on social support

Because, given past literature, we anticipated that social support would be an important source of coping resources for our participants, we asked participants in Study 2 more specifically who, other than coworkers (see Chapter 3), they had discussed their personal crisis with.

Discussing the crisis with family (87%) and friends (73%) were most frequently endorsed. Help-seeking from formal, professional sources was less prevalent, with 29% discussing their crisis with a physician, 25% with a therapist, and 11% with an Employee Assistance Program counselor (Table 2.2). Overall, 93% of participants had discussed their crisis with family or friends (informal sources), and only 46% had discussed their crisis with a formal source (55% if religious leaders are included as formal sources). Our data are remarkably consistent with the research on help-seeking, which has shown that people are at least twice as likely to seek help from

TABLE 2.2 Percentage of participants in Study 2 endorsing each response to the question: "I discussed my personal crisis with (check all that apply)."

Relationship	Percent endorsing
Family members	87%
Friends	73%
My physician (primary case/specialist)	29%
My religious leader(s)	25%
My therapist/psychiatrist	25%
Counselor via my organization's Employee Assistance Program	11%
None of the individuals above	4%

informal sources compared to formal sources and that 45–55% of people seek help exclusively from informal sources (Wills, 1987). And, as you will see in Chapter 3, the vast majority of leaders in Study 2 (97%) reported talking about the crisis with at least one person in their organization, suggesting that team members, colleagues, or supervisors might also serve as important sources of emotional or instrumental support. Furthermore, research consistently demonstrates that perceived availability of social support is among the most important buffers against negative outcomes, such as depression and anxiety, when people experience significant life stressors (Skinner & Zimmer-Gembeck, 2016; Taylor, 2011).

Leader coping strategies: summary

To summarize, a majority of leaders in Study 2 endorsed at least one strategy in each of the following clusters: seeking social support, staying engaged in non-crisis-related activities, respite, cognitive strategies (i.e., thinking about the situation differently) and self-care activities. When seeking social support, like people in general, a greater percentage of leaders sought help from informal sources rather than formal sources. Study 1 responses provided a glimpse into strategies that, in some cases, had not worked well, including seeking and receiving unhelpful social support, avoiding thinking or talking about the crisis, and using substances. To foreshadow, the overall patterns in our coping responses are consistent with prior literature on non-leaders.

Understanding the effects of crisis: Conservation of Resources Theory

To frame our broader discussion of what is known about coping responses, we draw upon the Conservation of Resources (COR) Theory of response to crisis events (Hobfoll, 2011; Hobfoll, Halbesleben, Neveu, & Westman, 2018). We chose COR theory as our organizing framework for a few reasons. First, COR theory is a theory of stress responses that has generated a wealth of research supporting its core tenets. Second, COR theory has been used extensively in organizational psychology and other leadership-adjacent disciplines, generating research findings that are particularly relevant to our topic. Finally, we find COR theory to be a validating and humanizing theory in that it emphasizes the actual losses and threats people experience during crises. It conceptualizes crises as understandably distressing and culturally meaningful rather than focusing on a person's interpretations of events as primarily responsible for their crisis-related distress. Thus, COR theory can help researchers and practitioners to avoid the pitfall of oversimplifying or minimizing the profound nature of personal crisis and proposing easy, quick-fix solutions (e.g., simple "positive thinking") while providing a useful framework for studying and understanding crises and their impacts. Figure 2.1 summarizes the key principles of COR theory, described in the following sections.

The basic tenet of COR theory is that people strive to "obtain, retain, foster, and protect those things they centrally value" (Hobfoll et al., 2018, p. 106). In COR

PRINCIPLES AND COROLLARIES OF CONSERVATION OF RESOURCES THEORY

Basic COR theory tenet: Individuals (and groups) strive to obtain, retain, foster, and protect those things they centrally value.

Principle 1: Primacy of loss principle. Resource loss is disproportionately more salient than resource gain.

Principle 2: Resource investment principle. People must invest resources in order to protect against resource loss, recover from losses, and gain resources.

Principle 3: Gain paradox principle. Resource gain increases in salience in the context of resource loss. That is, when resource loss circumstances are high, resource gains become more important-they gain in value.

Principle 4: Desperation principle. When people's resources are outstretched or exhausted, they enter a defensive mode to preserve the self which is often defensive, aggressive, and may become irrational.

Resource Caravans and Resource Caravan Passageways Principles

Resource caravans: Resources do not exist individually but travel in packs, or caravans, for both individuals and organizations

Resource caravan passageways: People's resources exist in ecological conditions that either foster and nurture or limit and block resource creation and sustenance.

Corollaries

Corollary 1: Those with greater resources are less vulnerable to resource loss and more capable of resource gain. Conversely, individuals and organizations who lack resources are more vulnerable to resource loss and less capable of resource gain.

Corollary 2: Resource loss cycles. Because resource loss is more powerful than resource gain, and because stress occurs when resources are lost, at each iteration of the stress spiral individuals and organizations have fewer resources to offset resource loss, and these loss spirals gain in momentum as well as magnitude.

Corollary 3: Resource gain spirals. Because resource gain is both of less magnitude and slower than resource loss, resource gain spirals tend to be weak and develop slowly.

FIGURE 2.1 Principles and Corollaries of Conservation of Resources Theory

Source: Republished with permission of *Annual Review of Organizational Psychology and Organizational Behavior* from "Conservation of resources in the organizational context: The reality of resources and their consequences" by Stevan E. Hobfoll, Jonathon Halbesleben, Jean-Pierre Neveu, and Mina Westman volume 5, 2018; permission conveyed through Copyright Clearance Center, Inc.

theory, these "valued things" are referred to as "resources" and include tangible object resources (a car, a computer), condition resources (employment, marriage), personal resources (skills, optimism), and energy resources (money, knowledge). Resources are those things necessary for survival or accomplishing major goals, and they are recognized as important and valuable by people who share the same culture. To be effective, leaders need to accrue and mobilize a wide array of resources (Byrne et al., 2014). For example, a manager of a department may need to use effective communication skills (personal resource) and tap his or her network of relationships in the field (condition resource) to gain additional knowledge (energy resource) about which type of technology (object resource) his or her workers will need to accomplish the department's goals. If the manager is successful, the workers view the manager as more competent and trustworthy (condition resource), and the department may perform better and generate more revenue (energy resource). Importantly, because investment of resources is necessary to acquire more resources, a crisis that threatens any aspect of the leader's resources – personal or professional – can impact the leader's functioning and her or his ability to retain and obtain resources.

Severe personal crises involve loss or threat of loss to more than one resource and more than one type of resource. COR theory contends that the degree of resource loss or threatened loss is often the best predictor of distress in response to a crisis and of subsequent difficulty in coping with and adapting to it (Hobfoll, 2011). Furthermore, COR theory's "Principle 1: Primacy of Loss" states that, "Resource loss is disproportionately more salient than resource gain" (Hobfoll et al., 2018, p. 106). This "losses loom larger than gains" principle is supported by extensive scholarship in psychology and behavioral economics, showing that in decision-making situations, people tend to be loss averse, valuing avoidance of loss more highly than the opportunity to obtain benefits (Kahneman & Tversky, 1979). Thus, compared to gains, the impact of losses is larger in magnitude, occurs more rapidly, and may gain in momentum (accelerate) over time (Hobfoll et al., 2018). In a sense, losses and threatened losses experienced during a crisis are "felt" more strongly and perceived as more urgent and attention-grabbing than gains or opportunities for gain.

Thus, people are motivated to stem the tide of impending loss or prevent it altogether and, to do so, they must invest additional resources. "Principle 2: Resource Investment Principle" states that, "People must invest resources in order to protect against resource loss, recover from losses, and gain resources" (Hobfoll et al., 2018, p. 106). For example, a leader in crisis may need to devote increased time and attention (energy resources) to dealing with the consequences of a personal crisis (e.g., planning a funeral; serving as executor for a parent's estate), which may leave fewer resources available for their leadership role. One implication of this principle is that crises are rarely single events that require only one type of resource invested over a short period of time. COR theory Corollary 2 describes "loss spirals" whereby initial losses require additional and accelerating amounts of resources over time. Thus, personal crises are often best understood as sequences of events and losses that require different types of resource investment at different times. For example, a child's health or mental health crisis may require an initial heavy investment of resources to stabilize the situation, but longer-term, even lifelong, resource investment may be needed to help the child thrive. Furthermore, the expenditure of resources (e.g., for caregiving) may create other resource deficits (e.g., burnout) that, in the long run, will need their own resource infusions. Thus, leaders and researchers who study leadership during personal crisis should view a personal crisis as an unfolding set of events over time – not a one-shot event with a simple solution that brings a tidy resolution.

But do leaders' personal crises actually have the potential to influence the health and profitability of their organizations? What evidence is there that the impact of a personal crisis on the leader has any relevance beyond the personal? An intriguing pair of studies suggests that when CEOs experience personal crises, the operating profitability of the firm is negatively impacted. Bennedsen, Pérez-González, and Wolfenzon (2010) merged data from all limited liability firms in Denmark from 1993 to 2003 with Danish civil registry data so that they could identify which firms experienced deaths of CEOs or the CEO's immediate family members.[1] Most

---

1 A total of 5,440 CEOs experienced family death (total N = 75,647) in the eight-year period covered by the study, which is 7.2% of the sample. Thus, .9% of CEOs per year experienced the stressful life event of death of a close family member, suggesting that such events, over time, are not uncommon for executive leaders.

pertinent to the effects of a personal crisis, they found that the death of a CEO's relative was associated with a significant decline in performance as measured by industry-adjusted operating return on assets, the ratio of gross earnings to value of firm assets, during the two-year window after the event compared to two years before the event. Similar to the broader literature on the relative stressfulness of life events (Dohrenwend, Askenasy, Krasnoff, & Dohrenwend, 1978), the effect was most pronounced when the CEO lost his or her spouse or child. Consistent with COR theory, the authors speculate that the effect of family death may occur because of the leader's reduced time and attention devoted to the firm – in other words, he or she must divert resources in order to cope with the crisis.

These authors subsequently analyzed the effect of CEO hospitalization[2] in the Danish limited liability firm dataset using national medical registry data (Bennedsen, Pérez-González, & Wolfenzon, 2012). They found that firms whose CEOs were hospitalized for more than five days had a significantly lower ratio of gross earnings to value of firm assets, underperforming industry standards by 1.2 percentage points and representing reductions in operating profitability of 14%. Interestingly, similar life events in firm board members in the family death study and non-CEO senior executives in the hospitalization study were not associated with differences in profitability, suggesting that the impact of personal crises on the top leader in the company may be associated with the largest organization-wide impacts. Taken together, these studies suggest that when CEOs understandably divert resources to manage their own illnesses or the loss of a close relative, such diversion has the potential to impact the broader organization. Yet COR theory suggests that such impacts are not the inevitable result of stressful events.

As discussed earlier, COR theory holds that stressful events produce losses of resources and that resource loss is more salient than resource gain. However, despite this imbalance in the perceived importance of loss vs. gain, COR theory holds that the salience of gains increases in the context of losses. "Principle 3: Gain Paradox Principle" states that, "resource gain increases in salience in the context of resource loss" (Hobfoll et al., 2018, p. 106). In other words, in situations that involve heavy resource losses, the relative value of gains or infusions of resources increases. For example, in a situation where a leader is struggling with losses of time, money, optimism, and physical energy when facing a serious illness, resource gains such as social support from family or coworkers or an increase in work flexibility take on a higher value than they would under conditions of resource stability. Thus, the Gain Paradox Principle suggests that, although losses will continue to be more salient than gains, under stressful conditions, resource gains take on increased power and influence. For example, research on burnout (further described next) has shown that job resources have their most powerful effects on motivation and engagement under conditions of high job demands (Bakker & Demerouti, 2016). Furthermore, resource gain spirals are possible (Corollary 3); however, they develop much more slowly than resource loss spirals.

---

2 A statistic of 6.5% of CEOs per year experienced at least one day of hospitalization, and 21% per year experienced five days or more.

What happens to the leader when, despite their efforts to shore up resource loss by investing other resources, their stores of resources are outstripped by the demands of the personal crisis? COR theory "Principle 4, the Desperation Principle," states that, "When people's resources are outstretched or exhausted, they enter a defensive mode to preserve the self which is often defensive, aggressive, and may become irrational" (Hobfoll et al., 2018, p. 106). In other words, when resources are severely depleted, emotion and motivation tend to shift to preserving what few resources are left rather than investing additional resources in problem-solving, looking for creative solutions to problems, or working to gain additional resources. Indeed, pervasive negative emotion is associated with a narrowed focus of attention to threat cues that can reduce a leader's ability to engage the self-regulation resources needed to lead effectively – resources that are particularly needed during difficult leadership tasks (Collins & Jackson, 2015). The resource-depleted leader may withdraw, spend less time investing energy and attention in his or her team members, become extremely risk-averse, or give up on certain aspects of his or her leadership role altogether.

This state of affairs is similar to the condition of "burnout," which has been studied extensively in the organizational literature. Burnout is characterized by emotional exhaustion related to one's work, depersonalization and disengagement from others at work, and reduced work self-efficacy and sense of accomplishment (Maslach & Jackson, 1984). Relating burnout to COR theory, as work stresses and crises deplete a worker's resources, additional resources must be recruited to cope with the loss, eventually leading to depletion, desperation, and burnout (Bakker & Demerouti, 2016; Harms, Credé, Tynan, Leon, & Jeung, 2017). Although we are not aware of any studies examining the contributions of leaders' personal crises to depletion and burnout, it seems reasonable to expect that the resource depletion inherent in coping with such personal life stressors would impact the resources available to the leader to successfully execute this resource-demanding role.

Importantly, research on burnout has also shown that job resources (e.g., autonomy, social support) can buffer the impact of job demands (e.g., work overload and work-home conflict) on the exhaustion and disengagement that characterize burnout (Bakker, 2005). These findings raise the possibility that availability of key resources for leaders might also serve to buffer the negative effects of a personal crisis on their health, motivation, and other capacities, which would be consistent with COR Theory Corollary 1: "Those with greater resources are less vulnerable to resource loss and more capable of resource gain" (Hobfoll et al., 2018, p. 106).

Leaders under stress: what do we know?

Resource loss as a result of coping with personal crisis, in combination with the self-preservation-oriented posture described in the Desperation Principle, may leave the leader in crisis with fewer resources to manage the demands of leadership. The interpersonal demands of effective but effortful leadership practices, such as inspirational motivation or individual consideration, may be particularly vulnerable to falling by the wayside (Byrne et al., 2014; Collins & Jackson, 2015). Although we were unable to locate any studies that directly address the question of whether leaders in personal crisis are more vulnerable to the effects of resource loss and the

Desperation Principle, a few studies have examined the relationship between work-related stress, burnout, or general psychological distress and leader behavior.

Harms and colleagues (2017) conducted a meta-analysis designed to examine the strength of the relationship between leadership and stress – both between leader stress and leader behavior and between leader behavior and team member stress. Most relevant to the current discussion, they found that, in five studies ($N = 492$), overall leader burnout was not related to transformational leadership behaviors ($r = 0.00$), although in two studies that reported burnout at the facet level ($N = 185$), all three facets of burnout were associated with less transformational leadership (emotional exhaustion $r = -.22$, depersonalization $r = -.20$, professional efficacy $r = -.43$). Leader work stress was related to more abusive supervision practices, although the relationship was stronger when both of these were self-reported by the leader (two studies, $N = 432, r = .34$) than when abusive supervision was reported by team members (three studies, $N = 471, r = .17$). In a separate meta-analysis, Zhang and colleagues (2016) found a small but significant relationship between leader stress and abusive supervision ($r = .16$). Thus, the available evidence points to a small association between leader stress/burnout and less positive and more negative leader behavior. Although the studies in this meta-analysis defined leader stress solely in terms of stress and burnout related to the workplace, leaders may also find it difficult to lead effectively when their resources are depleted by a personal crisis. However, the very small number of available studies suggests the need for more research and supports Harms et al.'s observation that there is a surprising lack of research on leader stress as an antecedent or contributor to leader behavior and effectiveness.

Likewise, Byrne and colleagues (2014) noted the surprising paucity of research on the relationship between leaders' psychological well-being and leader behaviors, speculating that there is perhaps an assumption that psychological distress in the leader does not impact his or her leadership, employees, or organization. Seeking to fill this gap, Byrne and colleagues (2014) specifically drew upon COR theory to study the relationship between leader resource depletion and transformational leadership and abusive supervision. They theorized that, in line with the Desperation Principle, leaders in a state of resource depletion would take a more passive and impersonal approach to leadership characterized by less transformational leadership. Similarly, they predicted that resource depletion might lower leader self-regulation, increasing vulnerability to abusive supervision practices. Byrne and colleagues (2014) used leaders' self-reported depression symptoms, anxiety, and workplace drinking as separate indicators of depleted resources. They found that, among 172 leader-team member pairs, each of these factors was separately related to lower transformational leadership ($r = -.31$ to $-.39$) and more abusive supervision ($r = .41$ to $.47$) as rated by the leaders' team members. These results suggest that the consequences of resource losses experienced during a personal crisis might reduce leader capacity to engage in effective practices, as suggested by COR theory.

To be clear, depletion of resources does not inevitably lead to compromised leadership nor is it the only condition that determines the occurrence of such extreme leader misbehavior as abusive supervision; yet, the presence of a depleted state may increase the risk for such behavior. Lam, Walter, and Huang (2017) found that increases in employee-rated abusive supervision in two studies – one in a manufacturing setting and the other in a customer service setting – were predicted by supervisors' emotional exhaustion, but only when combined with poorer employee performance (as rated by the supervisor) and the supervisor's self-reported tendency not to control her or his behavior strategically (a personal resource). Thus, leaders experiencing personal crises and resource loss as a result of a crisis may be more vulnerable to engaging in ineffective leadership practices – particularly if they are dealing with difficult employee behavior and tend to be less in control of their behavior to begin with.

In sum, the tenets of COR theory provide a framework for organizing, understanding, and investigating the effects of personal crises on leaders. Although research on this specific topic is virtually nonexistent, the tenets of COR theory and related studies on leaders suggest that personal crises have the potential to trigger resource losses that can accelerate, impacting the leader's ability to cope with the crisis and continue effective leadership. On the other hand, COR theory and research on successful coping, reviewed in the next section, also provide guidance for leaders wishing to enhance their resources and cope successfully with personal crises – even to learn and grow their organizational relationships and resources through the experience. For example, the Gain Paradox Principles means that even small gains in resources can have a meaningful impact when a person is in a state of resource loss – for example, small acts of kindness and social support can represent important resource gains to the person in crisis. In addition, Corollary 1 from COR theory states that those with more resources are less vulnerable to resource loss during a crisis. As such, leaders and organizations can build stores of specific object, condition, personal, and energy resources that can "shore up" the organization against the effects of resource loss when individuals – including leaders – inevitably experience personal crisis. We will review this and other key insights and principles from COR theory on building resource-resilient organizations in Chapters 4 and 6.

The science of effective coping

Recall that coping responses can be defined as a person's efforts to reduce the potential or actual harm or loss associated with a stressful event or efforts to reduce accompanying emotional distress. Because coping is a complex and highly contextual phenomenon, the study of coping has resulted in a dizzying array of proposals on how to categorize and study different coping strategies and their effects (see Skinner, Edge, Altman, & Sherwood, 2003). Here, we highlight two of the most frequent coping dimensions that have been used by researchers: problem- vs. emotion-focused coping and approach vs. avoidance coping (Figure 2.2). Although these ways of parsing coping responses do not provide a comprehensive account (Skinner & Zimmer-Gembeck, 2016), they do provide a user-friendly way of reflecting on key functions of coping for leaders in personal crises.

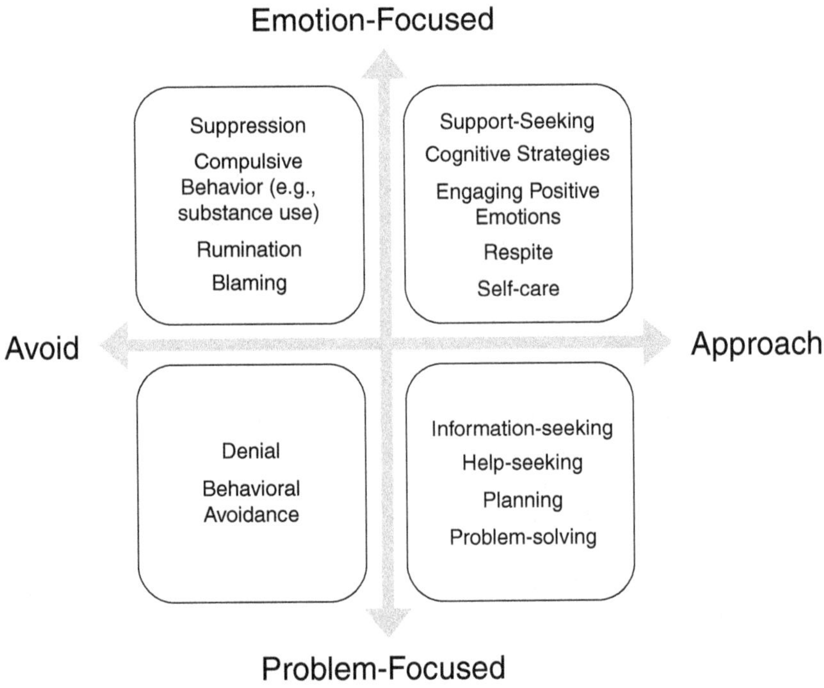

Emotion-Focused

FIGURE 2.2 Two Dimensions of Coping and Example Coping Responses

Problem- and emotion-focused coping

Problem-focused coping

The most long-standing distinction in modern coping research is coping that is problem-focused vs. emotion-focused (Lazarus & Folkman, 1984, as cited in Carver & Connor-Smith, 2010). This distinction focuses on the goal of the coping response. Problem-focused coping is directed at dealing with the threat or stressor to reduce or evade its impact. Examples of problem-focused coping include direct problem-solving efforts, seeking information or advice on how to handle the stressor, accumulating resources to prevent further loss, or making accommodations in other areas of life to facilitate adjustment to the stressor. Within problem-focused coping, researchers have sometimes distinguished between strategies directly targeted at controlling the stressor (primary control coping) and strategies meant to adjust or adapt to the presence of the stressor (accommodative coping) (Carver & Connor-Smith, 2010). For example, a leader facing a new cancer diagnosis may work closely with his or her medical team to rapidly determine a treatment plan while gathering as much information as possible to aid in decision-making (primary control coping). At the same time, he or she might request work schedule accommodations to enable attendance at scheduled medical appointments and to help accommodate the fatigue that comes along with chemotherapy treatments (accommodative coping). Yet both types of coping responses are directed at reducing the overall impact of the stressor itself, and both responses can be thought of as re-directing and deploying resources to stem the loss and potential loss associated with the stressor.

Emotion-focused coping

Emotion-focused coping responses are aimed at reducing or managing the distress associated with a stressful event. Emotions are complex responses to events that have physiological, cognitive, and behavioral components – in other words, emotional responses involve physical feelings, thoughts, and tendencies toward particular actions. As noted earlier at the outset of Chapter 1, emotions evolved as adaptations to particular kinds of threats and challenges to our ancestors, and each emotion can be associated with particular kinds of situations and responses. Emotions also serve an important interpersonal function, providing others around us with crucial information about what we need in a given situation (Lazarus, 2006). Emotions can also give the person experiencing them crucial information about what is needed and provide them with the motivation to take action – either to ensure their own well-being or the well-being of a relationship. As such, emotion researchers do not view emotions as "the opposite of" thinking and reason but as a complementary process that provides critical motivation for survival and preservation of resources. Furthermore, skillful management of one's own emotions and the emotions of others has been identified as a key skill for effective leaders (Collins & Jackson, 2015; Rajah, Song, & Arvey, 2011).

Distress experienced in response to a crisis may be emotional or physical and can cover a range of negative experiences that can shift and change over time. For example, a leader whose child is diagnosed with a serious illness may alternatively feel deeply fearful of the future, blindingly angry about the suffering the child must endure, and saddened by the loss of the future he or she had imagined for their healthy child. Particularly painful and distressing may be intense "self-focused emotions" such as shame and guilt, which include components of self-blame and a sense of failure to live up to one's own ideals or moral imperatives (Lazarus, 2006). Further complicating the emotional life of humans in distress is the fact that we are also capable of feeling shame or guilt about experiencing particular emotions and thoughts. For example, if the parent in the previous example learns that his or her child will lose the ability to have children in the future and feels sad at the thought of losing the opportunity for grandchildren someday, he or she might judge this sadness to be selfish or inappropriate, triggering feelings of guilt.

It is important to recognize that emotional responses are often associated with one's appraisal of the situation – that is, their assessment or interpretation about the degree of threat posed by the stressor combined with an assessment of their ability to cope (Lazarus, 2006). In other words, the cognitive filter through which a person views the situation can have an important impact on his or her emotional response. For example, if the leader in the previous example has little information about the child's illness and assumes that the prognosis is poor and, simultaneously, judges himself or herself ill-equipped emotionally to handle the situation, this leader is likely to experience more intense fear and helplessness regarding the situation than a leader who has more accurate information and a more optimistic appraisal of their coping resources. The role of appraisals in emotions and coping is important to recognize because some coping strategies rely on gaining additional information or changing one's appraisal of the situation or one's own resources as a way of reducing and managing distress.

Yet it is also important to recognize that, for most major personal crises, the stressors involved would be universally distressing regardless of one's appraisal because they actually involve profound resource loss or threatened loss (Hobfoll, 2011). As such, it is important to avoid "blaming the victim" by assuming that simple "positive thinking" or even reappraisal on its own will be sufficient to manage the powerful distress triggered in response to a personal crisis (Hobfoll et al., 2018). However, reappraising one's potentially catastrophic thoughts about a situation can be an effective emotion regulation strategy (Aldao, Nolen-Hoeksema, & Schweizer, 2010).

Emotion-focused coping responses include a broad array of conscious and nonconscious strategies aimed at reducing or managing distress, including efforts to escape the emotions (distraction, avoidance, suppression, denial, wishful thinking, social withdrawal); self-soothe (substance use, self-care, seeking emotional support from others); change one's way of thinking (re-appraisal, acceptance); or "think one's way out" (worry, rumination). Although some emotion-focused coping strategies are more strongly associated with adaptive outcomes than others, as discussed next, taken together emotion-focused coping is not considered any "worse" or "better" than problem-focused coping. It is widely recognized that these processes occur simultaneously and often complement one another (Lazarus, 2006). For example, problem-focused strategies that actually reduce the threat associated with the stressor will have the effect of reducing emotional distress, while coping strategies that effectively reduce negative emotions and increase positive emotions may enhance one's ability to think through problems strategically and formulate creative and effective solutions (Fredrickson & Joiner, 2018). In COR theory, positive emotions, effective emotion-focused coping skills, and other positive psychological qualities such as strong self-efficacy and optimism are considered personal resources that are useful in coping with and preventing resource loss (Hobfoll, 2011). As such, consistent with COR Theory Corollary 1, providing experiences that help leaders and team members to build emotional and esteem resources and creating supports to help them deploy such resources can make them more resilient to the resource losses that occur during personal crises. Such capacities can be considered critical resources, not just feel-good luxuries.

As mentioned previously with regard to COR theory, in the context of large resource losses, small resource gains take on increased salience. In addition, although loss spirals escalate and accelerate more quickly while gain spirals develop more slowly, there is growing evidence that gain spirals and their associated positive emotions can have a crucial impact during times of coping with crisis. Importantly, positive emotional experiences and gains can coexist with distress and loss, and this coexistence can have a meaningful impact, even in the midst of a crisis.

Perhaps not surprisingly, research on emotions in clinical psychology has focused largely on the impact of negative emotions while for many years largely ignoring the function and effects of positive emotions (Fredrickson & Joiner, 2018). Yet, like negative emotions, positive emotions have physiological, cognitive, and behavioral components (physical feelings, thoughts, and action tendencies) and probably represent adaptations that enhanced the survival of our ancestors, which may be linked to their functions today. For example, in her "Broaden and Build" theory of positive emotions, Fredrickson (1998) proposes that positive emotions share in common the effect of "broadening thought-action tendencies," including what we pay attention to, what we think about, who we associate with, and the extent to which we are willing to engage in a wider array of activities. By contrast, as noted earlier, negative emotions and "loss spirals" are associated with a narrowing of attention focus, thought, and action so that responses may become inflexible or irrational (see Desperation Principle, discussed earlier). The longer-term function of the more expansive thought-action tendencies associated with positive emotions is to build emotional, personal, social, and energy resources over time. For example, Fredrickson describes joy as being associated with a thought-action tendency of "free activation" and playfulness, interest as associated with the tendency to explore, and love with the tendency to form deeper attachments with others. She further proposes that the function, or ultimate result, of these broadened thought-action tendencies is the building of resources: building skills through play, building knowledge through exploration, and building social connections through the formation of attachments.

Studies based on the Broaden and Build model of positive emotions have demonstrated that even mild, everyday positive emotions are associated with greater cognitive flexibility in devising solutions to problems that, in turn, are associated with a greater experience of positive emotions over time (Fredrickson & Joiner, 2002, 2018). Thus, not unlike COR theory, the Broaden and Build theory identifies a process whereby gain spirals may develop over time when positive emotions broaden attention, thoughts, and actions toward the development of resource gains that potentiate additional resource gains.[3] Based on this research, leaders should consider the role of everyday positive emotional experiences in replenishing what is lost during a personal crisis and how these experiences may set the occasion for resource gains over time.

Researchers have begun to test a wide array of strategies for enhancing positive emotions that might be useful as coping strategy interventions. Moskowitz

---

3 Recall that, in COR theory, social supports, self-efficacy, coping skills, and knowledge can all be conceptualized as resources.

(2011) reviewed evidence for 11 different strategies for enhancing positive emotions and concluded that interventions targeting positive emotions are "feasible, acceptable, and in many cases efficacious and that many different approaches hold promise for increasing positive affect" (p. 407). For example, interventions based on scheduling and engaging in positive or pleasant activities are an integral part of many evidence-based treatments for depression (Cuijpers, van Straten, & Warmerdam, 2007). Furthermore, the way that positive events are experienced or re-experienced can enhance their effect on positive emotions. "Savoring" refers to an expressive experience where a person talks about, marks, or remembers and reflects on a positive event. Savoring is associated with enhanced positive emotions, suggesting that paying attention to and vividly remembering (but not over-analyzing) positive experiences can allow a person to extract a greater emotional benefit from such positive events (Moskowitz, 2011). Other strategies that may be useful in enhancing positive emotions include enhancing gratitude, engaging in acts of kindness, reappraising the situation, setting attainable goals, focusing on strengths, meditation, exercise/yoga, engaging with humor, and practicing forgiveness. We are not suggesting that leaders in crisis engage with all of these strategies, but the list represents an array of options for enhancing positive emotions in daily life throughout a crisis. As with all coping, leaders must find the subset of strategies that works well for them and adjust their approach over time as the situation dictates. In sum, leaders should consider including attention to emotions – including positive emotions – as part of an effective coping resource portfolio.

Approach vs. avoidance coping

Another important distinction in research on coping is that of approach coping vs. avoidance coping. This way of thinking about coping emphasizes the function of the response – that is, what the results of the coping action are with respect to the stressful event or distressing emotions. As the names suggests, approach coping responses result in the person in crisis engaging more directly with the stressor or resulting emotions, while avoidance coping results in pulling back from the situation or emotions. For example, a leader going through a lengthy divorce proceeding may attend meetings with her lawyer and attend counseling sessions to address her thoughts and feelings about the event (approach coping) while also putting off completing legal paperwork in a timely manner, instead spending time "zoning out" and watching Netflix rather than thinking about the situation (avoidance coping). As this example illustrates, like problem- and emotion-focused coping, the constellation of a person's coping responses often includes both approach and avoidance responses at different times and with respect to different aspects of the crisis. Each of these types of responses can serve important functions depending on the situation. Yet research has shown that when a person's repertoire of coping responses becomes dominated predominantly by avoidance responses, they are more likely to experience ongoing difficulties.

Approach coping

Approach coping responses involve the person in crisis dealing directly with the stressful situation or distressing emotions he or she is experiencing – a process that Skinner and Zimmer-Gembeck (2016, p. 43) refer to as "constructive engagement." Most problem-focused coping responses would also be approach responses, since problem-focused coping involves dealing directly with the threat or stressor to reduce its impact. Problem-solving, seeking information or advice, asking for help from others, and making and executing plans to cope with a crisis all require the person in crisis to approach the situation physically, mentally, and emotionally. Engaging in approach coping is often necessary for ultimately resolving the crisis and ending the resource losses associated with it. Yet problem-focused approach coping can be particularly difficult when the act of approaching and engaging triggers distressing thoughts and emotions. Going to the chemotherapy infusion center provokes fear and conditioned nausea. Planning a deceased parent's funeral triggers painful reminders and may require interacting with difficult family members. Attending therapy sessions or medical appointments requires thinking and talking about what is painful. In such situations, skillful methods for managing negative emotion in the service of approach coping may be required.

Many emotion-focused coping responses could also be described as approach coping, provided they promote constructive engagement. Emotion-focused approach coping can be described as responses that aid in the constructive processing, expression, and regulation of distressing crisis-related emotions (Stanton, 2011). A variety of different coping responses might fall under the heading of emotion-focused approach coping. Reappraisal[4] involves "cognitively transforming the situation so as to alter its emotional impact" (Gross, 1998, p. 284). For example, a leader going through a relationship breakup might come to view the event as not only a painful, stressful time of loss but also a life transition, a learning experience, or an opportunity to explore new possibilities. Such reappraisals may not erase painful emotions, but they may reduce emotional intensity or allow for other more positive emotions and actions to co-occur in the presence of distress. Acceptance, often facilitated by mindfulness strategies, is the intentional willingness to experience negative thoughts and feelings without trying to push them away or engage in other problematic behaviors to avoid them (Hayes, Strosahl, & Wilson, 2012). Efforts to increase positive emotions, mentioned earlier, could also be described as emotion approach strategies because they are directed at intentionally regulating emotional experiences in the face of a crisis situation. Strategies such as engaging in pleasant events and even what one might call "strategic distraction"[5] during times of high emotional distress

---

4 Because depression and anxiety are associated with overly pessimistic interpretations of and predictions about events as well as underestimation of one's coping resources, reappraising a situation in a more balanced and emotionally helpful manner is a key skill in cognitive-behavioral therapy for these disorders.

5 Distraction as an approach coping strategy does present some definitional difficulties because, on its face, distraction seems like a way to avoid negative emotion. By "strategic distraction," however, we are referring specifically to intentional efforts to move attention away from a distressing situation when further attention to that situation serves no current constructive purpose.

can represent methods of constructive engagement with emotions during a personal crisis. For example, a leader might prioritize maintaining his regular exercise schedule during a crisis – despite the time it consumes – because he is aware that exercise functions to help regulate his emotions as well as promote physical health.

Importantly, many approach coping strategies are neither easy to execute nor are they "natural" responses that occur in the absence of prior learning experiences to support them. Rather, it is only "natural" to want to avoid what is painful. The capacity to cope skillfully with a personal crisis is itself a resource that is developed as a result of other resource-rich experiences and contexts, such as a childhood free from trauma, a strong and supportive family, safe and effective schools, and the availability of mentors to model and teach effective coping skills (Hobfoll, 2011). As such, the skills and emotional resources necessary to engage in approach coping can be considered important resources within a COR framework – resources that can be actively enhanced and supported by wise organizations.

Help-seeking and social support

Help-seeking is a specific approach-oriented coping strategy that deserves special mention due to its importance in the coping research literature and its prominence in the coping responses reported by our participants in Study 2. Why is help-seeking such a prominent and important coping strategy? One reason may be that others can provide access to a variety of different resources that can help in stemming losses associated with a personal crisis (Wills, 1987) (see Box 2.1). People in crisis may seek concrete instrumental support from others in coping with a crisis, such as material help, financial assistance, or support in obtaining access to other resources. For example, a leader in crisis may obtain a personal referral from a colleague with prominent social connections to a highly regarded medical clinic or prominent attorney (condition resources) or may be able to stay in a family friend's vacation condo when traveling out of town for medical treatment (object resources). People in crisis may also seek informational support, seeking knowledge (an energy resource) to help them problem-solve with respect to the crisis. For example, a leader whose child is experiencing a serious illness might seek coping advice from parents of children who have experienced the same illness. People may also seek motivational support (personal resource) for their coping efforts, such as encouragement, reassurance, and help with reappraising a difficult situation. Finally, esteem or emotional support may be sought by people in crisis to remedy diminished self-worth, lowered self-efficacy, invalidation, a sense of disconnectedness, or to soothe negative emotions. Feeling heard, validated, worthy, and cared for by others can all be conceptualized as personal resources that can aid in coping and may need to be replenished throughout the coping experience.

Interestingly, research has shown that the belief or perception that social support is available is particularly important and can have greater effects on well-being than actual receipt of support (Taylor, 2011). In sum, effective help-seeking can give the person in crisis access to a wide array of resources that he or she might not otherwise be able to access, making effective help-seeking a crucial coping strategy, while the knowledge that such support is available represents a resource in its own right.

BOX 2.1 TYPES OF SOCIAL SUPPORT RESOURCES (WILLS, 1987; TAYLOR, 2011)

Instrumental Support – tangible assistance for coping with the crisis (services, financial support, other specific help)

Informational Support – knowledge or a new perspective that helps to determine a course of action for the crisis (advice, information on where to obtain resources)

Motivational Support – encouragement to continue coping efforts

Emotional (Esteem) Support – reassurance that the person in crisis is valued and cared for (e.g., that he or she is not alone)

Seeking social support, however, is not always effective. People in crisis may attempt to seek support from people who are unable or unwilling to give it. There may be a mismatch between the needs of the person in crisis and the type of support that is offered. Notably, in Study 1, unhelpful support from others was also among the most commonly mentioned less effective coping strategies for resolving the crisis, dealing with the crisis in the leadership role, and managing the crisis on one's own well-being. Not every person is capable of or willing to provide every kind of resource, and being "let down" or feeling invalidated by one's social network during a time of crisis can be a particularly painful experience. For example, research demonstrates that emotional support is most effective in the context of the closest relationships and that interactions in high-conflict relationships during times of crisis can exacerbate stress rather than decrease it (Taylor, 2011). In addition, "supportive" attempts in the workplace that call further attention to the stressful situation, that threaten the recipient's sense of autonomy, or are imposed and unwanted are associated with negative outcomes (Beehr, Bowling, & Bennett, 2010; Deelstra et al., 2003). We discuss in-organization support-seeking, disclosure, and related topics in Chapter 3, where we recommend that leaders in crisis strategically consider which types of social support they need and, importantly, which people are the best equipped to provide such resources. Importantly, there may be previously untapped resources and support available if the leader has the insight and willingness to access them.

Avoidance coping

Avoidance coping has the effect of helping the person in crisis escape from the threatening event or the distressing thoughts and emotions it provokes. As a short-term response, avoidance can be an effective way of temporarily "turning down the volume" on stressful experiences. In particular, unpleasant thoughts and emotions can motivate a natural process of pulling away from what is painful, and many avoidance responses are probably triggered by escape from such unpleasant internal experiences – a process referred to as "experiential avoidance" (Hayes et al., 2012). Avoidance coping can take a range of forms, including denial, minimizing, wishful thinking, and withdrawal from people and from activities and situations. In particular, people in crisis may refrain from taking steps necessary for effective problem-focused coping because taking those steps causes painful internal experiences, triggering experiential avoidance responses. For example, when considering disclosing a crisis to his staff in order to make supportive work arrangements, a leader feels embarrassment about his situation and has thoughts of being looked down upon by the employees, which prompts him to avoid seeking support. Human beings can be quite creative in devising ways to avoid distressing emotions and, to complicate matters, almost any behavior can serve an avoidance function. Using substances, eating high-calorie foods, sexual encounters, excessive use of technology – even seemingly "positive" behaviors such as exercise or socializing with friends – can all represent problematic avoidance coping if they have the function of allowing the person to escape from situations and experiences that are necessary to encounter in the process of coping with a personal crisis. Some other "mental" coping behaviors also seem to serve an avoidance function. For example, excessive worry can prolong emotional distress and prevent a person from either taking direct action that might address the stressful situation or prevent her or him from engaging in more effective emotion-focused coping strategies. (Worry can be quite pernicious in that it may sometimes masquerade as "planning," which is another example of a seemingly "positive" behavior actually serving an unhelpful avoidance function.) Another category of "mental" avoidant coping behavior is rumination, wherein a person repetitively focuses on his or her experience of negative emotion and tries to analyze its causes and consequences (Nolen-Hoeksema, Wisco, & Lyubomirsky, 2008). Similar to worry, excessive rumination may interfere with problem-solving and other approach coping efforts.

Notably, the avoidance coping responses just described bear a striking resemblance to the disengagement aspect of "burnout" in the organizational behavior literature and the outcomes of the Desperation Principle from COR theory – when resources are severely depleted after repeated loss cycles, people are more likely to engage in responses aimed at preserving what little they have left rather than approaching problems or emotions in a way that would require more resources. And in the context of loss spirals, avoidance responses may seem to make sense in the short term because potential gain spirals develop slowly, and thus potential gains are far away in time. In sum, it is important to recognize that pervasive avoidant coping may be both a symptom of resource depletion (Skinner & Zimmer-Gembeck, 2016) and a contributing factor in the failure to recover from resource loss.

How can leaders cope most effectively?

Multiple factors influence the outcome of successful coping with personal crisis. For example, a classic study that followed nearly 500 participants over the course of one year found that, in addition to the severity of stressors playing a role, a "resistance to stress" score composed of personal resources (easy-going personality, self-confidence), family support, and less use of avoidant coping predicted lower depression symptoms and, for women, fewer physical symptoms (Holahan & Moos, 1986). The study illustrates that multiple factors influence successful coping and these vary from person to person. Yet, coping research has identified important general patterns that predict more effective and less effective coping.

(Frequent) avoidance coping is to be avoided

As described earlier, avoidance coping functions to allow the person in crisis to escape from the threatening event or the distressing thoughts and emotions it provokes, and almost any behavior might function as avoidance, depending on the situation. Higher frequency of avoidant coping behavior has been shown to predict poorer outcomes when people are coping with a variety of stressful life events – for example, severe injury and interpersonal violence (Littleton, Horsley, John, & Nelson, 2007), HIV (Moskowitz, Hult, Bussolari, & Acree, 2009), and prostate cancer (Roesch et al., 2005). As reported earlier, our own Study 1 participants mentioned several avoidant coping responses as less helpful to their well-being and to resolving the crisis. There are several reasons why people who predominantly respond to a personal crisis with avoidance might be expected to have less favorable outcomes. First, when coping with a personal crisis, experiencing certain situations and emotions is often necessary in order to stem resource losses and solve problems. By chronically avoiding, the problem may get worse. For example, a leader who avoids recommended medical treatments and minimizes the severity of the problem in an effort to escape anxiety or reduce the anxiety of those around them may experience disease progression as a result of the avoidance strategies. When avoidant coping responses get in the way of needed approach strategies, they become more problematic than palliative.

Second, behaviors that are being used as avoidance tactics can, themselves, have problematic consequences. For example, heavy drinking, substance use, and both over-eating and under-eating behaviors that may help to ease negative emotions in the short term can become so frequent and impairing that they can constitute their own psychological disorders. Social withdrawal diminishes access to activities and social supports that might provide crucial resources for successful coping. Worry and rumination can be distracting, making it difficult to devote attentional resources to other pursuits. Even avoidance of distressing thoughts by denial or suppression can paradoxically make such thoughts even more intrusive (Wegner, Schneider, Carter, & White, 1987). (See what happens to the frequency of thoughts about white bears if you actively try NOT to think about white bears!)

Because avoidance tactics can block more effective coping responses and create problems of their own, high rates of avoidance in response to negative emotion may make emotional issues worse, not better. In a meta-analysis examining the relationship between six different emotion coping strategies and different forms of clinical distress, rumination and avoidance were the approaches most strongly related to anxiety (r = .42 and .37, respectively) and depression (r = .55 and .48) (Aldao et al., 2010). This means that if a person habitually thinks about the self-focused causes and negative effects of problems over and over (e.g., worrying or brooding) or avoids thinking about or dealing with important situations because of the negative emotional responses they provoke (avoidance), they are more at risk for anxiety and depression. If leaders find themselves unable to break out of cycles of negative, painful, and unproductive thoughts, this may leave them with fewer cognitive resources to devote to problem-solving regarding the crisis, engaging in leadership activities, or engaging in resource-restoring self-care activities. In addition, leaders who find themselves disengaging from necessary thoughts, activities, and relationships due to the provocation of painful emotions may also find that – over time – this avoidance impairs their ability to function. In addition, people may engage in other behaviors as a form of avoidance – such as substance use, excessive technology use, or other compulsive behaviors that allow one to "zone out" but can create their own problems over time. Leaders who find themselves drawn into such cycles of avoidance should seek help in finding alternative coping strategies that may not immediately reduce all emotional distress but, in the long run, may be more likely to resolve the crisis and restore the leader to health and constructive engagement.

Approach, with (self) care

Higher rates of coping strategies that promote constructive engagement have been associated with more favorable outcomes (Skinner & Zimmer-Gembeck, 2016). Approach-oriented strategies such as problem-solving, seeking social support, and reappraisal of situations and stressors have been associated with more successful coping and better emotional and physical outcomes (Aldao et al., 2010; Moskowitz et al., 2009; Roesch et al., 2005). Importantly, since approaching a situation through problem-solving or other strategies might actually increase the experience of negative emotion or physical strain, a problem-focused approach may need to be balanced with intentional emotion-focused strategies. For example, a leader who is expending resources (time, energy) in making arrangements for the long-term care of his medically vulnerable parent and recruiting help from other family members (problem-focused approach coping) might wisely keep up with his exercise and sleep schedules because he knows these activities typically soothe the anxiety, frustration, and sadness that arise during the course of addressing the problem. An executive going through a divorce may attend weekly therapy sessions, despite the immediate negative emotions they provoke, because she knows they will help her problem-solve and reappraise the situation. She might then wisely engage in the habit of a trip to the movies on the evenings of her therapy sessions because this allows her to experience rejuvenating positive emotions. (Perhaps she even joins a sci-fi fan meet-up and builds a network of new social supports.)

Responses from leaders in Study 2 are consistent with the research on the importance of approach-oriented strategies that are focused not just on problem-solving but also on managing emotions to promote well-being. As described earlier in the chapter, 71% of participants endorsed at least one cognitive strategy, such as engaging in reappraisal or calling to mind positive memories, as an effective strategy for them during the crisis. Sixty-one percent of participants endorsed at least one effective self-care strategy related to physical and personal well-being. Seventy-one percent also endorsed the effectiveness of some type of short- or long-term respite, while 70% reported that engagement in non-crisis activities (work, hobbies) had helped them preserve their well-being. It is interesting and important to note that strategies such as respite and engagement in other activities can "look like" avoidance responses. However, when coping strategies such as distraction and alternative engagement in non-stressor-related activities help to manage emotions effectively, support approach-oriented coping efforts, and do not produce problematic consequences, then they may help people restore important resources.

Thus, in the language of COR theory, although approach coping may require an additional investment of resources, wisely executed approach coping responses may also generate "gain cycles," such as increases in positive emotion, interpersonal connection, and new ways of viewing the world and one's self (personal resources). (Recall that the Gain Paradox Principle states that small infusions of resources can have disproportionate positive impacts when resources are low.) The field of psychology has increasingly recognized the growth and reorganization potential of coping with stressful life events and personal crises. As the noted stress and resilience scholar, Richard Lazarus, observed:

> Stress is, in effect, not necessarily a negative force. It can mobilize us to achieve more than we believed could be accomplished, and it can even lead to a greater appreciation of life. From crisis, too, can come a reorganization of our lives in ways that leave us more productive, engaged, and satisfied than before the crisis.
>
> *(Lazarus, 2006, p. 20)*

Experiencing such positive, life-affirming outcomes from a personal crisis is by no means a guarantee. Yet, current research on coping and the glimpses of insight from the leaders in our studies suggest that thoughtful, skillful, socially supported responses to personal crisis may increase the likelihood of regaining lost resources and (possibly) acquiring new ones (see Chapter 5).

"Organized, flexible, constructive"

Skinner and Zimmer-Gembeck (2016, p. 44) recently described what is known about effective coping using three adjectives: "organized, flexible, and constructive." They note that, when a person's coping seems to be disorganized, rigid, and habitual, this may be a sign that he or she has become overwhelmed by the stressor – in other words, that the person is experiencing resource depletion and desperation. Leaders who can reflect on their habitual ways of coping, assess the more and less effective aspects of those strategies, and remain open and flexible to integrating active problem- and emotion-focused strategies – including seeking out high-quality social support – may find themselves better able to cope with and reverse the resource losses inherent in the experience of a personal crisis. Because each crisis is a unique, evolving chain of events that requires changing resources over time, leaders must remain flexible and even entrepreneurial in their coping strategies with respect to their team members and their own well-being. Importantly, COR theory reveals that emotional health and social support are not simply pleasant "extras" when it comes to leader effectiveness during a crisis. They are crucial resources that may allow a leader to cope more effectively with a crisis. Wise leaders might also consider ways in which their organizations could be structured to provide resources to leaders and team members when or, ideally, before the onset of a personal crisis (Chapters 4 and 6).

Finally, leaders or practitioners who find the ideas in this final section of the chapter helpful (i.e., cognitive and behavioral approaches to coping and emotion regulation) may wish to learn more about cognitive-behavioral therapy (CBT), a family of therapy approaches from which many of these ideas are drawn. More information about CBT, including a therapist directory, can be obtained from the Association for Behavioral and Cognitive Therapies at www.abct.org.

Leaders coping with personal crisis: summary and conclusions

- Coping responses are attempts to avoid or reduce the impact of the crisis or effects on resulting negative emotions. People use different strategies throughout the evolution of a crisis, and there is no strictly "correct" or "incorrect" way to cope with a given crisis.
- Leaders in our studies used a variety of coping strategies to manage the impact of the crisis on their personal well-being, including seeking social support, staying engaged in non-crisis-related activities, respite, cognitive strategies, and self-care activities. A greater percentage of leaders sought help from informal sources than formal sources. Coping strategies that had not worked well included seeking and receiving unhelpful social support, avoiding thinking or talking about the crisis, and using substances.
- Conservation of Resources (COR) Theory is useful for understanding and studying the effects of personal crises on leaders and conceptualizes crises in terms of loss of a variety of resources. Losses trigger additional losses and, over time, the leader may become depleted, resulting in negative impacts on his or her ability to lead effectively.
- COR Theory also explains how infusions of resources during crisis events take on increased influence and importance. Leaders may receive resources, including instrumental and personal resources, from others in their organization.
- Two key dimensions of coping responses are problem- vs. emotion-focused coping and approach vs. avoidance coping. When people's coping responses are dominated by avoidant coping responses, they tend to experience poorer

outcomes. Leaders may need to engage in emotion-focused coping so that they can sustain their problem-focused coping efforts.

- Research on effective coping points to coping that is organized, flexible, and constructive. Leaders may need to flexibly employ different coping strategies throughout the evolution of a crisis and take an intentional, non-reflexive approach to handling it. Leaders should strive to be patient with themselves throughout the coping process and seek outside counsel and support for their efforts.

References

Aldao, A., Nolen-Hoeksema, S., & Schweizer, S. (2010). Emotion-regulation strategies across psychopathology: A meta-analytic review. *Clinical Psychology Review, 30*(2), 217–237. https://doi.org/10.1016/j.cpr.2009.11.004

American Psychological Association. (2019). The road to resilience. Retrieved August 4, 2019, from https://www.apa.org, website: https://www.apa.org/helpcenter/road-resilience

Bakker, A. B. (2005). Job resources buffer the impact of job demands on burnout. *Journal of Occupational Health Psychology, 10*(2), 170–180. https://doi.org/10.1037/1076-8998. 10.2.170

Bakker, A. B., & Demerouti, E. (2016). Job demands – Resources theory: Taking stock and looking forward. *Journal of Occupational Health Psychology, 22*(3), 273. https://doi.org/10.1037/ocp0000056

Beehr, T. A., Bowling, N. A., & Bennett, M. M. (2010). Occupational stress and failures of social support: When helping hurts. *Journal of Occupational Health Psychology, 15*(1), 45–59. https://doi.org/10.1037/a0018234

Bennedsen, M., Pérez-González, F., & Wolfenzon, D. (2010). *Do CEOs matter?* Retrieved from www0.gsb.columbia.edu/mygsb/faculty/research/pubfiles/3177/valueceos.pdf

Bennedsen, M., Pérez-González, F., & Wolfenzon, D. (2012). *Evaluating the impact of the boss: Evidence from CEO hospitalization events*. Retrieved from http://conference.iza.org/conference_files/Leadership_2012/perez-gonzalez_f7878.pdf

Byrne, A., Dionisi, A. M., Barling, J., Akers, A., Robertson, J., Lys, R., . . . Dupré, K. (2014). The depleted leader: The influence of leaders' diminished psychological resources on leadership behaviors. *The Leadership Quarterly, 25*(2), 344–357. https://doi.org/10.1016/j. leaqua.2013.09.003

Carver, C. S., & Connor-Smith, J. (2010). Personality and coping. *Annual Review of Psychology, 61*(1), 679–704. https://doi.org/10.1146/annurev.psych.093008.100352

Collins, M. D., & Jackson, C. J. (2015). A process model of self-regulation and leadership: How attentional resource capacity and negative emotions influence constructive and destructive leadership. *The Leadership Quarterly, 26*(3), 386–401. https://doi.org/10.1016/j. leaqua.2015.02.005

Cuijpers, P., van Straten, A., & Warmerdam, L. (2007). Behavioral activation treatments of depression: A meta-analysis. *Clinical Psychology Review, 27*(3), 318–326. https://doi.org/10.1016/j.cpr.2006.11.001

Deelstra, J. T., Peeters, M. C. W., Schaufeli, W. B., Stroebe, W., Zijlstra, F. R. H., & van Doornen, L. P. (2003). Receiving instrumental support at work: When help is not welcome. *Journal of Applied Psychology, 88*(2), 324–331. https://doi.org/10.1037/0021-9010.88.2.324

Dohrenwend, B. S., Askenasy, A. R., Krasnoff, L., & Dohrenwend, B. P. (1978). Exemplification of a method for scaling life events: The PERI Life Events Scale. *Journal of Health and Social Behavior, 19*(2), 205–229. https://doi.org/10.2307/2136536

Fredrickson, B. L. (1998). What good are positive emotions? *Review of General Psychology*, *2*(3), 300. https://doi.org/10.1037/1089-2680.2.3.300

Fredrickson, B. L., & Joiner, T. (2002). Positive emotions trigger upward spirals toward emotional well-being. *Psychological Science*, *13*(2), 172–175. https://doi.org/10.1111/1467-9280.00431

Fredrickson, B. L., & Joiner, T. (2018). Reflections on positive emotions and upward spirals. *Perspectives on Psychological Science*, *13*(2), 194–199. https://doi.org/10.1177/1745691617692106

Gross, J. J. (1998). The emerging field of emotion regulation: An integrative review. *Review of General Psychology*, *2*(3), 271. https://doi.org/10.1037/1089-2680.2.3.271

Harms, P. D., Credé, M., Tynan, M., Leon, M., & Jeung, W. (2017). Leadership and stress: A meta-analytic review. *The Leadership Quarterly*, *28*(1), 178–194. https://doi.org/10.1016/j.leaqua.2016.10.006

Hayes, S. C., Strosahl, K. D., & Wilson, K. G. (2012). *Acceptance and commitment therapy, second edition: The process and practice of mindful change*. New York: Guilford Press.

Hobfoll, S. E. (2011). Conservation of resources theory: Its implication for stress, health, and resilience. In S. Folkman (Ed.), *The Oxford handbook of stress, health, and coping* (pp. 127–147). New York: Oxford University Press.

Hobfoll, S. E., Halbesleben, J., Neveu, J.-P., & Westman, M. (2018). Conservation of resources in the organizational context: The reality of resources and their consequences. *Annual Review of Organizational Psychology and Organizational Behavior*, *5*(1), 103–128. https://doi.org/10.1146/annurev-orgpsych-032117-104640

Holahan, C. J., & Moos, R. H. (1986). Personality, coping, and family resources in stress resistance: A longitudinal analysis. *Journal of Personality and Social Psychology*, *51*(2), 389–395.

Kahneman, D., & Tversky, A. (1979). Prospect theory: An analysis of decision under risk. *Econometrica*, *47*(2), 263–291. https://doi.org/10.2307/1914185

Lam, C. K., Walter, F., & Huang, X. (2017). Supervisors' emotional exhaustion and abusive supervision: The moderating roles of perceived subordinate performance and supervisor self-monitoring. *Journal of Organizational Behavior*, *38*(8), 1151–1166. https://doi.org/10.1002/job.2193

Lazarus, R. S. (2006). Emotions and interpersonal relationships: Toward a person-centered conceptualization of emotions and coping. *Journal of Personality*, *74*(1), 9–46. https://doi.org/10.1111/j.1467-6494.2005.00368.x

Lazarus, R. S., & Folkman, S. (1984). *Stress, appraisal, and coping*. New York: Springer.

Littleton, H., Horsley, S., John, S., & Nelson, D. V. (2007). Trauma coping strategies and psychological distress: A meta-analysis. *Journal of Traumatic Stress*, *20*(6), 977–988. https://doi.org/10.1002/jts.20276

Maslach, C., & Jackson, S. E. (1984). Burnout in organizational settings. *Applied Social Psychology Annual*, *5*, 133–153.

Moskowitz, J. T. (2011). Coping interventions and the regulation of positive affect. In S. Folkman (Ed.), *The Oxford handbook of stress, health, and coping* (pp. 407–427). New York: Oxford University Press.

Moskowitz, J. T., Hult, J. R., Bussolari, C., & Acree, M. (2009). What works in coping with HIV? A meta-analysis with implications for coping with serious illness. *Psychological Bulletin*, *135*(1), 121–141. https://doi.org/10.1037/a0014210

Nolen-Hoeksema, S., Wisco, B. E., & Lyubomirsky, S. (2008). Rethinking rumination. *Perspectives on Psychological Science*, *3*(5), 400–424. https://doi.org/10.1111/j.1745-6924.2008.00088.x

Rajah, R., Song, Z., & Arvey, R. D. (2011). Emotionality and leadership: Taking stock of the past decade of research. *The Leadership Quarterly*, *22*(6), 1107–1119. https://doi.org/10.1016/j.leaqua.2011.09.006

Roesch, S. C., Adams, L., Hines, A., Palmores, A., Vyas, P., Tran, C., . . . Vaughn, A. A. (2005). Coping with prostate cancer: A meta-analytic review. *Journal of Behavioral Medicine, 28*(3), 281–293. https://doi.org/10.1007/s10865-005-4664-z

Skinner, E. A., Edge, K., Altman, J., & Sherwood, H. (2003). Searching for the structure of coping: A review and critique of category systems for classifying ways of coping. *Psychological Bulletin, 129*(2), 216. https://doi.org/10.1037/0033-2909.129.2.216

Skinner, E. A., & Zimmer-Gembeck, M. J. (2016). Ways and families of coping as adaptive processes. In E. A. Skinner & M. J. Zimmer-Gembeck (Eds.), *The development of coping* (pp. 27–49). Switzerland: Springer International Publishing. https://doi.org/10.1007/978-3-319-41740-0_2

Stanton, A. (2011). Regulating emotions during stressful experiences: The adaptive utility of coping through emotional approach. In S. Folkman (Ed.), *The Oxford handbook of stress, health, and coping* (pp. 369–386). New York: Oxford University Press.

Taylor, S. E. (2011). Social support: A review. In H. S. Friedman (Ed.), *The Oxford handbook of health psychology* (Vol. 1, pp. 189–214). New York: Oxford University Press.

Wegner, D. M., Schneider, D. J., Carter, S. L., & White, T. L. (1987). Paradoxical effects of thought suppression. *Journal of Personality and Social Psychology, 53*(1), 5–13. http://doi.org/10.1037/0022-3514.53.1.5

Wills, T. A. (1987). Help-seeking as a coping mechanism. In C. R. Snyder & C. E. Ford (Eds.), *Coping with negative life events: Clinical and social psychological perspectives* (pp. 19–50). New York: Plenum Press.

Zhang, Y., & Bednall, T. (2016). Antecedents of abusive supervision: A meta-analytic review. *Journal of Business Ethics, 139*(3), 455–471. https://doi.org/10.1007/s10551-015-2657-6

3

DECIDING TO DISCLOSE, ASKING FOR HELP

DISCLOSURE STORIES – QUOTATIONS FROM LEADERS

I don't want people to be nervous. You know everyone has enough concerns in their life . . . they don't need the additional burden of wondering if the leadership of the organization where they work is flawed physically and the security of their position may be jeopardized because of that. They don't need that.

– Study participant

I think it's very important to share certain events, certain aspects of what's going on in your life because it exposes you. Oh my gosh, there's a human being there. He's just like me! I remind people all the time, "Hey, I wake up in the morning and believe it or not, I haven't figured out how to levitate so my pants can go on both legs at the same time. I get dressed just like everybody else in the morning, and I have the same issues, just like everyone else. Maybe differences here and there, but we're all in this thing." We're trying to get through this thing we call life and make things better for our children and ourselves. So yeah, I'm just a person like everyone else. And I think that's what that does, it makes you more real.

– Study participant

I felt sharing with select people in my organization helped me to cope with my crisis. I was careful not to mention my problems with anyone else because I feel they would use it as an opportunity to ruin my hard-working reputation. My friends and co-workers that I did share with offered me advice on how to better deal with my issues.

– Study participant

I had one of the guys find me weeping, and he sent me home. And that was okay – I let them send me home. When I was not functioning, I needed to be told that I was not functioning and that I needed to go home. At first, that's what I needed to do.

– Study participant

I really did not give my work a chance to object. I came in, told my boss and a few superiors that I was going to take a step back, why I was going to do it, and a timeline of the transition. If they were not ok with it, I would have been ok to find another position.

– Study participant

Leader disclosure in our research

We asked the leaders in Study 2 to what extent they had disclosed their crisis to people in their organization – their staff/team members, their colleagues/peers, and the people to whom they reported (e.g., supervisor, board members). In Table 3.1, the majority of participants had disclosed to a few people in each category of organizational relationship, and only a minority of participants had disclosed to no one in each category. Between role categories, disclosing to at least some colleagues/peers was slightly more likely than to people in either staff or supervisor roles. Across categories, however, only 3% of participants (five people) had not disclosed their crisis to anyone in the organization. On the other hand, a similarly small percentage (2.4%; four people) had disclosed to everyone at each level of relationship in their organization. Taken together, these results suggest that the vast majority of leaders disclosed their crisis and did so at least somewhat selectively.[1]

Our results are largely consistent with a study of disclosure regarding psychiatric conditions in the workplace (Ellison, Russinova, MacDonald-Wilson, & Lyass, 2003). Surprisingly to the researchers, over 80% of workers surveyed in non-mental-health

TABLE 3.1 Degree to Which Leaders Disclosed by Organizational Relationship

	Staff/team members	*Colleagues/peers*	*People to whom you report*
None of them	19%	10%	21%
A few of them	60%	68%	49%
Most of them	11%	15%	14%
All of them	10%	7%	16%

1 Degree of disclosure did not differ according to leader gender (all $p < .05$).

related fields had disclosed their condition to someone at work. Although this was not exclusively a study of leaders (only about one-third were executives, managers, or "other administrative personnel"), the relatively high level of disclosure is notable given the severity of the conditions involved (79% of participants had been hospitalized at some point because of their condition) and the regrettable extent to which mental health conditions are stigmatized (Hinshaw & Stier, 2008). In this study, most participants had disclosed to their supervisor or a coworker, with only 22% disclosing to team members (although, given that the study included non-leaders, it is unclear how many participants had staff members). Feeling secure at work and feeling secure in managing the condition were related to the decision to disclose. Notably, 61% of participants had no regrets at all about disclosing, and only 7.7% had "a lot of" regrets or "completely" regretted it (Ellison et al., 2003). Thus, the results in our study of leaders are largely consistent with patterns of workplace disclosure for one of the most stigmatized personal crises, mental illness. In sum, most people in crisis disclose to someone in their organization.

Why did leaders in our study choose to disclose? Leaders in Study 2 reported on their reasons for disclosing to people in the organization using categories developed from our prior work in Study 1. Although these results will be more extensively discussed in Chapter 5, here we note that simply informing people was a motivation for disclosure for the majority of disclosers (60–74%), followed by the need to explain any changes in behavior (42–49%). Leaders also disclosed to gain instrumental support on the job (21–33%) and to obtain emotional support (17–29%).

Were leaders satisfied with the decisions they had made about disclosure of their personal crisis? On average, leaders rated their degree of satisfaction between "slightly satisfied" and "satisfied" ($M = 5.49$, $SD = 1.32$) on a scale ranging from "very dissatisfied" to "very satisfied," with "satisfied" being the most frequent response, and 77% of participants expressing some degree of satisfaction. Yet, despite a general trend toward satisfaction, 6.2% of participants endorsed some level of dissatisfaction with their disclosure decisions, and 16% felt neutral. These results suggest that some leaders had at least mixed feelings about their disclosure decisions.

Finally, we explored the relationship between extent of disclosure, represented by an average disclosure value across all three types of organizational relationships, and satisfaction with disclosure and found that these variables were positively correlated ($r = .30, p < .001$). In other words, leaders who disclosed their crisis more broadly in their organization tended to be more satisfied with their disclosure decisions.[2]

Exploring factors associated with disclosure

Leaders' willingness to disclose their crisis might depend on a number of factors – the nature of the crisis event, personality or personal trust beliefs, and the nature of the interpersonal environment of the organization in which they are embedded. For

---

2 Importantly, the positive association between extent of disclosure and satisfaction with disclosure persisted when controlling for key personality traits (neuroticism, agreeableness, extraversion) and propensity for trust/mistrust.

example, Mooradian, Renzl, and Matzler (2006) found that, among 64 employees in a software firm, the personality traits of agreeableness and propensity to trust were related to trust in peers within the organization, which was in turn related to knowledge-sharing within and across teams. In our Study 2 data, we explored these relationships by examining the correlations between the degree to which leaders disclosed across all three types of organizational relationships, represented by the mean disclosure score across these relationship types, and key factors in each category. For crisis-related factors, we examined the degree to which disclosure was associated with participants' degree of self-blame and embarrassment related to the crisis. We reasoned that fear of stigma regarding the crisis might relate to less propensity to disclose to others about it. For within-person factors, we examined personality traits of extraversion, neuroticism, agreeableness, and propensity for trust/mistrust related to disclosure.[3] We reasoned that these personality traits and beliefs – which represent somewhat stable patterns of behavior across settings and situations (Costa & McCrae, 1992) – might be related to the degree to which leaders chose to disclose. Finally, we examined the degree to which disclosure was related to describing one's self as a "private person." We did so based on our Study 1 research, wherein some participants invoked the concept of being a "private person" to describe their reasons for not disclosing. Because we were unable to locate specific academic literature on the idea of being a "private person," we conducted exploratory research on this description in Study 2.

Unexpectedly, none of the variables described in the previous paragraph were associated with the degree to which leaders disclosed their crisis ($r = -.07$ to $.06$; all $p > .39$).[4] In other words, leaders' shame and embarrassment about the crisis, their outgoingness (extraversion), tendency toward anxiety and stress (neuroticism), tendency toward being interpersonally agreeable, the extent to which they said they were a "private person," and their degree of general trust in others did not relate to the breadth with which they chose to disclose their crisis to others in their organization. In contrast, Mooradian and colleagues (2006) found that agreeableness and propensity to trust were related to greater sharing of general work-related (non-crisis) information with others in the organization. Because personality traits have the capacity to predict important interpersonal behavioral patterns, it is notable that – in the case of the extent of disclosure of leaders about their personal crises – we did not observe this pattern. While additional research will certainly be needed to replicate and extend our findings, they suggest that other situation-specific factors might be important in understanding leader disclosure in personal crisis situations.

---

3 While most readers are probably familiar with the concept of extraversion, neuroticism and agreeableness may be less familiar. Neuroticism reflects reactivity to stress and emotional instability, while agreeableness reflects kindness, trust, and concern for social harmony (Costa & McCrae, 1992).

4 Due to concerns about low internal consistency of items in our short personality scale, we examined disattenuated correlations of these variables with disclosure (see Appendix C). This analysis did not change our results and correlations between personality traits tested, and disclosure remained weak when correcting for measurement error ($rs = -.05$ to $.07$).

Finally, we considered the extent to which the nature of the work environment and its culture might influence the propensity to disclose, which will be considered more fully in Chapter 4. To foreshadow, we obtained much stronger evidence for a relationship between leader perceptions of the work environment and the extent to which participants disclosed their crisis.

Exploring the "private person" construct

As noted earlier, a few participants in Study 1 used the term "private person" to describe themselves or others with regard to willingness to disclose personal matters at work (e.g., "I'm generally a pretty private person, so I didn't want to spread my personal business further than I needed to."). We have also observed in our work as practitioners that people will sometimes use this phrase to describe themselves or others; yet, we were unable to find any scholarship regarding the construct of being a private person – that is, what people mean when they use this description and whether describing one's self as a private person is related to traits or behaviors that would be relevant to understanding disclosure in a personal crisis. As such, we included two questions in the Study 2 survey to explore this construct: "Please indicate to what extent you agree or disagree with the following statement: I would describe myself as a "private person," with a response scale ranging from "Strongly disagree" to "Strongly agree." We then asked participants, "What does being a 'private person' mean to you?" and allowed them to provide a free text response.

To explore how participants defined "private person," we subjected a subset of the free text responses ($n = 125$) to qualitative coding and found that the majority of participants (54%) described being a private person as "being hesitant to disclose about one's personal life" (e.g., "Work is separate from home. Only a few close friends know me well."). Another 21% described "being socially withdrawn" (e.g., "Shy, quiet, keep to themselves."), and 6% described "being reticent or reserved" (e.g., "Not talkative."), with another 19% of responses categorized as "Other" (e.g., "Depressed," "A person who is more laid back and calm."). Thus, this exploratory analysis suggests that people use the phrase "private person" to refer to related but distinct traits – reluctant to disclose, less socially interactive, or taciturn.

Seventy-five percent of participants endorsed considering themselves a "private person" to some degree (i.e., rated the statement as "agree a little" or above) with 29% of participants endorsing "Agree" and 17% endorsing "Strongly Agree." The average score corresponded to "Agree a little" ($M = 5.07$, $SD = 1.57$). Next, we explored the association between describing one's self as a "private person" and other traits and behaviors that might help us better understand the meaning of this term for participants. We found that describing one's self as a private person was associated with being less open to experience, less extraverted, less trusting of others, and feeling more socially constrained in disclosing or talking about the crisis with family and at work[5] (Appendix C, Table C.2). These relationships are consistent

---

5 The concept of "social constraints on disclosure" will be more fully discussed in Chapter 4.

with participants' conceptualizations of what it meant to be a "private person" in terms of hesitancy to disclose and introversion. Notably, however, being a private person was not correlated with the extent to which participants had disclosed their crisis to people in their organization ($r = .002, p = .98$).

In sum, when participants in the study endorsed describing themselves as a "private person" they seemed to be referring to introversion combined with the desire to conceal personal information from others, possibly related to a sense of mistrust. The relationships among these three constructs with respect to the idea of being a private person will need to be investigated in future research. Importantly, like the other factors described earlier, being a "private person" was not associated with the breadth of disclosure to others in the organization regarding the personal crisis.

Disclosure in the context of the organization

To foreshadow, in Study 2, there was evidence of an association between leaders' disclosure behavior and their perceptions of the interpersonal organizational context and culture, including ideas of trust, psychological safety, and a belief that disclosure would be met with acceptance. This topic will be fully covered in Chapter 4. Here, we report the associations between these contextual factors and disclosure. Leaders who endorsed more trust in their organizational peers (e.g., "If I got into difficulties at work, I know my colleagues would try and help me out.") reported wider disclosure in their organization regarding their personal crisis ($r = .37, p < .001$). Leaders who endorsed more trust in the management of the organization (e.g., "I feel quite confident that the organization will always try to treat me fairly.") were also more likely to report wider disclosure ($r = .26, p = .001$). Furthermore, leaders who endorsed a greater sense of "psychological safety" in their organization (e.g., "It is safe to take a risk in this organization.") reported disclosing more extensively to others about the crisis ($r = .27, p < .001$). These results suggest that the interpersonal organizational climate in terms of the leader's trust in others and his or her sense that the organization is safe for interpersonal risk-taking without fear of negative consequences may be important factors that facilitate greater disclosure regarding a personal crisis.

Disclosure of personal information: culture and context

Chapter 2 described the numerous coping strategies that leaders use to manage the impact of a personal crisis. Among these, seeking social support was one of the most frequently reported by our participants and among the most important to emerge from our review of the research literature on coping. As covered in Chapter 5, leaders also endorsed strategies at work that relied on changing work arrangements, executing specific plans to handle the impact of the crisis at work, and delegating to others. To deploy many of these strategies, leaders must first disclose information about the crisis and, in some cases, directly seek help from others within their organization. Yet, as one wise leader who participated in our research noted, managing a personal crisis is, for a leader, "psychologically complex." Cultural expectations of leaders and norms of leadership – both at the societal and local levels – collide with personal and professional need for support, need for privacy, and impulses toward impression management. Leadership traits and values reinforced by organizational culture in a Western cultural context – independence, competence, certainty – may seem to be contradicted by a leader's disclosure of a personal crisis. Yet a broad review of the literature on disclosure and help-seeking also reveals potential unexpected opportunities for leader-team member growth in these challenging circumstances and points the way toward recommendations for leaders navigating disclosure and help-seeking.

As emphasized in the prior chapter on coping, we believe that a thoughtful, flexible approach to leader disclosure and help-seeking is likely to be more effective than either a rigid, rule-based approach or an impulsive style. In this chapter, we synthesize literature from a variety of disciplines with insights from our own research participants to draw preliminary conclusions about the costs and benefits of disclosure and help-seeking for leaders, and suggest an approach to decision-making in these important moments. We first review literature on the potential costs and benefits of disclosure and then focus on the costs and benefits of help-seeking.

Like most human behaviors, behavior in organizations is heavily influenced by social norms, or the ways things are typically done in a given culture or group and what is considered appropriate behavior in that context (Goldstein & Mortensen, 2012). Social norms include explicit rules codified in law (e.g., drive your car on the (right or left) side of the roadway), commonly understood standards of behavior (e.g., don't pick your nose – at least not in public), and normative behaviors so ingrained and automatic that it goes unrecognized that they are, essentially, arbitrary (e.g., use the urinal or stall furthest away from other restroom users). Norms often serve a useful social function, for example, organizing and coordinating the behavior of groups, allowing one to predict what others will do in a given situation, or allowing one to determine an acceptable course of action by observing others (Goldstein & Mortensen, 2012). Yet norms can also constrain behavior in situations where flexibility is beneficial. Thus, it is important to recognize and identify the norms that may govern (or constrain) disclosure and help-seeking for leaders in a given culture.[6]

Like other social situations, workplace behavior is influenced by its own set of cultural norms, referred to as "workways" (Sanchez-Burks, 2005). Workways proscribe when, where, and how work is done as well as what is considered "professional" or "work-appropriate" in a given culture. For example, a frequently studied norm that influences workways in the United States is the Protestant Work Ethic in which work is valued as a praiseworthy activity outside of its actual utility or function (Sanchez-Burks & Uhlmann, 2013). Another prominent workway in

---

6 Our discussion will focus on cultural norms prevalent in "professional" settings in Western cultures because we anticipate that many of our readers may be embedded in such cultures. At the same time, we acknowledge the shortcomings of this culturally narrow focus and hope that future investigations of leadership in personal crisis will continue to expand cultural perspectives on this topic.

the United States is the Protestant Relational Ideology (PRI), which is the belief that focusing on relationships or emotions in the workplace is inappropriate or "unprofessional" (Sanchez-Burks, 2005). PRI dictates that work interactions should be polite, unemotional, and impersonal (Sanchez-Burks & Uhlmann, 2013). By extension, in the United States, referring to non-work life or other personal matters in certain work settings can be considered unprofessional. Evidence that such proscription is a U.S. cultural norm comes from studies showing that American workers rate others who make reference to non-work topics as less professional and that this effect is stronger for people who had lived in the United States the longest (Uhlmann, Heaphy, Ashford, Zhu, & Sanchez Burks, 2013). In addition, when U.S. participants read vignettes about hypothetical job candidates who did or did not discuss personal information when meeting with a client (e.g., information about children and family), they rated the candidates who mentioned their personal life as less professional. In contrast, these non-work disclosures had no effect on the ratings given by East Indian participants (Uhlmann et al., 2013).

Thus, the edict to "leave home at home and keep work at work" can be considered a U.S. cultural norm rooted in PRI. While a separation between work and home life may be beneficial in many circumstances, we believe it is important to acknowledge the strong and potentially arbitrary influence that PRI culture can have on leader (and team member) behavior. Organizational norms that prohibit discussion of the personal and emotional at work may, in some cases, impede leaders from accessing the social support and accommodations they need to effectively manage their personal crises and fulfill their leadership roles.

Disclosure of nonwork or private information in the workplace has also been explored in the field of communication. Communication researchers have studied how people conceive of and manage personal information in the context of their relationships. Communication privacy management (CPM) theory (Petronio, 2015) conceives of private information as a commodity controlled by the person who possesses or "owns" that information about themselves. It assumes that people believe they have a right to control this information and that they do so through the use of personal rules that aim to balance the risks and benefits of disclosure. People control the flow of personal information across the boundary between themselves and other people such that when someone else is told personal information, they become a co-owner of that information. Co-owners of information must negotiate privacy rules about when the information may cross additional boundaries and be disclosed to others (boundary coordination). Rule-breaking disclosures of personal information bring distress and conflict (boundary turbulence). In sum, CPM conceives of personal information as a commodity that disclosers attempt to coordinate across relationship boundaries to balance risk and reward.

Supporting the ideas of CPM theory, a focus group study of employees revealed that most believed respect for the privacy of their health information at work should be "a given" when disclosed to a supervisor (Westerman, Miller, Reno, & Spates, 2015). Many said that they would ask others not to disclose personal health information when it was shared, and some were skeptical about whether others would follow these "co-owner" rules. For example, some participants said they would never share personal information at work that they would not mind everyone in the workplace knowing. Participants cited reasons for disclosing personal health information, including inevitability of the information being known (due to illness-related absence, for example), to prevent rumors, to explain changes in workplace behavior or performance, to ensure safety to self and others, and to obtain social support from coworkers. Some participants described being employed in "close" workplaces where disclosure felt easy and extensive support was readily forthcoming. Greater disclosure also occurred in workplaces where employees were more interdependent on one other. In terms of disclosure risks, participants cited fear of losing opportunities at work or even being terminated and fear of stigma. With respect to formal structures in the organization, many employees were not aware of any formal policies governing the disclosure and re-disclosure of personal health information by supervisors. However, many strongly felt that there should be official, clearly communicated policies (Westerman et al., 2015).

Risks and benefits of leader disclosure: perceptions and findings

According to communication privacy management theory, people develop rules about disclosure that are designed to balance the potential risks and benefits of sharing information across boundaries (Petronio, 2015). As such, in this section, we review literature relevant to perceived risks to leaders of disclosing significant personal information, followed by evidence for potential benefits of disclosure, so that the leader in crisis can balance these considerations in making disclosure decisions.

Perceived risks of disclosure

"Breaking the rules"

As reviewed earlier, organizational culture in the United States is influenced by Protestant Relational Ideology, which proscribes impersonal, unemotional interactions in the workplace. It is important to acknowledge that disclosing personal information may violate these strong norms – in other words, break the rules – of "professionalism" that are often ingrained in workplace culture. In Study 1, several participants mentioned that rules such as "leave home at home" or "don't talk about personal matters at work" had influenced their behavior surrounding the personal crisis. We must acknowledge that people can face social consequences for violating norms. As demonstrated in the study on views of what is considered "professional" in the U.S. (Uhlmann et al., 2013), disclosure may change others' impressions of the leader. For the leader, the prospect of violating strong norms can give rise to feelings of discomfort, anxiety, and fear of shame or embarrassment that serve as a barrier to disclosure. Yet, as will be described throughout the rest of the chapter, benefits may outweigh the uncertain downsides of violating social norms.

Indeed, other psychological effects on the receiver may even mitigate the negative consequences of a norm-breaking disclosure.

Losing status and power

People have culture-bound expectations about who a leader is and what he or she should do. Common assumptions about leaders, as high-power individuals, include that they are more independent, more competent, and therefore superior to their team members (Lee, 1997). When information about a leader violates expectations of leaders, Status Distance Theory predicts that the perceived power distance between the team member and his or her leader will be reduced, resulting in perceptions of lower leader power (Phillips, Rothbard, & Dumas, 2009). Unfortunately, expectations of leaders are also biased by stereotypes that permeate the surrounding culture. Thus, information that contradicts biased team member expectations of who is powerful (ascribed status; Phillips et al., 2009) – including stereotypes based on gender, race, socioeconomic status, background, and disability status – can affect the perceived status of the leader.[7] For example, a team member who initially perceives the leader to be vastly superior in terms of status and power may learn that the leader received her or his college degree from a lower-ranked university after transferring from a community college. If this information violates the team member's expectations regarding the elite backgrounds of high-power individuals – which, unfortunately, may be the case – then the perceived status of the leader and the status distance between the leader and team member will be reduced.

Gibson, Harari, and Marr (2018) suggest that such disruptions in the status hierarchy may create disorder in task-oriented situations because such hierarchies coordinate action by dictating who should defer to whom. In a series of studies, when a higher-status task partner disclosed information indicating weakness (e.g., poor academic record; obesity-related illness; attending therapy) during a laboratory task, participants perceived the partner to be lower in status, had more conflict with the partner, and liked the partner less. In one study, the authors found evidence that perceived vulnerability of the high-status partner accounted for the effects. Importantly, these negative effects were observed during the initial stages of a relationship in which the participant had no other prior experience with the partner, which is consistent with prior research showing that personal disclosures to strangers are especially likely to result in negative impressions (Collins & Miller, 1995). Taken together, these findings suggest disclosing information that makes one seem vulnerable in the initial stages of a new relationship is probably ill advised. Thus, the effect of disclosing information that increases perceived vulnerability depends on the strength of the prior relationship (Gibson, 2018).

---

7 Philips and colleagues (2009) posit that the consequences of disclosure of information that reduces status distance may present more risk for leaders with lower ascribed status. For example, a white male executive who discloses that he was raised by a single mother is likely at a lower risk of status loss resulting from sharing this information than would be a black female executive.

Thus, information that contradicts team member expectations of powerful people may indeed result in lower perceived status and power for the leader. Yet the outcomes of reduced status distance may not be necessarily negative. As will be discussed in the section on benefits, disclosure and the reduced perceived status distance resulting from it may enable the formation of stronger relationships between team members and their leaders (Gibson, 2018; Nifadkar, Wu, & Gu, 2019; Phillips et al., 2009). In conclusion, it is likely that disclosure will change the way that others perceive the leader, but this change might have positive or negative consequences.

Stigma and rejection

Leaders who disclose information that makes them feel vulnerable may fear being stigmatized or rejected by others. While stigma is a rich, multi-faceted concept that would require much more space to fully discuss, one consequence of being stigmatized is that others may reduce contact with the stigmatized individual and reduce their willingness to lend support. In the workplace, Gibson (2018) speculates that receivers of disclosed information will consider the meaning of the disclosure for their own work-related goals. For example, a team member may wonder whether a leader's chronic illness will result in an increased workload or reduced availability of the leader for mentoring support. If receivers perceive that the disclosure conveys information out of line with their own work-related goals, Gibson suggests that the receiver may avoid the discloser. If Gibson's predictions bear out, leaders should craft their disclosures to include information about the expected impact of the personal crisis on team members and any plans the leader has to help mitigate these impacts.

In addition, leaders may fear losing control of their personal information and doubt whether others will honor their requests to maintain privacy boundaries (Petronio, 2015; Westerman et al., 2015). The more potentially stigmatizing the information, the greater the leader's concern is likely to be. Thus, leaders may need to carefully consider who can be trusted with disclosed information and should clearly communicate their expectations to receivers regarding confidentiality.

Causing instability and uncertainty

Leaders may fear that disclosure about personal crises will introduce uncertainty that can hinder their ability to effectively influence others. In a dramatic instantiation of this idea, CEO well-being and succession decisions can send powerful market signals, affecting company performance and stock prices. In particular, the perception of stability can have an impact on company performance. For example, when a CEO steps down due to illness, boards are more likely to re-appoint a former CEO, and markets tend to respond favorably to this stability-signaling action (Davidson, Tong, Worrell, & Rowe, 2006).

Although executive leaders may fear the impact of succession due to personal crises on the health of their companies, surprisingly, markets react more positively to unanticipated CEO succession announcements than anticipated ones (Rhim, Peluchette, & Song, 2006), and stock prices tend to rise after succession events, although overall firm value may remain flat (Adams & Mansi, 2009). However, poorly managed rumors of illness may have more negative consequences. For example, despite company denials, Apple stocks took a 10% loss after rumors surfaced of the return of Steve Jobs's cancer and then fell 17% when it was subsequently announced that Jobs would, in fact, take a leave of absence due to cancer relapse (Larcker & Tayan, 2011; Perryman, Butler, Martin, & Ferris, 2010). High-level leaders must weigh the costs of disclosure vs. the costs of uncertainty that can result from nondisclosure and consider ways to strategically manage disclosure to address the effects of uncertainty for the organization.

Conclusions about disclosure risks

In summary, leaders may hesitate to disclose their personal crises to others in their organization because they feel compelled to follow strong social norms against such disclosures; because they anticipate a loss of status and influence; because they predict rejection and social distancing due to stigma; or because they are concerned that the information will create a sense of uncertainty and instability for their team members and their organization. Concern about these risks is understandable, although it is important to note that most of the literature we were able to find about the negative consequences of disclosure in organizations was theoretical in nature, and few empirical investigations have documented the degree to which negative consequences are actually experienced by leaders who choose to disclose sensitive personal information. Yet these risks represent significant potential downsides to disclosure that leaders should take into consideration when deciding if, when, to whom, and how to disclose their personal crises. In addition, because humans tend to weigh potential costs more heavily in their decision-making than potential gains (Kahneman & Tversky, 1979), potential benefits should also be considered in the disclosure equation.

Benefits of disclosure, costs of concealment

In addition to risks of disclosure, leaders should be aware of the potential benefits of disclosure when planning their response to personal crises. From our review of the literature, the primary benefits of disclosure for leaders include access to social and other supports, strengthening of relationships with team members, and the ability to execute a well-planned response to the crisis. Our review of these benefits serves to highlight what leaders could potentially be "leaving on the table" by adhering rigidly to nondisclosure norms – in other words, there may be unseen costs of concealment of a crisis.

Social support and stress reduction

As described in Chapter 2, social support can provide access to critical coping resources such as information and advice, instrumental support, and emotional and "moral" support (see Box 2.1, page 59). A leader might disclose in order to make an explicit request for help or others may spontaneously offer support in response to a disclosure. As reviewed in the prior chapter, social support is among the most important factors that can mitigate the negative effects of stressful life events, and disclosure is often a prerequisite to accessing help. In one study of (non-leader) employees coping with chronic illness, the likelihood of fully disclosing difficulties to others in the organization was predicted by prior (presumably successful) disclosure to coworkers and the perceived importance of social support for coping with the illness (Munir, Leka, & Griffiths, 2005).

Intriguingly, there is also evidence that the effort involved in suppressing and concealing negative emotions can undermine team member perceptions of leader authenticity and even affect team member job satisfaction (see Rajah, Song, & Arvey, 2011 for a review). In one recent study of managers, Weiss, Razinskas, Backmann, and Hoegl (2018) hypothesized that, because surface acting and impression management require cognitive and emotional effort, less authentic leadership would be related to greater depletion of self-control resources, which would lead to increased job stress and decreased work engagement. They further reasoned that the effect of leader authenticity on depletion would depend on the degree to which leaders interacted with their team members. Using questionnaire data collected daily for ten days, Weiss and colleagues (2018) found that inauthentic leaders experienced more depletion and, in turn, more stress and less engagement, especially when they interacted more with their team members. By contrast, more authentic leaders were actually less depleted the more they interacted with team members on a given day. In the context of personal crisis, "putting on a brave face" for long periods of time with team members may deplete the leader and increase stress and disengagement. Therefore, leaders may want to consider the extent to which strategic disclosure might relieve a burden of inauthenticity. Selective disclosure to others in the organization may reduce the emotional and cognitive load, freeing the leader's personal and psychological resources for effective leadership in the organization and reduced stress.

Strengthened relationships

In contrast to the perceived risks of personal disclosure, research on personal disclosure in the field of social psychology highlights the relationship-building benefits of disclosure. Self-Disclosure Theory posits that disclosure of personal information is a primary mechanism by which relationships are built and strengthened – specifically, that sharing of information builds trust between people, which facilitates the development of mutually beneficial relationships (Nifadkar et al., 2019). As discussed in Chapter 4, trust in leaders is associated with a range of positive team member outcomes. Nifadkar and colleagues (2019) posited that supervisor disclosure about non-work matters would increase employee trust in supervisors about both work and non-work matters, which would increase employee information-seeking from the supervisor. They further hypothesized that this information-seeking from the leader would result in improved job performance, employee participation in decision-making, and greater intentions to stay in the job.

The authors obtained evidence for the components of their model across five studies and then tested the full model in a sample of 279 supervisor-staff member pairs. In this study, supervisor work disclosure interacted with non-work disclosure to enhance work-related trust in the supervisor. Enhanced trust was related to increased information-seeking and predicted positive outcomes of supervisor-rated job performance and self-reported intention to stay. Importantly, enhanced employee trust explained (mediated) the relationship between information-sharing and positive outcomes, supporting the idea that self-disclosure has the potential to enhance trust in leader-team member relationships in productive ways. Another recent cross-cultural study showed that trust in a leader was related to the leader's perceived emotional sincerity (Caza, Zhang, Wang, & Bai, 2015). To the extent that leader disclosure (non-concealment) enhances team member perceptions of sincerity, trust in the leader may be enhanced by this route as well.

At a more basic level, many studies in social psychology find that self-disclosure increases the extent to which the recipient of the information likes the discloser (Collins & Miller, 1995),[8] leading to the possibility that self-disclosure on the part of the leader may cause team members to like him or her more. Relevant to disclosures regarding personal crises, the power of the positive effects of disclosure on liking depend more on the depth (intimacy) of information disclosed rather than the breadth (amount). While the reasons for the effect of disclosure on liking are not entirely clear, it may be that recipients find disclosure more rewarding if they perceive that the discloser has singled them out to receive the information due to some special personal quality or the quality of their shared relationship[9] (Wortman, Adesman, Herman, & Greenberg, 1976). While more research into this possibility is needed, the existing research suggests that team members may like their leaders more when they disclose their personal crises – particularly if the leader discloses to them personally and emphasizes the importance of the team member to the leader and the importance of their relationship.

While disclosure of certain personal information has the potential to reduce a leader's perceived power, as discussed in the prior section, the effect of personal disclosure on perceived leader status may also have salutary effects. While Status Distance Theory predicts that personal disclosure of information inconsistent with expectations of leaders can reduce team member perceptions of leader power, the reduced status distance between the leader and team member may set the occasion for stronger relationships (Phillips et al., 2009), since high status distance can serve as a barrier to relationship formation. In other words, disclosure of certain information may signal to team members that the leader is "one of them," facilitating increased

---

8 In this analysis, although few gender differences were detected, women tended to benefit slightly more in terms of being liked when they self-disclosed (Collins & Miller, 1995).

9 One study even showed that men who are more interpersonally strategic and Machiavellian were especially likely to use self-disclosure strategically as an influence tactic when attempting to persuade others, perhaps capitalizing on the disclosure-liking effect (Dingler-Duhon & Brown, 1987).

trust and enhanced relationships across a reduced status divide. For example, a leader who discloses to his employee that he will need to take time off to help his adult child find treatment for substance abuse problems is – due to the stigmatized status of substance use disorders – disclosing a vulnerability that violates expectations regarding high-status individuals. Such a disclosure may result in the employee feeling closer – emotionally and status-wise – to the leader, providing the opportunity for increased trust and more meaningful interactions in the future (Gibson, 2018). The effect will probably be particularly powerful if the employee has experienced similar life circumstances.

Yet, as Phillips and colleagues (2009) emphasize, the extent to which leaders are comfortable disclosing status-distance-reducing information may depend upon other variables of ascribed status – gender, social class, race and ethnicity, disability status – and the extent to which these identities are considered to violate expectations for leaders within the organization. For example, a woman who is the only female leader in a traditionally male-dominated field (e.g., engineering) might conceal a personal crisis related to, for example, pregnancy because of concern that it confirms stereotypes about the suitability of women and mothers for leadership positions. As such, more research and careful consideration are needed when weighing the degree to which reduced status distance may be beneficial to specific leader-team member relationships embedded in particular organizational cultures.

In sum, disclosure of personal information by a leader has the potential to strengthen relationships by increasing trust, reducing status distance, and increasing liking of the leader, which may increase the likelihood of increased interactions and stronger relationships over time – all influenced, of course, by the way the disclosure message is crafted, the preexisting leader-team member relationship, the characteristics of the leader, and the culture of the organization.

Ability to execute planful responses

Strategic disclosure may enable leaders to plan and execute a more effective response to personal crises *vis-à-vis* their leadership roles. In the case of executive leaders such as CEOs, leaders and firms may have a fiduciary responsibility to disclose information about leader health and to judiciously and thoughtfully plan for possible threats to leader well-being. Importantly, the Securities and Exchange Commission (SEC) requires that publicly held companies disclose material information that can affect market valuation of the firm, although there are no specific SEC guidelines related to CEO health disclosures (Perryman et al., 2010). Thus, disclosure regarding executive leader health may, at times, be mandatory if the board decides that the CEO needs to be replaced. As articulated by Charles Elson, director of the Center for Corporate Governance at the University of Delaware, some corporate leaders believe that "When you go public and take public capital, one thing you agree to is you have less of an expectation of privacy than you would otherwise have" (as quoted in Larcker & Tayan, 2011, p. 2). As discussed in the prior section on the possible effect of leader personal crises on organization certainty and stability, there are potential costs to succession rumors for organizations. Thoughtful disclosure can help leaders formulate and communicate orderly plans for managing the impact of the crisis on their availability and performance.

In sum, leader disclosure of personal information in the context of a crisis may result in strategic benefits (e.g., ability to formulate and execute a planned response; ability to obtain requested help) and unanticipated side benefits (e.g., increased liking of and trust in the leader; unexpected social support).

Considerations for leader disclosure

From our own research and our review of the literature, we present a research-informed worksheet tool (Box 3.1) that leaders in crises can use to help guide their decision-making about disclosure. This worksheet is consistent with communication privacy management theory (Petronio, 2015) in that it recognizes personal information as a commodity that must often be managed strategically. The worksheet draws upon the research discussed earlier and on techniques from Motivational Interviewing (Miller & Rollnick, 2002), a set of interventions designed to help people resolve ambivalence and commit to thoughtful action.

Help-seeking: cultural context and power dynamics

In some cases, leader disclosure about a personal crisis is followed by requests for help and support. As reported in Chapter 5, up to 33% of leaders disclosed their crisis in order to obtain work or job support and up to 29% to gain emotional support. In this section we synthesize existing literature relevant to understanding the dynamics of leader help-seeking beyond disclosure.

As previously discussed, the cultural context in which leader help-seeking occurs may influence the impact of help-seeking behavior on others' impressions of the leader. In other words, help-seeking may have a different meaning when the seeker is a leader vs. a team member based on cultural context and norms. One important dimension of culture to consider is the extent to which cultural norms are individualistic vs. collectivistic. Cultures high in individualism highly value individual achievement, while those high in collectivism highly value group harmony and group success. The meaning of help-seeking can vary based on this dimension. Help-seeking may be more consistent with collectivist norms where the success of the group is paramount and interdependence is expected. In individualistic cultures, because leaders in particular are expected to be independent, superior, and competent, leader help-seeking may violate these norms. (Sandoval & Lee, 2006). Importantly, although the individualism-collectivism dimension has been most extensively examined with respect to cultures encompassing larger populations (e.g., "Western" vs. "Eastern" cultural contexts), organizations can be characterized according to the degree to which they emphasize individualism vs. collectivism, which may influence leader help-seeking behavior. Specifically, in organizational cultures characterized by individualistic norms, leaders may be less likely to ask

BOX 3.1 DISCLOSURE WORKSHEET FOR LEADERS

- Who are you considering disclosing to? For what purpose(s) (refer to Box 2.1, page 59)?

- What information will you disclose to accomplish the goal(s)?

- What will you ask of the recipient(s) in terms of confidentiality? How confident are you that it can be maintained?

- When and where will you make the disclosure?

- How will you personalize the communication to convey the value of the relationship to you?

- What will the recipient(s) need to know to understand the impact of the situation on them or the organization?

- What specific requests for help, if any, do you want to make at this time?

Using the chart provided, map out the possible benefits and costs of making vs. not making this disclosure.

	Benefits	Costs
Disclosing Information		
Concealing Information		

If you decide to follow through with the disclosure, what can you do to mitigate the COSTS of DISCLOSING that you listed on the worksheet?

others for help, whereas organizational cultures where the work structure is interdependent may pave the way for greater help-seeking.

Similar to the dynamics of disclosure, asking for and receiving help from others can change (or is perceived to change) the power dynamics of the leader's relationships. In a fascinating paper, Lee and Tiedens (2001) describe the seemingly paradoxical social and power status of leaders – specifically, leaders see themselves as more independent than non-leaders (independent self-construal), but they also have more extensive interdependent social networks. Lee and Tiedens (2001) describe how this state of affairs is not contradictory and assert that a rich interdependent social network allows for greater leader independence. Specifically, a richer and more well-connected social network may allow the leader to access a wide variety of resources and to be less dependent on any one relationship. This diffused dependence may allow the leader to wield more autonomous social influence. In turn, a leader's self-perception of independence may help him or her to work strategically to build relationships that will boost power and influence. Help-seeking during personal crises may threaten leaders' views of themselves as independent and, simultaneously, it may require them to make requests of people in their social networks that fall outside the bounds of their typical strategic use of those networks. For example, a CEO who wishes to take a leave of absence and requests support from the board of directors for the leave may feel that making such a request violates her perceived sense of independence, and she may be concerned that the request jeopardizes her ability to influence the board in the future. In other words, leaders may worry that help-seeking will diminish their power. As such, leaders may be more hesitant than others to request help and may perceive more negative consequences of such requests.

Furthermore, for some leaders, asking for help from others may "flip the script" of their more typical role as a help-giver to others. Helping is one way in which many leaders achieve their social status (Flynn, Reagans, Amanatullah, & Ames, 2006; Grant, 2013), and such leaders may continue to more often be the giver of help rather than the recipient. The role of help-giver may be particularly expected of certain types of leaders, such as religious leaders or leaders in nonprofit organizations. These types of leaders may have unique challenges in disclosing the crisis and asking for help (for an example, see Proffitt, Cann, Calhoun, & Tedeschi, 2007).

Who asks for help? Role of perceived social costs

In this section, we describe research by Fiona Lee (1997, 2002) that examines which people in organizations are most likely to ask for help and under what conditions. While these studies were not specifically conducted with leaders, they highlight several variables that may influence the propensity of leaders to request help. As discussed earlier, Lee (1997) describes how, in more individualistic organizational cultures, leader help-seeking may be perceived as acknowledging inferiority, incompetence, and dependence, which may undermine the leader's efforts at impression management. The motivation to maintain a powerful public and self-image may therefore inhibit help-seeking, and so in cultures and situations where gaining and maintaining power is salient, fewer help-seeking behaviors may occur. Lee first hypothesized that demographic (gender), relational (status), and contextual (organizational culture) factors affect power motivation and, in turn, help-seeking. Across a laboratory and a field study, Lee (1997) found that, while women were just as likely to engage in help-seeking in cultures with individualistic or collectivistic norms, men's help-seeking was substantially influenced by organizational norms – they engaged in substantially more help-seeking under collectivistic norms and less help-seeking when norms were individualistic. Power differential was also important to help-seeking: equal status people were more likely to seek help from one another.

Why might men's help-seeking behavior be particularly influenced by organizational norms? Lee (2002) hypothesized that men may be less likely to seek help because the perceived social costs for help-seeking are higher for men, as help-seeking may be seen to violate masculine gender norms – particularly in individualistic cultural contexts. This notion is supported by extensive literature showing that men are less likely than women to seek professional help for a variety of problems and that men who endorse more traditional ideas about masculinity have more negative attitudes toward help-seeking (Addis & Mahalik, 2003). The effect of gender on help-seeking may also be stronger for "masculine" gender-typed occupational roles.

Lee (2002) tested her hypothesis that perceived social costs influence help-seeking by conducting a field study in a hospital that was adopting a new computerized medication system and measuring patterns of help-seeking during the transition. Lee predicted that employees who rated individualistic norms (competence, superiority, independence) as more important to them would perceive higher social costs for help-seeking, and these employees were indeed less likely to seek help. Gender and gender-typed occupational role were related to help-seeking in that women (who were disproportionately nurses) were more likely than men (who were disproportionately physicians) to seek help. Perceived social costs mediated (explained) this effect. As in the prior study, help-seeking was most likely to be lateral; in other words, people sought help most frequently from people at their same level of status in the organization (their peers). With respect to higher-status individuals, seeking help from their staff, Lee (2002) speculated that such requests for help may violate leaders' self-conceptions as higher-status individuals who should be more competent and independent than their staff members. Lee concluded that perceived social costs are an important factor in predicting who will seek help when and from whom.

Taken together, these results suggest that, because of their status in the organization, leaders may perceive greater social costs as a result of seeking help. Perceived costs of help-seeking may be higher for men, for people in masculine-typed professions, and for people in organizations that subscribe to strong individualistic norms. Because leaders are, by definition, at or near the "top of the heap" in terms of status, they may have fewer peers and mentors from whom to seek help and thus are faced with the more seemingly costly prospect of seeking help from staff members. Such perceived constraints on help-seeking may extend to help-seeking in the context of leader personal crisis – a possibility that will need to be investigated in future research.

Importantly, Lee's (1997, 2002) work does not speak to the results of help-seeking or to the actual social costs of asking for help – only to the influence of perceptions of social costs on help-seeking behavior. As such, leaders should consider the possible benefits of help-seeking in addition to the perceived social costs of asking for help. In other words, perception with regard to social costs may or may not reflect the reality of the net effect of help-seeking for the leader and on his or her relationships. The final section of the chapter seeks to compare perceptions of the costs of help-seeking with the available evidence.

Perceived costs of help-seeking: perceptions and findings

Status loss

As described earlier, based on the work of Lee (1997, 2002), leaders may be concerned that they will lose status by asking for help based upon violation of individualistic leader norms of competence, independence, and superiority. What is the evidence for status loss as a result of leader help-seeking? Although there are very few studies on this important topic, the handful of studies available suggest that risk of status loss is mixed but may depend on gender and organizational norms.

A series of studies by Rosette, Mueller, and Lebel (2015) addresses the impact of help-seeking behavior on views of leaders according to gender. In a field study of a leadership development workshop that took place during an outdoor excursion, greater help-seeking was related to lower perceived competence for male leaders but not for female leaders. In two laboratory studies, participants who read descriptions of leader behavior rated males as less competent if they asked for help, but help-seeking had no effect on competence ratings for female leaders. The authors found that their results were consistent with role congruity theory, such that male help-seeking behavior is seen as less gender typical and therefore viewed more negatively in male leaders than in female leaders. The authors conclude that, "These findings represent a paradox for male leaders. Specifically, a large body of literature has shown that help-seeking behaviors contribute to positive functioning in a host of domains, including leadership" (Rosette et al., 2015, p. 760). They recommend that men in leadership roles consider ways to mitigate the effect of help-seeking on perceptions – for example, attributing the need for help to external rather than internal factors.

A study examining the relationship between receiving help from team members and team member perception of leader behavior also suggests that gender may play a role (Hoption, 2016). In a sample of 45 staff-supervisor pairs, leaders' reports of seeking help from their team members was not related to staff ratings of transformational leadership behaviors. However, in analyses that controlled for leader liking, leaders' ratings of receiving help from the staff were associated with lower ratings of transformational leadership by team members if the supervisor was male. However, there are a number of caveats to this finding that should be noted, including the fact that the analysis controlled for liking of the leader with no clear rationale and the fact that team members' ratings of their help provision to leaders was not reported or analyzed. Furthermore, extending the results of this study to leaders requesting help in personal crises is difficult because the study focused on how much team members were providing help to the leader on an ongoing basis that may or may not have been solicited. In contrast, help-seeking by the leader in the context of a personal crisis would likely involve more specific requests associated with the special circumstances of the event. In addition, it is important to note that leaders who reported receiving more help from team members were better liked by their team members ($r = .38$), consistent with social psychology research showing that people tend to like others for whom they have done favors (Jecker & Landy, 1969).

Taken together, the studies by Rosette et al. (2015) and Hoption (2016) suggest that male leaders may be at a greater risk of status loss than female leaders when they seek help, but no study has yet specifically examined leader help-seeking during a personal crisis. Help-seeking may have benefits for the leader and his or her relationships that could offset the costs of status loss.

A study by Lee (1999) suggests that leaders might consider using particular verbal strategies when requesting help and that using such strategies may be more common when one is a leader vs. a team member. Across both a laboratory and a field experiment, when asked to make a request for help, the use of verbal strategies, including enhancing the other (being polite, complimentary, deferential), minimizing the imposition of the request, and focusing on explaining the task (giving reasons, intensifying interest), was related to increased ratings of likability of the requestor and desirability as a colleague. Participants engaged in more of these interpersonal help-seeking verbal strategies under collectivistic norms. Under individualistic norms, men used more strategies when they were in the follower role, but women used strategies most often with peers. Lee's (1999) work suggests that leaders may wish to do perspective-taking when crafting their requests for help and consider framing requests in a way that will enhance the relationship, make requests seem reasonable, and communicate how providing help may enhance common goals. In addition, fostering collective organizational norms may boost the use of effective help-seeking strategies (Chapter 6).

In sum, a few studies suggest that male leaders who engage in help-seeking may be at increased risk of status loss but that leaders might consider help-seeking strategies to temper such potential losses. In addition, future studies should examine the extent to which collectivistic organizational norms might mitigate the risk of status loss.

Social rejection

Asking for help and being rejected is a painful potential cost of help-seeking. Yet, social psychology research suggests that people tend to overestimate the likelihood that their request for help will be rejected. In a series of studies, people systematically underestimated the extent to which strangers would comply with their requests for help. They tended to discount how much others are motivated to conform to altruistic norms and underestimate how awkward it feels to refuse direct requests for help. Thus, people may be more willing to comply with direct requests for help than help-seekers might assume (Flynn & Lake, 2008). Conversely, people assume it is easier than it really is for people in need to request help because they do not perceive how awkward and anxiety-provoking it can be to make such requests (Bohns & Flynn, 2010). As a result, people may be less likely to ask others who are in a personal crisis what they need because they assume it is easy for people to voice their requests. ("If they need something, they'll just ask.") In the specific case of leaders in crisis, team members may underestimate how hard it is for their leader to ask for help, since they are accustomed to the leader frequently giving work-related directives. Staff may not spontaneously reflect on how difficult it is for leaders to "cross the line" and become help-seekers – an intriguing possibility that requires further research.

Importantly, Bohns and Flynn (2010) suggest that people can better encourage help-seeking if they acknowledge and normalize the discomfort involved in making a help-seeking request ("Asking for help can feel awkward, which is totally normal."), rather than simply emphasizing its instrumental benefits ("Just ask so you can get what you need!"). As such, leaders themselves should be aware that help-seeking is likely to feel uncomfortable and out-of-role, but that in certain cases, the benefits may outweigh the costs.

Leader disclosure and help-seeking: summary and conclusions

- Most leaders in personal crises disclosed to someone in their organization, disclosed selectively, and were satisfied with their disclosure decisions, though some remained dissatisfied. Leaders disclosed for both informational and instrumental (i.e., help-seeking) purposes.
- Personality traits, being a "private person," and general degree of trust in others were less strongly related to disclosure than were factors more directly related to the interpersonal environment of the organization (Chapter 4).
- Cultural and organizational norms may create prohibitions on disclosure and help-seeking, while perceptions of leader help-seeking may depend on the leader's gender.
- Leaders in crisis may be concerned that disclosure will result in loss of status, experience of stigma or rejection, and an increase in uncertainty and instability for the organization. On the other hand, disclosure may also lead to access to resources, reduced stress, strengthened relationships, enhanced ability to plan and execute a response to the crisis and fulfillment of one's fiduciary responsibility to the organization.
- Leaders should carefully consider both the costs and benefits of disclosure and be strategic about to whom they disclose and for what purpose(s). Strategic disclosure

includes what information to disclose, the purpose, delivering the information in a way that helps team members understand how they will be impacted, and deciding how to coordinate boundaries after information is shared.

- Barriers to leader help-seeking include individualistic norms, concerns about loss of social status, and fear of rejection. Although there is very little research on the impact of leader help-seeking (and none on its impact in the context of personal crisis), leaders can consider crafting their requests for help in a way that strengthens relationships and should be aware that people will probably be more willing to provide help than they anticipate.
- Leader feelings of awkwardness and anxiety around disclosure and help-seeking are very normal and understandable, given the leader's typically expected role as competent, independent help-giver. Acknowledging these feelings may lower perceived barriers to sharing important information and asking for help.

References

Adams, J. C., & Mansi, S. A. (2009). CEO turnover and bondholder wealth. *Journal of Banking & Finance, 33*(3), 522–533. https://doi.org/10.1016/j.jbankfin.2008.09.005

Addis, M. E., & Mahalik, J. R. (2003). Men, masculinity, and the contexts of help seeking. *American Psychologist, 58*(1), 5. https://doi.org/10.1037/0003-066X.58.1.5

Bohns, V. K., & Flynn, F. J. (2010). "Why didn't you just ask?" Underestimating the discomfort of help-seeking. *Journal of Experimental Social Psychology, 46*(2), 402–409. https://doi.org/10.1016/j.jesp.2009.12.015

Caza, A., Zhang, G., Wang, L., & Bai, Y. (2015). How do you really feel? Effect of leaders' perceived emotional sincerity on followers' trust. *The Leadership Quarterly, 26*(4), 518–531. https://doi.org/10.1016/j.leaqua.2015.05.008

Collins, N. L., & Miller, L. C. (1995). Self-disclosure and liking: A meta-analytic review. *Psychological Bulletin, 116*(3), 457. https://doi.org/10.1037/0033-2909.116.3.457

Costa, P. T., & McCrae, R. R. (1992). Four ways five factors are basic. *Personality and Individual Differences, 13*(6), 653–665. https://doi.org/10.1016/0191-8869(92)90236-I

Davidson, W. N., Tong, S., Worrell, D. L., & Rowe, W. (2006). Ignoring rules of succession: How the board reacts to CEO illness announcements. *Journal of Business Strategies; Huntsville, 23*(2), 93–113.

Dingler-Duhon, M., & Brown, B. B. (1987). Self-disclosure as an influence strategy: Effects of machiavellianism, androgyny, and sex. *Sex Roles, 16*(3), 109–123. https://doi.org/10.1007/BF00289643

Ellison, M. L., Russinova, Z., MacDonald-Wilson, K. L., & Lyass, A. (2003). Patterns and correlates of workplace disclosure among professionals and managers with psychiatric conditions. *Journal of Vocational Rehabilitation, 18*, 3–13.

Flynn, F. J., & Lake, V. K. B. (2008). If you need help, just ask: Underestimating compliance with direct requests for help. *Journal of Personality and Social Psychology, 95*(1), 128–143. https://doi.org/10.1037/0022-3514.95.1.128

Flynn, F. J., Reagans, R. E., Amanatullah, E. T., & Ames, D. R. (2006). Helping one's way to the top: Self-monitors achieve status by helping others and knowing who helps whom. *Journal of Personality and Social Psychology, 91*(6), 1123–1137. https://doi.org/10.1037/0022-3514.91.6.1123

Gibson, K. R. (2018). Can I tell you something? How disruptive self-disclosure changes who "we" are. *Academy of Management Review, 43*(4), 570–589. https://doi.org/10.5465/amr.2016.0317

Gibson, K. R., Harari, D., & Marr, J. C. (2018). When sharing hurts: How and why self-disclosing weakness undermines the task-oriented relationships of higher status disclosers. *Organizational Behavior and Human Decision Processes, 144,* 25–43. https://doi.org/10.1016/j.obhdp.2017.09.001

Goldstein, N. J., & Mortensen, C. R. (2012). Social norms: A how-to (and how-not-to) guide. In D. T. Kenrick, N. J. Goldstein, & S. L. Braver (Series Eds.), *Six degrees of social influence: Science, application, and the psychology of Robert Cialdini.* New York: Oxford University Press.

Grant, A. M. (2013). *Give and take: Why helping others drives our success.* New York: Penguin Books.

Hinshaw, S. P., & Stier, A. (2008). Stigma as related to mental disorders. *Annual Review of Clinical Psychology, 4*(1), 367–393. https://doi.org/10.1146/annurev.clinpsy.4.022007.141245

Hoption, C. (2016). The double-edged sword of helping behavior in leader-follower dyads. *Leadership & Organization Development Journal; Bradford, 37*(1), 13–41.

Jecker, J., & Landy, D. (1969). Liking a person as a function of doing him a favour. *Human Relations, 22*(4), 371–378. https://doi.org/10.1177/001872676902200407

Kahneman, D., & Tversky, A. (1979). Prospect theory: An analysis of decision under risk. *Econometrica, 47*(2), 263–291. https://doi.org/10.2307/1914185

Larcker, D. F., & Tayan, B. (2011). CEO health disclosure at apple: A public or private matter? *Stanford Closer Look Series,* 1–7.

Lee, F. (1997). When the going gets tough, do the tough ask for help? Help seeking and power motivation in organizations. *Organizational Behavior and Human Decision Processes, 72*(3), 336–363. https://doi.org/10.1006/obhd.1997.2746

Lee, F. (1999). Verbal strategies for seeking help in organizations. *Journal of Applied Social Psychology, 29*(7), 1472–1496. https://doi.org/10.1111/j.1559-1816.1999.tb00148.x

Lee, F. (2002). The social costs of seeking help. *The Journal of Applied Behavioral Science, 38*(1), 17–35. https://doi.org/10.1177/0021886302381002

Lee, F., & Tiedens, L. Z. (2001). Is it lonely at the top?: The independence and interdependence of power holders. *Research in Organizational Behavior, 23,* 43–91. https://doi.org/10.1016/S0191-3085(01)23003-2

Miller, W. R., & Rollnick, S. (2002). *Motivational interviewing: Preparing people for change* (2nd ed.). New York: Guilford Press.

Mooradian, T., Renzl, B., & Matzler, K. (2006). Who trusts? Personality, trust and knowledge sharing. *Management Learning, 37*(4), 523–540. https://doi.org/10.1177/1350507606073424

Munir, F., Leka, S., & Griffiths, A. (2005). Dealing with self-management of chronic illness at work: predictors for self-disclosure. *Social Science & Medicine (1982), 60*(6), 1397–1407. https://doi.org/10.1016/j.socscimed.2004.07.012

Nifadkar, S. S., Wu, W., & Gu, Q. (2019). Supervisors' work related and nonwork information sharing: Integrating research on information sharing, information seeking, and trust using self disclosure theory. *Personnel Psychology, 72*(2), 241–269. https://doi.org/10.1111/peps.12305

Perryman, A. A., Butler, F. C., Martin, J. A., & Ferris, G. R. (2010). When the CEO is ill: Keeping quiet or going public? *Business Horizons, 53*(1), 21–29. https://doi.org/10.1016/j.bushor.2009.08.006

Petronio, S. (2015). Communication privacy management theory. In *The international encyclopedia of interpersonal communication* (pp. 353–360). New York: John Wiley and Sons. https://doi.org/10.1002/9781118540190.wbeic132

Phillips, K. W., Rothbard, N. P., & Dumas, T. L. (2009). To disclose or not to disclose? Status distance and self-disclosure in diverse environments. *Academy of Management Review, 34*(4), 710–732. https://doi.org/10.5465/amr.34.4.zok710

Proffitt, D., Cann, A., Calhoun, L. G., & Tedeschi, R. G. (2007). Judeo-Christian clergy and personal crisis: Religion, posttraumatic growth and well being. *Journal of Religion and Health, 46*(2), 219–231.

Rajah, R., Song, Z., & Arvey, R. D. (2011). Emotionality and leadership: Taking stock of the past decade of research. *The Leadership Quarterly, 22*(6), 1107–1119. https://doi.org/10.1016/j.leaqua.2011.09.006

Rhim, J. C., Peluchette, J. V., & Song, I. (2006). Stock market reactions and firm performance surrounding CEO succession: Antecedents of succession and successor origin. *American Journal of Business, 21*(1), 21–30. https://doi.org/10.1108/19355181200600002

Rosette, A. S., Mueller, J. S., & Lebel, R. D. (2015). Are male leaders penalized for seeking help? The influence of gender and asking behaviors on competence perceptions. *The Leadership Quarterly, 26*(5), 749–762. https://doi.org/10.1016/j.leaqua.2015.02.001

Sanchez-Burks, J. (2005). Protestant relational ideology: The cognitive underpinnings and organizational implications of an American anomaly. *Research in Organizational Behavior, 26*, 265–305. https://doi.org/10.1016/S0191-3085(04)26007-5

Sanchez-Burks, J., & Uhlmann, E. L. (2013). Outlier Nation: The cultural psychology of American workways. In M. Yuki & M. Brewer (Eds.), *Culture and group processes* (pp. 121–142). Oxford: Oxford University Press. https://doi.org/10.1093/acprof:oso/9780199985463.003.0006

Sandoval, B. E., & Lee, F. (2006). When is seeking help appropriate? How norms affect help-seeking in organizations. In V. Aleven & L. Alexitch (Eds.), *Help seeking in academic settings: Goals, groups, and contexts* (pp. 151–173). Mahwah, NJ: Lawrence Erlbaum.

Uhlmann, E. L., Heaphy, E., Ashford, S. J., Zhu, L. [Lei], & Sanchez-Burks, J. (2013). Acting professional: An exploration of culturally bounded norms against nonwork role referencing. *Journal of Organizational Behavior, 34*(6), 866–886. https://doi.org/10.1002/job.1874

Weiss, M., Razinskas, S., Backmann, J., & Hoegl, M. (2018). Authentic leadership and leaders' mental well-being: An experience sampling study. *The Leadership Quarterly, 29*(2), 309–321. https://doi.org/10.1016/j.leaqua.2017.05.007

Westerman, C. Y. K., Miller, L. E., Reno, K. M., & Spates, S. A. (2015). Sharing personal health information at work: What is appropriate and expected in organizations? *Communication Studies, 66*(3), 378–397. https://doi.org/10.1080/10510974.2015.1019157

Wortman, C. B., Adesman, P., Herman, E., & Greenberg, R. (1976). Self-disclosure: An attributional perspective. *Journal of Personality and Social Psychology, 33*(2), 184–191.

4

THE ORGANIZATION'S
INTERPERSONAL ENVIRONMENT

STORIES OF PSYCHOLOGICAL SAFETY AND TRUST (OR LACK THEREOF) – QUOTATIONS FROM LEADERS

And they [staff] responded as you would have expected . . . with a lot of concern. . . . I didn't have the same kind of reaction in the peer group or the CEO level, and I would attribute that more to the politics of the environment. A lot of people were more worried about their own skin than anything else . . . they were kind of looking out for what was best for them and so their willingness to step up and help somebody else out; that's unfortunate. That's something that the organization I work for needs to have a much more keen feel for, but they haven't got it yet.

– Study participant

My organization has always been committed to family – and so my supervisor was the one who first suggested that I work half-days so that I could provide my part of the care for my daughter.

– Study participant

In response to: do you think this environment helped or hindered your efforts to handle the crisis?

Definitely hindered! After 18 years of being a "top" performer and leader it took me a while to handle the "cold" nature of the corporation and the vice president I reported to. Loyalty and "respect for the individual" is not the norm of the corporate culture anymore. Only, who is "left on the bench to produce."

– Study participant

> Almost everyone had gone through losing a parent and many had trouble with alcohol or drugs afterwards to cope. They had a good understanding of where I was coming from and some even said that I just needed to get it out of my system. My supervisors are close friends and were only a phone call away for me to cry and ramble to.
>
> *– Study participant*

People's actions are heavily influenced by their environment and their past experiences in particular environments. A leader's choices about how to handle a personal crisis likely depend on their perception of the organizational culture and the possible interpersonal consequences of using particular coping strategies. The success of chosen strategies also depends on the responses of people surrounding the leader. Personal crises are times of vulnerability – particularly for leaders who are often expected to be less vulnerable than others (see Chapter 3). As such, a full understanding of leadership during a personal crisis must take into account the interpersonal climate and culture of the organization – in particular, whether leaders believe it is "safe" to be vulnerable and reach out to others when coping with the crisis and whether they generally trust the intentions of others in the organization. We first present relevant results from Study 2, followed by a theoretical perspective on the role of the organization's interpersonal context from Conservation of Resources Theory. Finally, we review and integrate research on the three key interpersonal environment concepts measured in Study 2 and suggest directions for future research.

The role of interpersonal environment in our studies

We examined three constructs related to leader perceptions of their organizational environment: psychological safety, trust in peers and the organization, and social constraints about discussing the crisis with others in the organization. In this section, we briefly describe each concept and our results from Study 2. More extensive background information about each concept is provided in the third section of this chapter.

Psychological safety

Psychological safety is the extent to which people perceive that it is safe to engage in interpersonal risk-taking in a team or organization (Edmondson, 1999). Psychologically safe teams are characterized by open communication, valuing of members as individuals, interpersonal supportiveness, and the ability to engage in constructive conflict (Newman, Donohue, & Eva, 2017). Psychological safety was measured using a modification of the seven-item scale by Edmondson (1999; see Appendix C).

On average, participants agreed slightly that their organizations were psychologically safe ($M = 4.62$, $SD = 0.99$; significantly higher than the scale midpoint of 4, $t(166) = 8.14$, $p < .001$). Yet 20% of participants had average scores in the strongly disagree to slightly disagree range (below the scale midpoint) and only 14%

of participants had average scores that indicated agreement to strong agreement. Ratings of organizational psychological safety given by middle managers $(M = 4.49, SD = 0.91)$ were lower than those given by executive leaders $(M = 4.81, SD = 1.06)$, $t(165) = 2.08, p = .04, d = 0.32$. However, middle managers, on average, still "agreed slightly" that their organizations were psychologically safe. Thus, participants in our study reported a range of perceptions regarding the extent to which they felt, in general, interpersonally safe in their organizations.

Trust in peers and the organization

We measured leaders' faith in the intentions of their colleagues and of the organization using two three-item scales adapted from Cook and Wall (1980) and reported in Mooradian, Renzl, and Matzler (2006). For trust in work colleagues, on average, participants agreed that they had faith in the intentions of their peers $(M = 5.57, SD = 1.15$; significantly higher than the scale midpoint of 4, $t(166) = 17.77, p < .001)$. Only 4% of participants had average scores in the strongly disagree to slightly disagree range. For trust in the organization and its management, on average, participants slightly agreed that they had faith in the intentions of the organization and management $(M = 4.96, SD = 1.23$; significantly higher than the scale midpoint of 4, $t(166) = 10.11, p < .001)$. Sixteen percent of participants had average scores in the strongly disagree to slightly disagree range. Participants endorsed significantly greater trust in their colleagues than in the overall organization, $t(166) = 7.07, p < .001$, and trust in peers and trust in the organization were moderately correlated $(r = .55, p < .001)$.

Social constraints on disclosure in the organization

People experiencing stressful life events vary in the extent to which they feel socially constrained about discussing the event with others – for example, the extent to which they find others receptive to their disclosures and feel they can speak freely (Lepore, Silver, Wortman, & Wayment, 1996). Social constraints on talking about the personal crisis when interacting with others in the organization was measured using a four-item scale adapted from Lepore et al. (1996; see Appendix C). On average, participants sometimes experienced social constraints related to talking about and receiving support for their personal crisis in the organization $(M = 2.79$ on a five-point scale, $SD = 0.91)$, but responses ranged widely from the minimum (endorsing no social constraints at all) to the maximum (always experiencing social constraints on all items). Thus, similar to psychological safety, participants in our study reported a range of perceptions regarding the extent to which they felt they could freely speak about the crisis to others in their organization.

Hindrance vs. support by the organization

We asked participants whether they believed their organization had "hindered [them] a great deal in coping with [their] personal crisis." On average, participants disagreed somewhat with this statement $(M = 3.68, SD = 2.00$; significantly lower than the scale midpoint of 4, $t(166) = -2.09, p = .04$). Yet 38% of participants agreed with this statement to some extent. We also asked participants whether their organization is supportive of people experiencing personal crisis. On average, participants agreed with this statement ($M = 5.55, SD = 1.39$; significantly higher than the scale midpoint of 4, $t(166) = 14.41, p < .001$). Nine percent of participants disagreed with this statement to some extent, and another 10% neither agreed nor disagreed. Taken together, these results demonstrate some variability (and even ambivalence) across leaders in our survey regarding the extent to which they believed their organization supported them and others in personal crises.

Exploring interpersonal environment and disclosure[1]

As noted in Chapter 3, we examined the association between work environment variables and the extent to which leaders reported disclosing their crisis to others in the organization. Overall breadth of disclosure was associated with greater psychological safety ($r = .27, p < .001$), and more trust in peers ($r = .37, p < .001$) and in management ($r = .26, p = .001$). There was a trend toward disclosure being associated with the perception of fewer social constraints on disclosure to others in the organization ($r = -.13, p = .10$). Therefore, leaders who had disclosed to more people perceived their organizations to be more tolerant of interpersonal risk-taking and had greater trust in colleagues and in the organization as a whole. Because we measured these variables at the same time point, we are unable to pinpoint the direction of the effects. Perhaps leaders with greater trust and perception of psychological safety in their organizations felt more comfortable disclosing, but it is also possible that the act of disclosing (and, presumably, being met with support) promoted leaders' sense of trust and safety. Future studies following participants over time will be needed to tease apart the direction of these effects.

We also examined the association between these organizational environment variables and participants' satisfaction with the decisions they made about disclosure. As with disclosure itself, greater psychological safety[2] ($r = .34, p < .001$), more trust in peers ($r = .30, p < .001$) and in management ($r = .24, p = .002$), and fewer social constraints in the organization ($r = -.25, p = .001$) were associated with greater leader satisfaction with disclosure decisions.

Exploring interpersonal environment and outcomes

We examined the extent to which organizational environment variables were related to leaders' perceptions of the supportiveness of their organization and to

---

1   Because internal consistency for some of these scales was lower than ideal, we calculated disattenuated correlation coefficients for values in this section so that the reader can gauge the possible impact of measurement error (see Appendix C for further explanation). These are: Psychological Safety ($r = .33$), Trust in Peers ($r = .40$), Trust in Management of the Organization ($r = .33$), and Social Constraints on Disclosure in Organization ($r = -.16$).

2   Disattenuated correlations are: Psychological Safety ($r = .41$), Trust in Peers ($r = .32$), Trust in Management ($r = .30$), and Social Constraints in Organization ($r = -.31$).

TABLE 4.1 Correlations between Organizational Environment Factors and Leader Perceptions of the Organization and Their Handling of the Crisis

	Psychological safety	Trust in colleagues	Trust in organization	Social constraints in organization
1. Organization hindered me in coping	−.28**	−.03	−.35**	.42**
2. Organization supportive of those in crisis	.51**	.57**	.53**	−.31**
3. Perceived effectiveness of handling crisis in leadership role	.29**	.26**	.27**	−.31**
4. Satisfaction with handling crisis in leadership role	.25**	.27**	.26**	−.32**

Note: *p < .05; **p < .01 for a two-tailed test. See Table C.3 in Appendix C for disattenuated correlations.

their overall evaluation of and satisfaction with their handling of the crisis *vis-à-vis* their leadership role (see Table 4.1).

Nearly all organization environment variables were related to perceptions of the organization and to leaders' perceptions of their own coping in their leadership role, with the exception of trust in colleagues and believing the organization had hindered coping. Notably, greater psychological safety and trust and experience of fewer social constraints were associated with more positive perceptions of overall leader effectiveness and satisfaction in handling their crisis in the leadership role.[3]

In sum, leaders varied in their perception of psychological safety in their organizations, in their trust in colleagues and management, and especially in the extent to which they felt they could speak freely about the crisis in their organizations. They expressed greater trust in their colleagues than they did in the organization and management as a whole. Most importantly, leaders who endorsed greater psychological safety, trust, and ability to speak freely about the crisis in their organization were more likely to report that they had been able to handle the crisis effectively in their leadership role and that they were satisfied with their ability to do so.

Importance of organizational culture

For the leaders in our studies, the nature of their organizational environments was related to the degree to which they felt they had successfully navigated the personal crisis in their leadership role. Although this result is, in hindsight, not surprising – most readers can probably give many examples of how their workplace culture affects them personally and professionally – the implications of the finding for

3 Notably, the significant association between these work environment variables and effectiveness and satisfaction persisted when controlling for key personality variables (neuroticism, agreeableness, overall trust/mistrust).

leadership practice are no less profound. If these findings are replicated, they suggest that helping leaders cope effectively with personal crises may not only be a function of choosing the "right" leaders who possess some internal quality of "resilience" but also a function of embedding leaders in the "right" environments (i.e., those that facilitate resilience and thriving.)[4]

To frame our discussion of the critical role of the organizational environment, we draw on two key concepts from the organizational and leadership studies literature: an organization's climate and its culture. Organizational or work group climate has been described as the "feel" of the organization or group that can be readily perceived by a newcomer (Schein, 2004). The physical environment and the behavior of individuals and how they interact with one another contribute to a sense of climate. Culture, however, is a much more deeply embedded aspect of an organization or group that is manifested in an observable climate. Schein (2010, p. 18) defines organizational culture as,

> a pattern of shared basic assumptions that the group has learned as it solved its problems of external adaptation and internal integration, that has worked well enough to be considered valid and, therefore, to be taught to new members as the correct way to perceive, think, and feel in relation to those problems.

This rich definition describes what culture is, how it develops, and how it can evolve over time – that is, via new experiences in which the group encounters and solves problems, both internal and external. Schein (2004) emphasizes that the tacit assumptions that constitute organizational culture are distinct from an organization's explicitly stated values and rules. Rather, culture is composed of those assumptions so basic that they mostly operate outside of awareness, shaping the actions and perceptions of group members. Culture shapes routine, day-to-day procedures, social interactions, and which actions are rewarded and which are punished by others. For example, as discussed in Chapter 3, organizations can vary in the extent to which the tacit assumption, "It is unprofessional to discuss one's personal life at work," is part of organizational culture (Sanchez-Burks & Uhlmann, 2013). In an organizational culture where such an assumption is strongly present, individuals will probably be less likely to disclose their personal crises because they (perhaps rightly) anticipate that disclosure may be punished with subtle interpersonal disapproval, loss of status, or other consequences.[5]

---

4 The juxtaposition of personal traits and qualities vs. the influence of the work environment is reminiscent of the classic "person vs. situation" debate in psychology and leadership studies, which pitted traits and situational factors against each other as the most powerful predictors of human behavior. Importantly, more recent work highlights the role of each factor in explaining within-person variation (situation) and between-person variation (traits) (Fleeson, 2004).

5 Thus, the concept of organizational culture includes the idea of "norms" discussed in Chapter 3 – i.e., what is commonly done in a situation or commonly approved of (Schein, 2010).

Because of its pervasiveness and its tacit nature, culture has the capacity to exert powerful effects on individual and group behavior within an organization, and these effects can extend to the actions of the leader. When groups are forming, leaders have much more power to influence and shape the organizational culture than when the leader is working within a mature group with established cultural assumptions (Schein, 2004). Thus, most leaders are likely to be subject to the influence of the organization's culture, particularly if they have risen to their leadership position from within that organization. Yet leaders have the capacity to change and manage culture, provided that they can stand outside of it just enough to perceive its assumptions and identify which may need to be changed (Schein, 2004). As we discuss in Chapter 6, we believe that there are key assumptions underlying organizational culture which, if promoted, might support maximal resilience for leaders in crisis and their team members.

Organizational culture, in theory, has the capacity to influence the extent to which leaders in crisis are able to successfully cope with personal crises in their leadership role. Data from our studies so far lends preliminary support to this notion. In the next section, we present a theoretical framework that leaders and researchers can employ to better understand the influence of organizational culture in the context of crisis events.

Theoretical framework: organizational culture and interpersonal resources

In this section, we return to Conservation of Resources (COR) Theory (see Chapter 2) to present a conceptual framework toward understanding the importance of the organizational environment to leaders experiencing personal crises. We also integrate research from a resource-based theory of workplace burnout to describe additional ways in which the organizational environment might provide resources to leaders in crises.

As described in Chapter 2, COR theory is concerned with explaining what occurs when people and organizations experience stressful events. Its basic tenet is that people strive to retain and protect things that they value, their resources (Hobfoll, Halbesleben, Neveu, & Westman, 2018). Resources include tangible object resources (a car, a computer), condition resources (employment, marriage), energy resources (money, knowledge), and personal resources (skills, optimism, self-worth). Crisis events cause the loss of different kinds of resources, losses which are more salient than gains and which require investment of additional resources with which to cope and from which to recover. When considering patterns of resource distribution, Hobfoll (2011; Hobfoll et al., 2018) observed that resources tend to "travel in packs" and correlate with one another. For example, personal resources such as optimism, self-esteem, and confidence are highly correlated, and individuals who have higher levels of object and energy resources are more likely to have access to these personal resources. Furthermore, those rich in resources can use them to obtain additional resources, as stated in Corollary 1 of COR theory (see Chapter 2).

Hobfoll calls this "rich get richer" pattern a resource caravan. He also observed that certain social structures protect and grow an individual's resource caravan and dubbed sets of these protective social structures "resource caravan passageways." For example, families rich in resources can give their children access to social structures (e.g., schools, tutors, professional network) that serve to protect and grow a variety of resources. Families with fewer resources have more limited access to these privileged and protective caravan passageways.

Building organizational caravan passageways

When applied to organizations, Hobfoll (2011) describes how some organizations provide caravan passageways that help individuals grow their resources, while other organizations deplete the resources of their members without replacement. As such, the concept of caravan passageways in COR theory emphasizes the powerful role of the environment in creating or inhibiting the personal resources and capacities of individuals and groups. Organizations should consider the ways in which their structures and cultures promote resource growth for individuals vs. depletion. As Hobfoll (2011) notes,

> Organizational support, stability, safety (ranging from safety from violence to safety to express ideas openly) are all aspects of resource caravan-creating and sustaining organizational ecologies. These ecologies can be seen to be creating passageways in which resources are supplied, protected, shared, fostered, and pooled.
>
> *(p. 118)*

Support from others in the organization as well as supportive policies and procedures within the formal organizational culture may create caravan passageways that help leaders (and non-leaders) protect against resource loss during personal crises and, potentially, grow new resource capacities in the process.

In addition to formal policies and institutional structures, Hobfoll et al. (2018) propose that the interpersonal process of "crossover" may support and sustain resource caravan passageways. Crossover is the process by which one person's emotional or psychological state – positive or negative – influences another. This process may occur directly via empathy, by the emotion-influenced actions of one person triggering the emotions of another, or as a result of the same environmental conditions (e.g., stressors) causing similar emotions in both persons (spurious crossover; Westman, 2013). Although frequently studied with respect to negative emotions, research has also investigated crossover of positive personal resources from one person to another, such as self-efficacy and work engagement, defined as a sense of vigor, absorption, and dedication to one's work (Chen, Westman, & Hobfoll, 2015; Schaufeli & Bakker, 2004). Both burnout and its antithesis, engagement, seem capable of crossing over between coworkers (Bakker, Emmerik, & Euwema, 2006). Hobfoll et al. (2018) suggest that finding ways to increase crossover of engagement and positive emotions among individuals and work teams might be a method of building more resilient organizations.

With respect to leaders in crisis, those who are embedded within a social network of engaged and well-resourced colleagues may experience crossover of engagement such that they find it easier to become absorbed in their work despite the psychological distress provoked by the personal crisis event. Leaders surrounded by staff and peers who experience and express more frequent positive emotions may likewise experience crossover of positivity and more frequent moments of emotional respite, consistent with the "broaden and build" theory of positive emotions (Fredrickson, 2000). Thus, crossover of engagement, positive emotion, and other personal resources may be another way that organizations can create caravan passageways of resources to benefit leaders in crisis. Much additional research will be needed to determine the optimal ways that organizations can support leaders in crisis and promote their resilience.

Two distinct functions of resource caravan passageways for leaders in crisis

We propose that caravan passageways of resources in organizations can serve two distinct supportive functions for leaders in crisis. First, organizations can support leaders to develop resources a priori – skills, strong relationships, rich social networks, a sense of autonomy and self-worth – that can be deployed in the event of a personal crisis. As Hobfoll et al. (2018) describe this function of caravan passageways, "Social and environmental conditions create resilience or fragility, social skillfulness or social awkwardness, tolerance or intolerance, among the individuals who are exposed to such environments" (p. 107). As such, organizations that provide opportunities for leaders to learn, grow, connect, and thrive not only promote personal well-being, but help to "shore up" leader resources in the event of a personal crisis, increasing the likelihood that the leader can navigate the crisis with less impact on their leadership performance.

As described in Chapter 2, many studies on burnout have shown that job resources buffer the effect of job demands on the exhaustion and disengagement that characterize the state of burnout, which is a core proposition of job demands-resources theory (JD-R; Bakker & Demerouti, 2016). This theory proposes that all aspects of a job can be categorized as either demands or resources and makes predictions about their impact on risk of burnout. Job demands have been shown to have direct effects on worker exhaustion while, in contrast, job resources have direct effects on worker engagement and motivation. The effects of resources on engagement are particularly strong under conditions of high job demands such that resources reduce the risk of burnout when demands are high (Bakker, 2005; Bakker & Demerouti, 2016). For example, in a study of 1,012 university employees, autonomy, quality of relationship with supervisor, and quality of feedback and communication buffered the negative impact of work-home interference (e.g., the extent to which the work schedule interferes with home obligations) on exhaustion and disengagement (Bakker, 2005). Based on JD-R theory, we propose that pre-existing job resources[6] might also buffer the effect of personal crises on exhaustion and disengagement in leaders. However, like other research questions in this book, we are unaware of research studies that specifically apply JD-R theory and test its predictions with respect to burnout in leaders or with respect to the effects of personal crisis.

A second function of organizational caravan passageways in the event of a personal crisis is the provision of "just in time" access to resources during all stages of the personal crisis. Ideally, leaders would have easy access to a variety of resources, knowing which are available, how to access them, and trusting that they will not experience negative consequences for doing so. Formal policies and procedures might facilitate access. However, the tacit assumptions that constitute organizational culture would also be important to promoting access. For example, cultures that assume that people's personal well-being is an important concern of the organization or that help-seeking is a smart and praiseworthy course of action would be expected to facilitate access to crisis-relevant resources. And, consistent with the concept of crossover, leaders surrounded by teams of engaged members frequently expressing positive emotions may find it easier to stay engaged when focus on work is necessary or helpful in coping with the crisis.

In sum, by applying the caravan passageway concept from COR theory to understanding the role of organizational culture in supporting leaders in crisis, we identify two distinct but related roles that the organization can play: fostering development of resources in the leader that will promote coping in the event of crisis and providing just-in-time access to resources for leaders actively navigating crisis. From the perspective of COR theory, then, the individual leader's ability to effectively respond to a personal crisis is as much a function of the resources provided by the organization and its culture – including permission for the leader to access those resources – as it is about the resources the leader brings to the organization. As such, we argue that some responsibility for leader resilience falls squarely in the purview of the organization.

Potentially important features of the interpersonal environment for leaders in crisis

In this section, we discuss in more detail the concepts we explored in Study 2 that point to effects of the organizational environment on leaders in crisis – psychological safety, trust in the organization, and social constraints regarding discussion of the crisis with others. Each of these concepts has fairly extensive literature supporting its validity and its importance in understanding behavior in organizations (psychological safety; colleague and organizational trust) or its role

---

6 Importantly, because findings from the JD-R perspective show weaker direct effects of resources on exhaustion, reduced job demands may also be needed to help depleted leaders in crisis.

in coping and recovering from stressful experiences (social constraints on disclosure). The application of these concepts to leader well-being is novel, and so our goal in this section is to provide an overview of each concept, describe how it can be applied to understanding leaders in crisis, and describe future research directions for each.

Psychological safety

Psychological safety is the extent to which people perceive that it is safe to engage in interpersonal risk-taking in a team or organization (Edmondson, 1999; Edmondson & Lei, 2014). The concept of psychological safety has its roots in the organizational change work of Schein and Bennis (1965), but more recent scholarship has been spurred by Amy Edmondson's qualitative and quantitative work on factors promoting creativity and productivity in work teams (Edmondson, 1999). Because sharing creative ideas and advocating for innovative courses of action increases the risk of being viewed negatively or judged harshly by others, members of teams that are characterized by low psychological safety – for example, teams where members perceive that they are likely to be undermined, judged, or discounted by others – may be less likely to share openly and collaborate fully with one another. In contrast, teams in which members collectively believe that their opinions are valued, that they are respected, and that they can make mistakes and reveal their true selves without fear of negative judgment (i.e., teams high in psychological safety) tend to be more creative and innovative, perform better, and have members that are more likely to participate and give voice to important information (e.g., safety concerns) (Newman et al., 2017).

We were interested in measuring leader perceptions of psychological safety in their organizations because of observations we made in earlier stages of our research. In the interview work that preceded our survey studies and in open-ended responses given by participants in Study 1, some participants discussed the extent to which they felt as though disclosing their crisis would cause them to lose face within the organization, and others mentioned fears that the information would be used against them in some way. These participants were giving voice to the idea that, in their interpersonal contexts, it was interpersonally risky and psychologically unsafe to disclose and that disclosure would make them socially and professionally vulnerable. For example, one participant reported that the unspoken rule in her organization seemed to be, "to act like even though this [personal crisis] is going on in your life that it's not affecting you, everybody knows that it has to be, but it's sort of an unwritten code of conduct depending on where you are and what you do." Thus, in designing Study 2, we went to the literature in search of research concepts that would tap into this sense of vulnerability. Although prior studies have examined leadership behaviors that seem to foster a sense of psychological safety in teams and organizations, we did not find any studies that examined leader perceptions of the psychological safety of their surrounding environments. Interestingly, we also did not encounter studies that examine personal well-being as an outcome of workplace psychological safety, which is a future direction for research on both leaders and non-leaders.

As reported at the outset of this chapter, leaders' perceived psychological safety of their organizations was associated with the extent to which they disclosed their crisis in their organization, their satisfaction with those disclosures, and their perception that the organization was helpful in managing the crisis and that they themselves were effective and satisfied with the outcome. Therefore, although none of the content of the items in the scale refers to personal disclosures or personal crisis, leader ratings of psychological safety were associated with key variables surrounding the experience of a personal crisis in the leadership role. As with any correlational study, we are unable to determine the direction of the effects observed here. For example, it is possible that leader experiences, positive or negative, with handling personal crisis in their role affected their perceptions of how psychologically safe their organization is generally. It is also plausible that leaders in psychologically safe organizations are more likely to disclose because they perceive fewer risks and that such disclosure enables them to obtain support and recover better from the personal crisis. Additional longitudinal and multi-level research is needed to determine the direction of these effects and to better understand the interplay among work environment variables and personal well-being outcomes, not just measures of workplace functioning.

Leaders occupy a unique position with respect to the psychological safety of the work environment because, while they are certainly embedded within the work environment and affected by it, they also have more capacity to influence the psychological safety of the environment, at least to some degree. Leadership factors most strongly associated with increased perceptions of psychological safety by team members include transformational leadership practices, trust in the leader, leader-member exchange, and inclusive leadership practices (Frazier, Fainshmidt, Klinger, Pezeshkan, & Vracheva, 2017). For example, a recent study found that employee perception of leader-member caring behavior was associated with stronger perceptions of psychological safety one month later (Binyamin, Friedman, & Carmeli, 2017). Thus, leaders who work to build psychological safety in their teams through positive and nurturing leader behaviors not only contribute to the enhanced performance of their team but may also create social structures that can provide support to them in the event of a personal crisis. In the language of COR theory, leaders who invest in creating psychologically safe environments are creating caravan passageways of resources not just for their staff but also for themselves.

Yet no leader has total control over organizational policies or culture, and so it is important to recognize that certain supportive organization-wide practices contribute to psychological safety and its associated outcomes. For example, perceived organizational support and access to mentoring have been identified as correlates of psychological safety in past studies. In addition, the frequency and quality of interpersonal interactions among team members and the social network connections of those team members with others has also been associated with psychological safety, suggesting that leaders and workplace policies that foster collegial interactions, cross-unit communication, and rich social networks may also have a positive impact on psychological safety and its downstream effects (Newman et al., 2017).

In sum, this brief review of the construct of psychological safety in conjunction with our preliminary findings from Study 2 suggests that the psychological safety of a leader's surrounding work environment may increase his or her access to resources during a personal crisis – a model that will need to be evaluated in future research. In addition, as noted by Edmondson and Lei (2014), very few studies have taken a dynamic approach to understanding how psychological safety develops. Future studies could investigate whether personal crisis events serve as critical periods for the development of psychological safety such that the interpersonal outcome of personal disclosure might strongly influence resulting perceptions of psychological safety (as suggested by Gibson, 2018). Because disclosure and help-seeking during times of personal crisis may be interpersonally risky, as described in Chapter 3, the interpersonal outcomes of these events should strongly influence perceptions of safety and willingness to trust in the future. If the leader in crisis receives resources and subsequently invests more trust and resources in his or her team, this may create a "gain spiral" that could enrich the entire team.

Trust in peers and the organization

Trust can be defined as the "willingness to be vulnerable to another person based on the expectation that the other person will act positively" (Halbesleben & Wheeler, 2015, p. 1633). Trust is a frequently studied concept in leadership studies, although investigations seem to focus mostly on the degree to which team members trust their leader and the consequences and causes of that trust (e.g., Burke, Sims, Lazzara, & Salas, 2007). Trust in leadership is associated with positive organizational outcomes. For example, across 106 studies, trust in leadership was most strongly associated with team member job satisfaction ($r = .51$) and organizational commitment ($r = .49$) and was also significantly associated with job performance ($r = .16$) (Dirks & Ferrin, 2002). Relationships to job satisfaction and performance were stronger when team members rated their trust in their direct supervisor rather than general trust in organizational leadership, suggesting that the trust quality of the one-to-one team member-leader relationship has a substantial effect on desirable team member outcomes.

Trust in one's peer colleagues is also associated with work-related outcomes (Colquitt, Scott, & LePine, 2007). For example, a meta-analysis of 112 studies found that greater trust among team members was associated with better team performance (De Jong, Dirks, & Gillespie, 2016) and trust in work peers has been positively associated with job satisfaction (Matzler & Renzl, 2006). Our exploratory analyses suggest that, for leaders, trust in organizational peers may be related to leader satisfaction and effectiveness with handling a personal crisis in the leadership role, as well as greater breadth of disclosure. Similarly, leader trust in the overall organization (i.e., management) was also related to these outcomes.

As is the case for psychological safety, the associations between trust and leaders' perceived satisfaction and effectiveness in handling the crisis could be interpreted in several ways. Perhaps leaders who had greater trust in peers and their organization were more likely to disclose their crises and to request and receive help and social and emotional support (resources), contributing to more positive outcomes. Conversely, leaders who found they could rely on their peers or their organization in a time of need developed deeper trust, while leaders who struggled and did not receive needed support had their trust in others shaken by the experience. As described earlier, it seems plausible, based on the narrative responses of some study participants, that team member behaviors of "stepping up" to support the leader would also increase the leader's trust in team members. In retrospect, it would have been wise for us to also measure leader trust in team members to evaluate this possibility. Perhaps our oversight reflects a general bias in the field to focus on trust in either "lateral" or "upward" directions. Future studies should more fully consider the role of mutual trust between leader and team.

In particular, mutual trust may play a critical role in the development and maintenance of resource caravan passageways that could buffer the effects of a personal crisis. An intriguing study found that reciprocal trust plays a critical role in the development of gain spirals of resource exchange between coworkers (Halbesleben & Wheeler, 2015). One hundred seventy-seven pairs of coworkers completed online surveys each day for five days and reported on the degree of help they gave their coworker, their perception of social support received from their coworker, and their degree of trust in the coworker. Halbesleben and Wheeler (2015) found that help given on a particular day was associated with greater perceived social support, which increased the likelihood that the supported coworker would reciprocate with help on the next day. Importantly, the relationship between perceived social support and subsequent reciprocal help-giving was mediated by the reciprocator's degree of trust. In other words, when coworkers were helped, they were more likely to trust that they would receive help from their partner in the future, and subsequently reciprocate the helping behavior. Thus, this study provided support for an interactive, reciprocal gain spiral of resource exchange between coworkers mediated by trust. Perhaps, then, leaders who have established reciprocal trust relationships with team members and colleagues – a resource caravan passageway – have more ready access to resources with which to navigate personal crisis.

Taken together, these findings also raise the intriguing possibility that leader personal crises present a window of opportunity for the development of greater trust between leaders and their team members. As discussed in Chapter 3, there is emerging evidence that non-work information sharing by leaders and perceived emotional sincerity of the leader can enhance trust, suggesting two routes by which more open leader behavior during a personal crisis might contribute to more trusting relationships with team members (Caza, Zhang, Wang, & Bai, 2015; Nifadkar, Wu, & Gu, 2019). From the leader's perspective, as we proposed with respect to psychological safety, if leaders are met with supportive and competent responses from their staff during personal crises, these experiences may deepen their trust in the team. Thus, while personal crises are painful and, by definition, involve deep losses for the leader, future research should investigate whether there are circumstances in which leader personal crisis leads to team relationship growth through deepening trust (see Chapter 5).

Social constraints on disclosure

People in crisis vary in the extent to which they perceive that others around them want to hear about their struggles and are interested in providing support. Lepore and Revenson (2007) define social constraints on disclosure as, "both objective social conditions and individuals' construal of those conditions that lead individuals to refrain from or modify their disclosure of stress- and trauma-related thoughts, feelings, or concerns" (p. 315). For example, a leader who talks about his or her crisis to colleagues and is met with unsupportive, dismissive, or awkward responses may "get the message" that it is better not to talk about the situation. Important in the previous definition is the idea that social constraints on disclosure result from both the actions and responses of others surrounding the potential discloser and the discloser's perception of those actions (Lepore & Revenson, 2007).

Social constraints on disclosure may prevent people from coping effectively with a stressful event. Drawing upon social cognitive processing theory, Lepore and Helgeson (1998) described how cognitive processing of stressful events, defined as active contemplation of the meaning of the event, is associated with better outcomes than is avoidance of thoughts and feelings (see Chapter 2). One way in which people experiencing stressful events such as cancer can engage in cognitive processing is by talking about the crisis with others. Speaking with others about the crisis can validate the feelings of the person in crisis, help her or him engage in reappraisal of the stressful event, and reduce emotional arousal (Lepore & Helgeson, 1998). However, if potentially supportive people have negative reactions to these disclosures, the person in crisis may be less likely to talk about the crisis and therefore be unable to reap the benefits of social cognitive processing. Therefore, Lepore and colleagues hypothesized that people with cancer or those experiencing other stressful life events (e.g., bereavement following miscarriage, Lepore et al., 1996) who reported greater social constraints on talking about the event would experience greater distress – particularly if they were also experiencing frequent intrusive thoughts about the event.

Social constraints have been studied most frequently in the cancer literature, where a recent meta-analysis demonstrated a moderately strong link between social constraints and cancer-related distress across 30 studies (Adams, Winger, & Mosher, 2015). More recently, social constraints on disclosure have been studied in other types of stressful life events such as relationship breakup (Harvey & Karpinski, 2016) and bereavement following suicide of a loved one (Groff, Ruzek, Bongar, & Cordova, 2016). Given these prior findings, we included measures of social constraints with respect to friends and family and with respect to others in the leaders' organizations to explore the association of perceiving constraints on talking about the crisis on other key variables.

As reported earlier, we found that leaders varied widely in their perceived social constraints on disclosure about their crisis to others in their organization. People who reported more social constraints on disclosure were less satisfied with their decisions about disclosure with a trend toward having disclosed less widely. If some leaders found the responses of others in their organization unsupportive or dismissive, that experience may have contributed to less satisfaction with disclosure. Perceived social constraints were also related to less overall effectiveness and satisfaction with handling the crisis in the leadership role. Although these findings are only correlations and we cannot determine the reason for the associations, these results support further investigation of the role of social constraints on disclosure for leaders in crisis.

We propose that social constraints on disclosure in their organizations might have different consequences for leaders than social constraints in their personal life. Social cognitive processing theory, as the name implies, focuses on the cognitive processing function of talking about the crisis with others. While this function could certainly apply to talking to others in one's organization, social constraints on disclosure in the organization may also reduce the leader's access to other resources or hamper their efforts to cope with the crisis in the ways in which leaders in our study endorsed – for example, changing work arrangements or delegating work. Yet perceived social constraints in the organization were strongly correlated with perceived social constraints on disclosure from family and friends ($r = -.67, p < .001$), and constraints from family and friends showed a similar pattern of associations with many of the variables described earlier. The strong correlation between organization and family/friend social constraints raises the unresolved question of whether social constraints are more a function of the assumptions of the prospective discloser vs. the result of actual negative experiences when disclosing (Lepore & Revenson, 2007). Examining the association between an individual's perceived social constraints among different groups may help to address this question. More broadly, we are unaware of any other research specifically examining social constraints on disclosure in the workplace, and so this is an area in need of additional research with respect to both leaders and non-leaders.

Summary and implications

- Leaders varied in their perception of psychological safety in their organizations, in their trust in colleagues and management, and especially in the extent to which they felt they could speak freely about the crisis in their organizations. Leaders who endorsed greater psychological safety, trust, and ability to speak freely about the crisis in their organization were more likely to report that they had been able to handle the crisis effectively in their leadership role and that they were satisfied with their ability to do so.
- Organizational culture may have a powerful influence on the extent to which leaders can survive and thrive during personal crises. Organizations and their

leaders may be able to build protected collections of resources shared among individuals (resource caravan passageways) that "shore up" leaders in advance of personal crises. Just-in-time access to crisis support resources and positive cultural attitudes toward accessing those resources would also support leaders in crises (see Chapter 6).

- Psychological safety is a key resource among members of teams and organizations that is associated with positive organizational outcomes. Our studies suggest that psychological safety in the organization may also benefit leaders in crisis. Leaders should engage in supportive behaviors that have been shown to foster psychological safety, and researchers should investigate the relationship between this factor and personal well-being for team members and leaders as well as workplace functioning.

- Trust between individuals in organizations is also consistently related to positive outcomes. Leader personal crises may present a window of opportunity for the development of greater trust between leaders and their team members. Future research should investigate whether there are circumstances in which leader personal crisis leads to team relationship growth through deepening trust.

- Social constraints on disclosure are related to distress and coping following stressful events such as cancer, and we found preliminary evidence that it could play a role in leaders coping with personal crises. Future studies on constraints on disclosure to coworkers and team members are recommended. Organizational practices that foster psychological safety and mutual trust may decrease social constraints on disclosure and improve leaders' and team members' access to resources for successful coping.

References

Adams, R. N., Winger, J. G., & Mosher, C. E. (2015). A meta-analysis of the relationship between social constraints and distress in cancer patients. *Journal of Behavioral Medicine, 38,* 294–305. https://doi.org/10.1007/s10865-014-9601-6

Bakker, A. B. (2005). Job resources buffer the impact of job demands on burnout. *Journal of Occupational Health Psychology, 10*(2), 170–180. https://doi.org/10.1037/1076-8998.10.2.170

Bakker, A. B., & Demerouti, E. (2016). Job demands – Resources theory: Taking stock and looking forward. *Journal of Occupational Health Psychology, 22*(3), 273. https://doi.org/10.1037/ocp0000056

Bakker, A. B., Emmerik, H. van, & Euwema, M. C. (2006). Crossover of burnout and engagement in work teams. *Work and Occupations, 33*(4), 464–489. https://doi.org/10.1177/0730888406291310

Binyamin, G., Friedman, A., & Carmeli, A. (2017). Reciprocal care in hierarchical exchange: Implications for psychological safety and innovative behaviors at work. *Psychology of Aesthetics, Creativity, and the Arts, 12*(1), 79. https://doi.org/10.1037/aca0000129

Burke, C. S., Sims, D. E., Lazzara, E. H., & Salas, E. (2007). Trust in leadership: A multilevel review and integration. *The Leadership Quarterly, 18*(6), 606–632. https://doi.org/10.1016/j.leaqua.2007.09.006

Caza, A., Zhang, G., Wang, L., & Bai, Y. (2015). How do you really feel? Effect of leaders' perceived emotional sincerity on followers' trust. *The Leadership Quarterly*, *26*(4), 518–531. https://doi.org/10.1016/j.leaqua.2015.05.008

Chen, S., Westman, M., & Hobfoll, S. E. (2015). The commerce and crossover of resources: Resource conservation in the service of resilience. *Stress and Health: Journal of the International Society for the Investigation of Stress*, *31*(2), 95–105. https://doi.org/10.1002/smi.2574

Colquitt, J. A., Scott, B. A., & LePine, J. A. (2007). Trust, trustworthiness, and trust propensity: A meta-analytic test of their unique relationships with risk taking and job performance. *Journal of Applied Psychology*, *92*(4), 909–927. https://doi.org/10.1037/0021-9010.92.4.909

Cook, J., & Wall, T. (1980). New work attitude measures of trust, organizational commitment and personal need non-fulfilment. *Journal of Occupational Psychology*, *53*(1), 39–52. https://doi.org/10.1111/j.2044-8325.1980.tb00005.x

De Jong, B. A., Dirks, K. T., & Gillespie, N. (2016). Trust and team performance: A meta-analysis of main effects, moderators, and covariates. *Journal of Applied Psychology*, *101*(8), 1134–1150. https://doi.org/10.1037/apl0000110

Dirks, K. T., & Ferrin, D. L. (2002). Trust in leadership: Meta-analytic findings and implications for research and practice. *The Journal of Applied Psychology*, *87*(4), 611–628. https://doi.org/10.1037/0021-9010.87.4.611

Edmondson, A. C. (1999). Psychological safety and learning behavior in work teams. *Administrative Science Quarterly*, *44*(2), 350. https://doi.org/10.2307/2666999

Edmondson, A. C., & Lei, Z. (2014). Psychological safety: The history, renaissance, and future of an interpersonal construct. *Annual Review of Organizational Psychology and Organizational Behavior*, *1*(1), 23–43. https://doi.org/10.1146/annurev-orgpsych-031413-091305

Fleeson, W. (2004). Moving personality beyond the person-situation debate: The challenge and the opportunity of within-person variability. *Current Directions in Psychological Science*, *13*(2), 83–87. https://doi.org/10.1111/j.0963-7214.2004.00280.x

Frazier, M. L., Fainshmidt, S., Klinger, R. L., Pezeshkan, A., & Vracheva, V. (2017). Psychological safety: A meta-analytic review and extension. *Personnel Psychology*, *70*(1), 113–165. https://doi.org/10.1111/peps.12183

Fredrickson, B. L. (2000). Why positive emotions matter in organizations: Lessons from the broaden-and-build model. *The Psychologist-Manager Journal*, *4*(2), 131–142. https://doi.org/10.1037/h0095887

Gibson, K. R. (2018). Can I tell you something? How disruptive self-disclosure changes who "we" are. *Academy of Management Review*, *43*(4), 570–589. https://doi.org/10.5465/amr.2016.0317

Groff, E. C., Ruzek, J. I., Bongar, B., & Cordova, M. J. (2016). Social constraints, loss-related factors, depression, and posttraumatic stress in a treatment-seeking suicide bereaved sample. *Psychological Trauma: Theory, Research, Practice, and Policy*, *8*(6), 657. https://doi.org/10.1037/tra0000128

Halbesleben, J. R. B., & Wheeler, A. R. (2015). To invest or not? The role of coworker support and trust in daily reciprocal gain spirals of helping behavior. *Journal of Management*, *41*(6), 1628–1650. https://doi.org/10.1177/0149206312455246

Harvey, A. B., & Karpinski, A. (2016). The impact of social constraints on adjustment following a romantic breakup. *Personal Relationships*, *23*(3), 396–408. https://doi.org/10.1111/pere.12132

Hobfoll, S. E. (2011). Conservation of resource caravans and engaged settings. *Journal of Occupational and Organizational Psychology*, *84*(1), 116–122. https://doi.org/10.1111/j.2044-8325.2010.02016.x

Hobfoll, S. E., Halbesleben, J., Neveu, J.-P., & Westman, M. (2018). Conservation of resources in the organizational context: The reality of resources and their consequences.

Annual Review of Organizational Psychology and Organizational Behavior, 5(1), 103–128. https://doi.org/10.1146/annurev-orgpsych-032117-104640

Lepore, S. J., & Helgeson, V. S. (1998). Social constraints, intrusive thoughts, and mental health after prostate cancer. *Journal of Social and Clinical Psychology, 17*(1), 89–106. https://doi.org/10.1521/jscp.1998.17.1.89

Lepore, S. J., & Revenson, T. A. (2007). Social constraints on disclosure and adjustment to cancer. *Social and Personality Psychology Compass, 1*(1), 313–333. https://doi.org/10.1111/j.1751-9004.2007.00013.x

Lepore, S. J., Silver, R. C., Wortman, C. B., & Wayment, H. A. (1996). Social constraints, intrusive thoughts, and depressive symptoms among bereaved mothers. *Journal of Personality and Social Psychology, 70*(2), 271–282. https://doi.org/10.1037/0022-3514.70.2.271

Matzler, K., & Renzl, B. (2006). The relationship between interpersonal trust, employee satisfaction, and employee loyalty. *Total Quality Management and Business Excellence, 17*(10), 1261–1271. https://doi.org/10.1080/14783360600753653

Mooradian, T., Renzl, B., & Matzler, K. (2006). Who trusts? Personality, trust and knowledge sharing. *Management Learning, 37*(4), 523–540. https://doi.org/10.1177/1350507606073424

Newman, A., Donohue, R., & Eva, N. (2017). Psychological safety: A systematic review of the literature. *Human Resource Management Review, 27*(3), 521–535. https://doi.org/10.1016/j.hrmr.2017.01.001

Nifadkar, S. S., Wu, W., & Gu, Q. (2019). Supervisors' work-related and nonwork information sharing: Integrating research on information sharing, information seeking, and trust using self-disclosure theory. *Personnel Psychology, 72*(2), 241–269. https://doi.org/10.1111/peps.12305

Sanchez-Burks, J., & Uhlmann, E. L. (2013). Outlier Nation: The cultural psychology of American workways. In M. Yuki & M. Brewer (Eds.), *Culture and group processes* (pp. 121–142). Oxford: Oxford University Press. https://doi.org/10.1093/acprof:oso/9780199985463.003.0006

Schaufeli, W. B., & Bakker, A. B. (2004). Job demands, job resources, and their relationship with burnout and engagement: A multi-sample study. *Journal of Organizational Behavior, 25*(3), 293–315. https://doi.org/10.1002/job.248

Schein, E. H. (2004). Organizational climate and culture. In G. Goethals, G. Sorenson, & J. Burns (Eds.), *Encyclopedia of leadership* (Vols. 1–4, pp. 1113–1117). https://doi.org/10.4135/9781412952392

Schein, E. H. (2010). The concept of organizational culture. In *Organizational culture and leadership* (4th ed., pp. 7–22). San Francisco, CA: Jossey-Bass.

Schein, E. H., & Bennis, W. G. (1965). *Personal and organizational change through group methods: The laboratory approach.* New York: John Wiley & Sons.

Westman, M. (2013). Crossover of positive states and experiences. *Stress and Health: Journal of the International Society for the Investigation of Stress, 29*(4), 263–265. https://doi.org/10.1002/smi.2535

5

RESPONSIBILITY FOR LEADERSHIP

Adaptive approaches

DANIEL'S STORY

The most memorable crisis is clearly a cardio-vascular event where I was experiencing something that I would call a minor discomfort in my chest over a period of about a month and I was heavily involved in doing a myriad of things. . . . I had three blocked arteries, one about 90%, one in the 80's and the other was about 70% and they put three stints in and kept me over night because I kept having these awful responses. . . .

I think people were very concerned. Here we had just taken over a company . . . there were just a multitude of negatives and then I had this situation one year after we take over; we had gone through some financial challenges as an organization, people weren't feeling real secure to begin with, then I'm heading up this organization, and we're trying to completely revamp the culture from an evil, distrustful place to work to one where people are really part of the organization and respectful of one another and that seemed to be working and then I had this episode and it adds to the insecurity of the entire group.

And you know, I came back to work; I think I missed a day of work during this whole experience . . . maybe two days . . . and I came back and people knew what had happened and I gathered everyone together and reminded them that the stories of my untimely death were greatly exaggerated. . . . We still had a business to run and we were growing it and, you know, I still had a dissertation to finish. I still had a couple of organizations I was chairing; I had a lot of work that needed to be done and I didn't have time for this.

I knew I had to make people feel more secure and that I was going to be around and everything's fine and so using humor as I did, that's where I met everyone, reminded them that reports of my untimely death were greatly exaggerated and I'm fine, let's keep this thing going, let's keep working, we're coming out of the doldrums here. Interestingly enough, at that same period, in July [year deleted], things were starting to look a lot better. . . .

Well I think it made the vision of my personal crisis much clearer. There was no gray area there. I knew that my personal crisis had to be addressed and outwardly I had to put on a performance for everyone because they needed leadership at that time. They did not need someone with a label of "sick," you know physically sick. There was just no room for it. . . .

"Okay, I've got this little vulnerability" and how important the collaboration among everyone is became so clear because if I dropped out of the picture, the organization was still there; it still had to exist and we still had at that time 240 people and we had to make sure that they were cared for. So let's band together, let's make sure we keep [name omitted] on course here, we're in the midst of a remarkable, 180-degree cultural shift and it's beginning to take hold, let's not lose ground because of a health issue of the leader. Let's keep this thing going.

But I walked through the plant all the time and I talked to people all the time and it was brought up by people time and time again with that sort of shy look, you know, "how are you feeling today?"

For me, I felt good that they were concerned because it's a sense of belonging to the group and it gave me another opportunity to reinforce what I've already said. A minor plumbing problem. . . .

I am a model for them when it comes to security and health and where we're going as an organization. No one worries about my health in terms of he's going to drop off the planet.

Adaptive approaches

Focusing on work

Daniel's story demonstrates his passionate need to focus on work and protect his company and its members during a potentially life-threatening personal crisis. Daniel insisted that his leadership must go on even while undergoing a crisis involving his own health (see Chapter 6 for information on reciprocal care of the leader). We asked our Study 2 participants, what work-related approaches were most effective in helping to manage the impact of the crisis. Participants were given the choice to identify all approaches they found effective. Among the seven response choices in Figure 5.1, the most frequent reply from leaders was that they "focused on work" (54%) – for example, "keeping my mind focused on work," "keeping myself working" and "working as normal, worked for me." Some leaders focused on work as a distraction from the crisis, especially in situations where the crisis was other-focused;

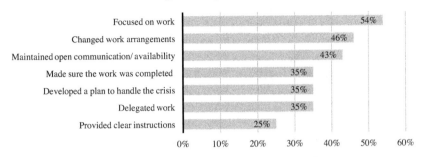

What work-related approaches were most effective in helping to manage the impact of the crisis?

FIGURE 5.1 Most Effective Work-Related Approaches to Manage Personal Crisis

that is, where the crisis happened to a family member and did not involve their own illness or injury. A study by Stoner and Gilligan (2002) found this same pattern of focusing on work among the 35 senior executives that they interviewed about leaders' ability to rebound from personal and business adversity (p. 20). This possibly beneficial focus on work may relate to the concept of "engagement" often investigated in research on burnout (Schaufeli & Bakker, 2004). Engagement, characterized by a sense of vigor, absorption, and dedication to one's work, is a protective factor for burnout that may also be useful as leaders navigate personal crises. In particular, if leaders engage at work in ways that increase positive emotion and offer a cognitive respite (Chapter 2), focus on work could have salutary effects.

Based on their interviews (Colbert, Bono, & Purvanova, 2015), researchers identified three stages of rebound when leaders face adversity: the disillusionment stage – where leaders feel the presence of their emotions, for instance, feeling down, confused, shocked, angry or worried and may immerse themselves in work and seek support from family, friends and spouses; the reflection stage – where leaders search for meaning through introspection and seek input from others (e.g., trusted colleagues, peers, and recognized experts) to gain perspective; and the transformation stage – where learning from adversity and change take place through five frequently overlapping steps: cognitive reframe, (stepping back to see the big picture), challenge reframe (reframe adversity into a challenge), control reframe (gaining a sharper focus on what they can and cannot control), courage (demonstrating the courage to change and adjust in the midst of fear), and seeking help and support (Stoner & Gilligan, 2002).

Focusing on work is much more difficult when the crisis disables leaders due to their own illness or injury, or the crisis of a family member requires them to spend time away from the office. Leaders in our survey reported various approaches were effective to keep their organization or division running, such as: changing their work arrangements (46%) (e.g., altering their work schedule, working from home, or scheduling time off or leave); maintaining open communication and availability

(43%); using technology and telephone calls ("I worked remotely by computer and stayed in touch with the people in my department and my supervisor by phone to get work done"); making sure the work was completed (35%), delegating work (35%); and providing clear instructions (25%) (see Figure 5.1). There were two areas where middle managers and executive leaders differed slightly. More middle managers (50%) than executive leaders (34%) endorsed maintaining open communication and availability ($p = .037$); and more middle managers (31%) than executive leaders (17%) endorsed providing clear instructions ($p = .035$). This difference may be due to the variance in experience levels and capabilities of the individuals that middle managers supervise contrasted with individuals that executive leaders supervise.

Delegating

Delegating work often served the dual purpose among our participants of continuing the functions for which they were responsible and developing leadership capacity in other team members. One leader in Study 1 commented, "I delegated responsibility to my team members. I had evening calls with most of them to keep in touch but I trusted them and it worked well," while another remarked, "I was able to see two [women] in my department really step up during this time."

In a few cases, leaders complained that delegating did not produce the results they expected, perhaps because team members were not prepared or trained to take on higher-level responsibilities. One study respondent commented," I tried to make my subordinates share some of my responsibilities and duties which [had] a big impact [on] the quality of the end product [but they were] not up to the mark or at least what we had before I had this crisis." Despite these comments, most participants in Study 1 who chose to delegate responsibilities did not express dissatisfaction in their comments about the outcome of their decision.

Developing a personal crisis plan

One significant approach identified by leaders was the development of a flexible plan to handle the crisis (35%). While many leaders learn to develop plans for handling organizational crises, it is less common to see them generate an explicit personal crisis plan. Participants did not report on their crisis plans in detail due to time constraints and space limitations in the survey; however, one respondent provided an example of several components of her or his plan:

> In my role as a leader, I knew that I was working half-days for the first several weeks. Thus, I tried to delegate to my team more so that I was able to be less involved in the day to day commitments. I also had my work computer with me and when I had breaks in caring for my [sick child], I tried to stay up-to-date with work issues and communicated guidance or direction to my team that way as opposed to face-to-face guidance or direction.

Survey participant

Based on various responses from participants in Study 1, a personal crisis plan may:

- Identify the leader's modified work schedule or time off;
- Identify which team members (or positions) will be delegated responsibility for work while the leader is away;
- Include a timeframe for the leader to check-in or keep updated on work progress and/or identify an alternate leader to contact for unforeseen events or questions;
- Provide information on how and when to communicate with or seek input from the leader and/or identify an alternate leader to contact for unforeseen events or questions; and
- Provide a tentative timeline for the leader's full or part-time return.

A personal crisis plan with these components may work best in situations where the leader is responding to a family members' crisis or has the capacity to focus on work during his or her own crisis. The organization becomes responsible for devising a crisis plan (e.g., a succession plan) in cases where the leader is incapacitated by illness or injury. Chapter 6 includes more details on the issue of succession planning.

Making use of workplace relationships

Another adaptive response to personal crisis by leaders in our study was to rely on relationships at work. Though we would not classify reliance on work relationships as an approach or strategy, these relationships provide a significant form of social and job-related support for the leader in crisis. In our opening scenario, Daniel was a new leader in the organization who made several difficult and unpopular decisions to restructure the company and dismiss employees at the beginning of his time in the organization. He was just starting to build trust and relationships in an environment that he referred to as "evil" because of the negative experiences employees had just lived through. His goal was to rebuild a viable company and establish trustworthy relationships with new and remaining team members. Consequently, he had limited opportunity to establish long-term, reliable relationships prior to his personal crisis.

Ragins and Dutton defined positive, high-quality work relationships as "a reoccurring connection between two people that takes place within the context of work . . . and is experienced as mutually beneficial" (as quoted in Colbert et al., 2015, p. 1199). Most leaders did in fact discuss their crises with team members, peers, and individuals to whom they report despite concerns about disclosure, detailed in Chapter 3. Their reasons for disclosure provide insight into the role of relationships in helping support both job-related and emotional needs at work.

As detailed in Figure 5.2, a majority of the leaders who disclosed their crisis told people at work in order to "inform them" (or essentially to communicate the fact that a personal crisis was taking place) as staff/team members (59%), colleagues/ peers (62%), and people to whom they report (74%). More middle managers (69%) than executives (52%) disclosed to colleagues or peers at work for the purpose of informing them ($p = .03$). A smaller percentage of leaders disclosed to staff/team members (21%), colleagues/peers (27%), and people to whom they report (33%) to gain "help with job support." Several survey participants told the people to whom they report for the purpose of "arranging accommodations" such as taking time off, changing their work schedules, or working from home (38%).[1]

Leaders in our survey reported that they relied on work support from team members, colleagues, and individuals to whom they report during their personal crises, (see Figure 5.2). Studies on workplace relationships associate positive work relationships with significant benefits for the organization, including enhanced performance, productivity, and task assistance (Colbert et al., 2015; Rumens, 2017). Leaders often turn to people with whom they have developed positive relationships for support to accomplish work objectives during times of personal crisis.

Relationships play a vital role in the quality of life at work for leaders, like other individuals in the workforce. In many cases, leaders understood that their behavior may be different from usual due to the personal crisis and wanted to "explain their behavior" to staff/team members (49%), colleagues/peers (42%), and the people to whom they report (42%).

Leaders wanted other people at work to know about their personal crises because "they were friends" with staff/team members (43%), colleagues/peers (43%), and people to whom they report (21%). We discovered some differences between executive leaders and middle managers with regard to disclosing the crisis because they were friends. There was a trend toward more executive leaders (52%) disclosing

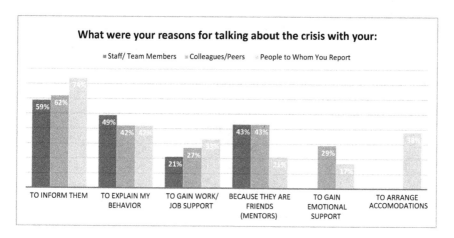

FIGURE 5.2 Reasons Leaders Discussed Personal Crisis at Work

Note: Percentages are calculated within leaders who reported disclosing to someone in each relationship category. The item "to gain emotional support" was inadvertently omitted from the survey for Staff/Team Members. "To arrange accommodations" was only asked for People to Whom You Report.

1 The staff/team members and colleagues/peers' categories were intentionally omitted from the responses available.

to their staff/team members because they were friends than did middle managers (37%) (p = .08). This is an interesting discovery because people may not expect leaders at the top to develop workplace friendships due to popular notions that executive leaders are isolated or that members of the organization cannot or should not become friends with "the boss." Though a lower number of participants in the survey overall disclosed to the people to whom they report than to team members or peers, more executives (32%) than middle managers (12%) disclosed to people to whom they report because of friendship (p = .005).

Leaders in the survey also disclosed to others in the workplace for "emotional support" – colleagues/peers (29%) and people to whom they report (17%).[2] Thus, as described in Chapter 2, social support seemed to be an important source of resources for many leaders.

Net effect of crisis on relationships

In Study 2, we asked participants what impact going through the crisis had on their relationships with others in the organization (Table 5.1). Participants could respond on a scale from "Very Negative Impact" to "Very Positive Impact" for work-oriented relationships and, separately, friendships. In Table 5.1 mean scores were significantly higher than the scale midpoint (all p values < .001) and indicated a "slightly positive" mean net effect on each type of relationship. It is important to note, however, that we did not observe this effect at the group level in our much smaller (n = 49) Study 1,[3] where mean scores of relationship impact tended to fall at the "no impact" mark. Yet some participants in Study 1 did report positive effects on relationships (20–31%), and narrative responses in our preliminary studies and in Study 1 indicated that some

TABLE 5.1 Mean participant responses to, "How did the personal crisis impact your (work relationships or friendships with ___."

	Work relationship impact M (SD)	Friendship impact M (SD)
Staff or team members	4.85 (1.26)	5.11 (1.37)[1]
Colleagues or peers	4.90 (1.24)	5.03 (1.35)[1]
People to whom you reported	4.80 (1.25)	5.01 (1.32)[2]

Note: 1 = very negative impact; 7 = very positive impact. All mean values are significantly higher than the scale midpoint of 4 "no impact" (all p < .001 using a single sample t-test). [1]n = 160 for these analyses because some participants indicated that they did not have friendships with people in these roles; [2]n = 162 because some participants indicated that they did not have friendships with supervisors.

2 The staff/team member category was unintentionally omitted from the responses available to participants.
3 In addition, in Study 1 we did not require that participants be at least one year out from the onset of their crisis, which was required in Study 2. Perhaps relationship benefits of navigating a crisis accrue over time, as predicted by the Conservation of Resources Theory (Hobfoll, 2011), which might explain why these were less frequent in Study 1.

participants had seen deepening relationships in their organization as one outcome of going through their crises. Although these findings require additional study and replication, we have dubbed the potential effect of enhanced relationships following personal crises as the "relationship growth benefit" (RGB) of leader personal crisis.

A "relationship growth benefit?"

We hypothesize that coping with crises prompts leaders to disclose and seek help from their team members in ways that have the potential to grow the level of trust in their relationships (Chapter 4). If others in the organization respond with emotional and instrumental support, leader trust is increased, leading the leader to confide in and rely on these relationships even more in the future. The receiver of the leader's trust may increase their liking of the leader as a result of the disclosure and the perception of reduced status distance between them (Chapter 3), resulting in increased trust on the part of the person trusted. Although we unfortunately do not know the degree of trust in specific relationships in our studies, we propose that increased trust would be one key mechanism of RGB.

To explore our data in Study 2 from the perspective of RGB, we examined whether the degree of disclosure for each relationship category was associated with the effect of the crisis on each relationship type. In other words, did leaders who disclosed more broadly to people in a given category (e.g., staff or team) tend to experience more positive relationship outcomes? We reasoned that, if leaders had disclosed more broadly and placed more trust in the people around them, this would increase the likelihood of reaping a relationship growth benefit. We indeed found that people who reported a more positive relationship impact had disclosed more widely ($r = .28$, .30, .30 for team member, peer, and supervisor work relationships, respectively; $r = .27, .33, .19$ for friendships; all $p < .05$). Because we only measured these variables as one time-point, however, we are unable to make claims about a causal connection between wider disclosure and more positive effects on relationships. For example, it is possible that workplaces greater in psychological safety (Chapter 4) might account for both increased disclosure and better relationship outcomes. Additional research will be needed to refine and test our RGB hypothesis.

Are relationship outcomes associated with leaders' views of the overall outcomes of their personal crisis with respect to their leadership role? If leader relationships in the organization are as influential as theory and research suggest, then we might expect that leaders who report RGB would rate themselves as having been more effective in handling the crisis and being more satisfied with the ultimate outcome. We found small but significant associations between impact on work relationships in each relationship category and overall leader perceived effectiveness ($r = .17, .23$, .17 for team member, peer, and supervisor work relationships, respectively; all $p < .05$) and satisfaction ($r = .23, .25, .23$; all $p < .05$). Crisis impact on personal relationships or friendships was less consistently related to overall effectiveness ($r = .19$, .14, .14 for team member, peer, and supervisor work relationships, respectively, $p = .02, .07, .07$) satisfaction ($r = .21, .21, .15, p = .01, .01, .05$). Taken together, these results lend preliminary support to the idea that the "relationship outcomes" of crisis for leaders may be a critical part of an overall successful outcome of personal crisis. As documented by numerous scholars in leadership studies, relationships matter for leadership, and this seems to extend to the leader's navigation of a personal crisis.

Workplace friendships

Workplace friendships may enhance quality of life for leaders and other members of the organization beyond support for accomplishing organization objectives. Colbert et al. (2015) observe that organizations in contemporary society are flatter (less hierarchical), increasingly utilize teams to accomplish tasks, and perform work more interdependently (p. 1199). Just as these new work arrangements blur the lines between work roles in formerly hierarchical structures, they also often blur the lines between work and nonwork (or personal) relationships among organizational members. These workplace relationships frequently generate meaningful friendships. Most leaders in our survey reported having workplace friendships among staff/team members, colleagues/peers, and individuals to whom they report (see Table 5.1 note). However, leaders were less likely to report that they had disclosed to their supervisors because of friendship (Figure 5.2).

Seminal research on workplace friendships distinguishes them from other workplace relationships using two key factors: friendships are "voluntary" and they are "personalistic" – meaning workplace friends interact with each other as "whole" persons, not simply as individuals in a role (Sias & Cahill, 1998). Most relevant to our study, Sias and Cahill (1998) explain:

> Because it is impossible to leave one's personal life "at the office door," life events (e.g., marital problems, health issues, etc.) likely influence workplace friendships. This notion is supported by a large body of literature that indicates coworkers are often a valuable source of emotional support when individuals are dealing with important events in their personal lives.
>
> *(p. 277)*

The researchers found several transitions in friendships over time: from "acquaintance to friend" – often caused by working with the other person for extended periods of time in close proximity or working on shared projects and extra-organizational socializing such as going to lunch together or going out for drinks after work; from "friend to close friend" (they became a trusted source of support) – driven by personal life events and work-related problems where extra-organizational socializing becomes more intimate, involving meeting each other's' families or going on vacations together; and from "close friend to 'almost best' friend" – associated with extra-organizational socializing, life events, and work-related problems where perceived similarity contributes to work friends becoming an important part of each other's personal and work lives (Sias & Cahill, 1998).

Recent studies on workplace relationships in the management literature and workplace friendships in the sociology of friendship research examine the broader meaning and dimensions of workplace friendships in the lives of employees. Colbert et al. (2015) conducted a two-part study to discover the broad range of functions that workplace relationships serve. In the first study, they identified six relationship functions in current workplaces:

- Task Assistance – helped me get my work done by answering questions, providing feedback, or assisting with a specific task;
- Career Advancement – helped me to advance my career by providing advice or access to contacts and other career-related resources;
- Emotional Support – helped me cope with stress by listening to my problems and responding in a supportive way;
- Friendship – became a friend or companion;
- Personal Growth – helped me grow and develop as a human being; and
- Giving to Others – provided me the opportunity to assist, mentor, support or care for others.

(Colbert et al., 2015, p. 1203)

The researchers found several functions of work relationships among the six components that were not common in existing literature – personal growth; friendship and companionship (the most frequently observed function); and giving to others. Participants in their study indicated that friendship and companionship connoted "people they enjoyed being around, whom they could share anything with, and whom they spent time with outside of work" (Colbert et al., 2015, p. 1204).

In their second study, the researchers aimed to discover which relationship functions were most associated with "flourishing." "To be flourishing . . . is to be filled with positive emotion and to be functioning well psychologically and socially" (Keyes, 2002, p. 210). Drawing insight from Keyes' work on flourishing, Colbert et al. (2015), identified indicators of workplace flourishing (meaningful work, positive emotions at work, and life satisfaction) and examined them in relation to their six relationship functions using a survey of participant pairs from Study 1. They discovered that "task assistance was most strongly associated with job satisfaction, giving to others was most strongly associated with meaningful work, friendship was most strongly associated with positive emotions at work, and personal growth was most strongly associated with life satisfaction" (Colbert et al., 2015, p. 1199). The researchers emphasize that these findings enhance our understanding of how workplace relationships might function to promote growth, well-being, and flourishing at work.

Rumens (2017) draws on the sociology of friendship literature to advocate for studying the social and personal significance of workplace "friendships in their own right." Much like Colbert et al., Rumens (2017) asserts that researchers have a responsibility to attend to "how workplace friendships can contribute to human flourishing, helping individuals to pursue a meaningful existence along preestablished and new pathways" (p. 1151). Based on work from the sociology of friendship, the researcher affirms that friendships are not simply individual relationships, but they help shape wider social structures and extend over time and space (Rumens, 2017).

There can be downsides to workplace friendships – distraction from work tasks; inter-role conflict between informal and formal roles; lower-quality decision processes where situations may benefit from more diverse perspectives; exclusion of others resulting in inhibited knowledge-sharing; and perceived threats to merit-based procedures and bureaucratic objectivity (Pillemer & Rothbard, 2018). Yet, leaders in our study identified workplace relationships, including friendships, as a significant reason for disclosing their personal crisis to team members, peers, and, to a lesser extent, individuals to whom they report. The studies reviewed previously support the perception that workplace friendships provide value to friends' lives, including supporting them through a personal crisis and ultimately contributing to their flourishing.

Advice to others concerning responsibility for leadership

Disclosing crisis

Consistent with their own selective disclosure (Chapter 2), participants in our survey advised other leaders to use discretion regarding disclosure of a personal crisis at work. As we will explain in the next chapter, leaders at the CEO level must be concerned about their own job vulnerability during a serious illness or injury due to the impact of their absence on the organization's profitability and the reactions of investors during their illness or injury. Even the leader's bereavement due to the death of a loved one may affect productivity and profitability as we note in Chapter 6. They must also consider the level of psychological safety, social constraints, and trust in their organizational culture and climate from the board level through the entire organization.

When asked if people in leadership positions should disclose their personal crises at work, our participants responses in Figure 5.3 clearly recommended forethought – disclose selectively (53%); it depends (31%); yes, always disclose personal crises (14%); and no, never disclose personal crises (2%). Leaders who replied "it depends" indicated that disclosure depends on the nature of the crisis (65%); the person's need for privacy (63%); the person's relationship with her or his team members/staff or supervisor (47%); and/or the organization's culture (33%) (see Figure 5.4). There was a trend toward more middle managers (76%) than executive leaders (50%) responding that disclosure should depend on the nature of the crisis ($p = .056$) regarding whether they would disclose their personal crisis to others in the workplace.

Leaders' concerns about disclosure of personal crises at work, however, should be balanced with findings in Chapter 3 on the benefits of sharing the leader's crisis in the workplace consisting of greater access to social support, enhanced relationships, and fulfilling fiduciary and planning responsibilities.

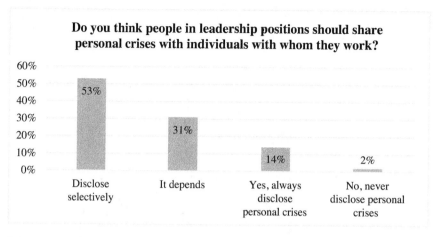

FIGURE 5.3 Advice on Disclosure of Personal Crisis at Work

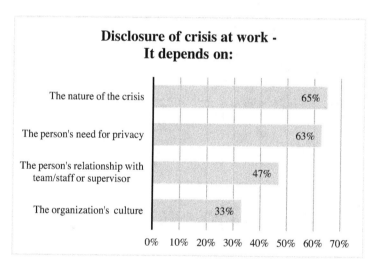

FIGURE 5.4 Advice from Respondents Who Said "It Depends"

Note: Participants could select more than one response.

Handling leadership responsibilities

Figure 5.5 shows the advice that survey participants endorsed for handling leadership responsibilities during a personal crisis. They proposed that other leaders develop a plan to handle the crisis (57%); maintain open communication and availability (51%); change work arrangements (44%); focus on work (38%); provide clear instructions (38%); delegate work (35%); and make sure the work is complete (35%). With regard to providing clear instructions, slightly more middle managers (45%) than executive leaders (30%) endorsed this advice ($p = .046$). Again, this difference

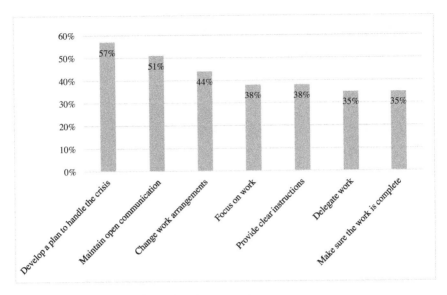

FIGURE 5.5 Advice on Effective Work Approaches

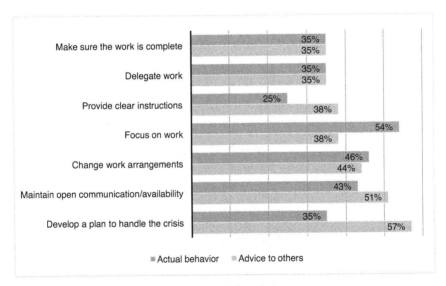

FIGURE 5.6 Advice vs. Leaders' Actions: Most Effective Work Approaches

may be due to the variance in experience levels and capabilities of the individuals that middle managers supervise contrasted with the individuals that executive leaders supervise.

Remarkably, the most highly endorsed advice (develop a plan to handle the personal crisis) was reported as an effective strategy used by only 35% of survey participants, while 57% of them advised other leaders to develop a plan for the crisis (see Figure 5.6). Leaders had the reverse pattern of responses to focusing on work. While more than half of the leaders in our survey (54%) nominated focusing on work as an effective strategy they had used, only 38% of them advised other leaders to focus on work.

There were two areas where leaders' advice and their own experiences were comparable – make sure the work is complete and delegate the work. In both cases, 35% advised others to take these actions, and 35% practiced the behaviors themselves and found them effective. Advice to change work arrangements was also closely aligned with leaders' actions, where 44% of participants advised others to alter their work schedule, work from home, or schedule time off; and 46% of leaders took the same action and rated it effective. There were moderate differences in leaders' advice vs. effective actions in several other areas – 38% advised others to provide clear instructions, while 25% took this action and found it effective; and 51% endorsed maintaining open communication and availability, while 43% of leaders engaged in the same effective behavior.

We surmise that differences in our participants' advice to other leaders vs. their own effective actions or behaviors may be due to their reflection on the personal crisis and their ability to gain insight and perspective over time. In the prescreening portion of Study 2, participants were able to complete the full questionnaire only if their personal crisis occurred at least one year prior to taking the survey. Research by Stoner and Gilligan (2002) concluded that leaders "must spend time in reflection, wrestling with the impact of the hardship. Reflection is a period for immersing oneself in a search for meaning. It demands self-confrontation and generates self-awareness" (p. 20).

Conclusion

Leaders recognize that the work of leadership must go on even when they are affected by personal crises. Our survey participants identified work-focused means to keep the organization stable or moving forward by focusing on work, changing their work arrangements, maintaining open communication or availability, making sure the work is completed, developing a plan to handle the crisis, delegating work, and providing clear instructions. Yet, leaders recommended that others prioritize these strategies or approaches differently from the way they did during their crisis. Notably, only 38% of leaders recommended focusing on work as an adaptive approach to leadership responsibilities during personal crises vs. 54% of leaders in our survey who actually spent time focusing on work and claimed that it was effective. These leaders advised that others develop a plan to handle the crisis, maintain open communication with people at work, and change their work arrangements as top priorities.

Leaders in crises also rely on robust relationships and friendships to provide work-related assistance and social support to prevail during their crises. Yet leaders first had to disclose the crisis to work friends and others in the workplace to benefit from their support. Over half (53%) of these leaders advised others to disclose their crisis selectively, and with good reason. We found very preliminary but interesting support for a relationship growth benefit (RGB) associated with wider leader disclosure in the organization, which requires additional study. And leaders who reported more positive effects on work relationships also reported higher overall effectiveness in and satisfaction with handling the crisis.

References

Colbert, A. E., Bono, J. E., & Purvanova, R. K. (2015). Flourishing via workplace relationships: Moving beyond instrumental support. *Academy of Management Journal, 59*(4), 1199–1223. https://doi.org/10.5465/amj.2014.0506

Hobfoll, S. E. (2011). Conservation of resources theory: Its implication for stress, health, and resilience. In S. Folkman (Ed.), *The Oxford handbook of stress, health, and coping* (pp. 127–147). New York: Oxford University Press.

Keyes, C. L. M. (2002). The mental health continuum: From languishing to flourishing in life. *Journal of Health and Social Behavior, 43*(2), 207–222. https://doi.org/10.2307/3090197

Pillemer, J., & Rothbard, N. P. (2018). Friends without benefits: Understanding the dark sides of workplace friendship. *Academy of Management Review, 43*(4), 635–660. https://doi.org/10.5465/amr.2016.0309

Rumens, N. (2017). Researching workplace friendships: Drawing insights from the sociology of friendship. *Journal of Social and Personal Relationships, 34*(8), 1149–1167. https://doi.org/10.1177/0265407516670276

Schaufeli, W. B., & Bakker, A. B. (2004). Job demands, job resources, and their relationship with burnout and engagement: A multi-sample study. *Journal of Organizational Behavior, 25*(3), 293–315. https://doi.org/10.1002/job.248

Sias, P. M., & Cahill, D. J. (1998). From coworkers to friends: The development of peer friendships in the workplace. *Western Journal of Communication, 62*(3), 273–299. https://doi.org/10.1080/10570319809374611

Stoner, C. R., & Gilligan, J. F. (2002). Leader rebound: How successful managers bounce back from the tests of adversity. *Business Horizons, 45*(6), 17–24. doi: 10.1016/S0007-6813(02)00256-2

6

TOWARD A CULTURE OF RECIPROCAL CARE

Advice and recommendations

JENNIFER'S STORY

I had a baby, that was a planned child, addition to our family . . . I was working 60 hours a week [as a partner in a law firm], I had a great deal of responsibility, I was in court trying a case the day before my child was born and went to the doctor for my regular weekly check-up because I was near my due date, and my blood pressure was sky-high and he induced labor the next day. After that, I guess my whole concept of what a maternity leave would be like and should be like, and what my return to work would be like and should be like was absolutely thrown out the window. I thought that I would be rested and restored to health by the time I went back to work, and that was certainly not the case.

And I felt a lot, just an enormous amount of pressure from all fronts; from my home, from my marriage, from my career to adjust to this very dramatic change. I returned to work and had a lot of problems with maintaining child care arrangements which I dealt with almost exclusively by myself because my husband works in the neighborhood of eighty to one hundred hours a week. I got no support almost from my coworkers because none of them were in a similar situation, they were either older males, childless males, or childless females. I began to have health problems which, at first, I did not associate with this status, and finally could no longer ignore the health problems, and once I associated them with the stress that was going on in my life at that time, I decided to resign. . . . It went on for eight months, until I finally quit.

Generating a culture of reciprocal care

Purpose: reciprocal care for all members

Jennifer's story illustrates the need for an organizational culture of reciprocal care. She encountered a neutral to uncooperative culture toward work-family support where the organization lost a valuable, experienced, and committed senior leader due to unimaginative solutions, inflexibility, and absence of care.

Generating a culture of reciprocal care in the organization begins with the purpose that its members intend to achieve. Allen and colleagues (1998) suggest that the purpose of leadership in the 21st century is "to create communities of *reciprocal care* and shared responsibility, where every person matters and each person's welfare and dignity is respected and supported" (p. 41) [italics added]. The concept of reciprocal care applies to leaders as vigorously as other members of the organization. While leaders are accustomed to caring for the organization and its members, a culture of reciprocal care assures that the leader-as-person in crisis is similarly cared for through its people, culture, policies, and practices.

Fuqua and Newman (2002) use the term caring organizations "to refer to systems where personal concern about the welfare of others and self is the norm" (p. 134). The concept of care in organizations seems to be an idea whose time has come. It has entered the literature and lexicon in disciplines as varied as ethics, psychology, and management. Rynes, Bartunek, Dutton, and Margolis (2012) observe:

> New scientific discoveries and conversations are causing scholars to reevaluate what we think we know about human motivations and behavior. A sharpened focus on care and compassion in organizations is consistent with a paradigm shift in the social sciences that emphasizes neurological, psychological, and sociological bases of human interrelating that have other-interest as opposed to self-interest at their core.
>
> *(p. 503)*

Gössling and van Liedekerke (2014) concur that:

> These [caring] organizations have understood that neglecting care and compassion equals neglecting a major driver of human interaction and that it is better to address this driver directly and make it a part of the fabric of the firm however strange the logic of care might seem to a profit driven organization.
>
> *(p. 438)*

Cultures of reciprocal care are environments where a "psychosocial safety climate" permeates the organization. A psychosocial safety climate mitigates risk factors for poor psychosocial health (e.g., emotional exhaustion, psychological distress, work overload, and emotional demands) by generating, "organizational policies, practices, and procedures for the protection of worker psychological health and safety. . . . Workers reporting high levels of psychosocial safety climate feel that their psychological safety and well-being is protected and supported by senior management" (Zadow & Dollard, 2015, p. 416). Further, as a tenet of reciprocal care, senior leaders receive psychological health and safety support, which may entail a new role for board committees and other members of the organization.

We propose that cultures of reciprocal care accept and anticipate that most members will experience personal crisis at some point during their tenure in leadership roles. In Study 1, we found that more than 70% of leaders had experienced a personal crisis while in that role. Thus, while personal crisis events are (hopefully) rare in the life of an individual, a culture of reciprocal care recognizes that personal crisis is an expected circumstance across the life cycle of teams and team members. As such, in a culture of reciprocal care, such "personal issues" are not treated as surprising anomalies but, rather, unfortunate facts of life which the organization is prepared to support the leader or team member in navigating. Communicating to individuals in the organization that such disruptions are expected and accepted can reduce barriers to disclosure and help-seeking. Furthermore, consistent with Conservation of Resources (COR) theory (Hobfoll, Halbesleben, Neveu, & Westman, 2018), organizations can build pre-crisis resource capacities in their organizations to reduce loss and potentiate gain.

Zooming in from the organizational level to the level of teams and dyads, we believe that psychological safety and mutual trust between leaders and their team members and among team members are necessary for a culture of reciprocal care and psychosocial safety climate across the organization. In other words, if individual members do not trust those with whom they interact on a daily basis and do not feel safe to reveal vulnerabilities and take interpersonal risks with those with whom they work most closely, the likelihood of reciprocal care actions between people shrinks nearly to zero. Because people experiencing crisis will act to preserve their remaining resources, people embedded within teams low in trust will be unlikely to take on further risk by seeking care when they need it. Therefore, a culture of reciprocal care cannot be conjured into existence by declarations from management or even the creation of new programs aimed to provide additional care resources. People within the organization must trust, respect, and value one another, and leaders must take actions that increase trust and psychological safety. Research has shown that supportive leadership behaviors such as inclusiveness and behavioral integrity are associated with enhanced psychological safety (Newman, Donohue, & Eva, 2017). These actions will, as described in Chapter 4, grow the team's pool of personal and interpersonal resources that can be used to support the leader or any team member in the event of a personal crisis.

We examine several approaches that organizations may use to create a culture of reciprocal care based on the results of our study, advice and reflections from our participants, and existing literature. We suggest that these approaches should comprise personal crisis support, personal crisis workshops and training, work-life support,

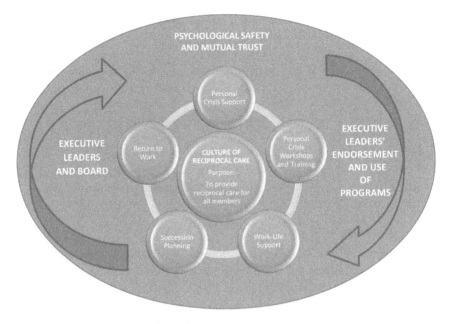

FIGURE 6.1 Culture of Reciprocal Care

succession planning and return-to-work programs (see Figure 6.1). Critically in our model, the engine that drives the success of these support efforts is psychological safety and trust between individuals at all levels of the organization. One key factor for embedding a culture of reciprocal care in the organization appears to be authentic communication from executive leaders and board members who endorse and support the culture, practice its tenets, and personally make use of its benefits, as depicted in Figure 6.1.

Creating programs for reciprocal care

Personal crisis support

Our research found that when leaders experience loss of family members, their own illness or injury, a family member's illness or injury, or a divorce/relationship breakup, they need personal, social, and organizational support. We asked participants in our survey to offer advice to current and prospective leaders based on their insights concerning personal crises. Leaders contributed their guidance on maintaining personal well-being.

Figure 6.2 depicts advice from our survey participants on personal well-being. We divided their recommendations into several categories – social support, healthy initiatives, spiritual practices, cognitive strategies, mindfulness, time away, family/

ADVICE ON HOW TO HANDLE PERSONAL CRISIS WITH REGARD TO THEIR OWN WELL-BEING

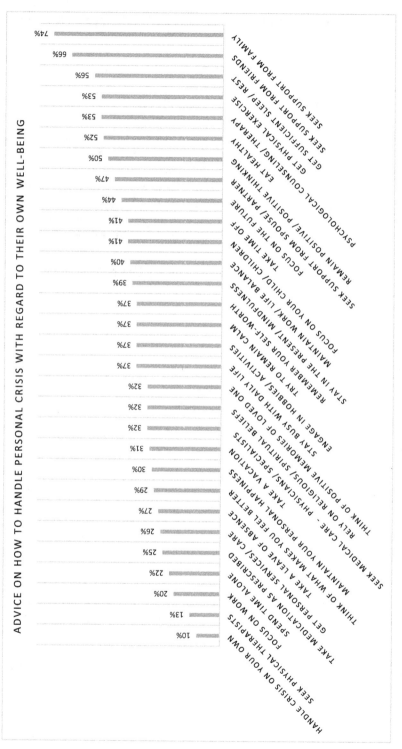

Advice	Percentage
SEEK SUPPORT FROM FAMILY	74%
SEEK SUPPORT FROM FRIENDS	66%
SEEK SUPPORT SLEEP / REST	56%
GET PHYSICAL EXERCISE	53%
GET SUFFICIENT SLEEP / THERAPY	53%
PSYCHOLOGICAL COUNSELING / THERAPY	52%
EAT HEALTHY	50%
REMAIN POSITIVE / POSITIVE THINKING	47%
FOCUS ON SPOUSE / PARTNER	44%
SEEK SUPPORT FROM SPOUSE / PARTNER	41%
TAKE TIME OFF	41%
FOCUS ON THE FUTURE	40%
FOCUS ON YOUR CHILD / CHILDREN	39%
MAINTAIN WORK / LIFE BALANCE	37%
REMEMBER YOUR SELF-WORTH	37%
STAY IN THE PRESENT / MINDFULNESS	37%
TRY TO REMAIN CALM	37%
ENGAGE IN HOBBIES / ACTIVITIES	32%
STAY BUSY WITH DAILY LIFE	32%
THINK OF POSITIVE MEMORIES OF LOVED ONE	32%
RELY ON RELIGIOUS / SPIRITUAL BELIEFS	31%
TAKE A VACATION	30%
SEEK MEDICAL CARE - PHYSICIANS / SPECIALISTS	29%
MAINTAIN YOUR PERSONAL HAPPINESS	27%
TAKE A LEAVE OF ABSENCE	26%
THINK OF WHAT MAKES YOU FEEL BETTER	25%
GET PERSONAL SERVICES / CARE	22%
SPEND TIME ALONE	20%
FOCUS ON WORK	13%
TAKE MEDICATION AS PRESCRIBED	10%
SEEK PHYSICAL THERAPISTS	
HANDLE CRISIS ON YOUR OWN	

FIGURE 6.2 Advice on Handling Leaders' Own Well-being

home life, and daily functioning. Leaders endorsed effective approaches to well-being that encompass:

- Seeking social support from family (74%), friends (66%), and spouse or partner (47%);
- Engaging in healthy initiatives, including getting sufficient sleep or rest (56%), physical exercise (53%), psychological counseling or therapy (53%), eating healthy (52%), engaging in hobbies or activities (37%), seeking medical care where applicable (32%), and taking medication as prescribed (25%);
- Relying on spiritual practices based on religious or spiritual beliefs (32%);
- Engaging in cognitive strategies (or changing the way they thought about the crisis) by remaining positive/positive thinking (50%), focusing on the future (44%), remembering your self-worth (37%), trying to remain calm (37%), maintaining your personal happiness (30%), and thinking of what makes you feel better (29%) (see also Chapter 2 for more details on cognitive strategies);
- Practicing mindfulness by staying in the present (39%), and thinking of positive memories of loved one (32%) (marginally more middle managers [38%] recommended thinking about positive memories of loved ones than executive leaders [24%], $p = .06$);
- Spending time away by taking time off (41%), taking a vacation (31%), taking a leave of absence (27%), and spending time alone (22%);
- Focusing on family/home life by concentrating on your child/children (41%) and maintaining work/life balance (40%); and
- Maintaining daily functioning through staying busy with daily life (37%); and focusing on work (20%).

We compared the advice from our survey participants with the actions they found effective during the personal crisis in Figure 6.3. There are a few areas where leaders' advice and successful actions align quite closely. For example, their most frequently endorsed advice to other leaders was to seek social support from family (74%) and friends (66%), which they consistently demonstrated by seeking advice from their own family (71%) and friends (62%). They also endorsed seeking support from one's spouse or partner (47%), and 41% demonstrated this behavior themselves and found it to be helpful.

Leaders were consistent with their advice and practices in the lowest endorsed behaviors — that is, they advised others to seek physical therapists where applicable (13 %) vs. 11% who took this action themselves; 10% advised others to handle the crisis on your own vs. 12% who took this action. A significant outcome for the purpose of our study is that very few participants advised others to handle the crisis on their own *and* very few leaders actually felt that handling the crisis by themselves had been a good strategy for them. This finding suggests that most leaders recognize the need for social support in order to navigate personal crises.

In three areas, there were disparities between leaders' advice and their own successful strategies — 41% of leaders in our survey said that focusing on work during

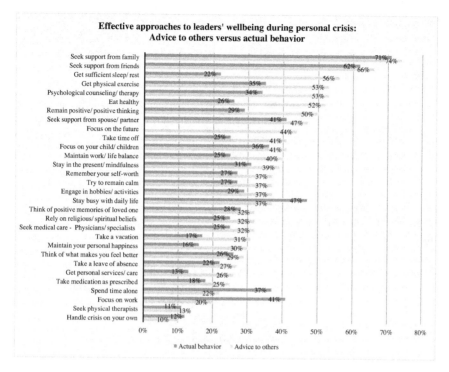

**Effective approaches to leaders' wellbeing during personal crisis:
Advice to others versus actual behavior**

FIGURE 6.3 Advice vs. Leaders' Actions: Well-being during Personal Crisis

Note: "Focus on the future" category was inadvertently omitted from the choices given to participants for the strategies that they found effective.

the crisis was helpful, while only 20% advised the same for others; 47% of leaders stayed busy with daily life, while 37% advised the same for others; and 37% spent time alone, while 22% advised others to do the same.

Organizational support for personal crisis care can take several forms, including referrals to psychiatrists or therapists, bereavement support groups or specialists, divorce support groups, and caregiver services. A study by Byrne et al. (2014, p. 353) concurs with the need for such organizational support concluding that, "organizations must not only take responsibility for communicating the importance of leaders' well-being, but also provide resources such as employee assistance programs or psychological counseling to all employees." The organization may also offer accompanying benefits programs for medical specialists or treatment centers, mental health care, legal services, elder care, long-term care, and fiduciary services; and they need to provide supportive polices on bereavement, sick leave, family leave, and flexible work arrangements that can be "tailored" to the needs of the person in crisis.

With regard to mental health, leaders are in an especially precarious position because their mental health affects not only their well-being but the well-being of their team members and organization. Yet, the persistent stigma surrounding mental illness contributes to a lack of disclosure and treatment for leaders and other members of the organization. A culture of reciprocal care could help generate interventions in support of mental health care for leaders and members. Barling and Cloutier (2016) report that

> Workplace interventions to reduce stigma associated with mental illness are effective, and even cost effective. . . . What is missing to date, however, is a concerted effort by organizations to take care of those who bear responsibility for the well-being of the organization and its employees.
>
> *(p. 401)*

The researchers cite a meta-analysis of 55 interventions which showed that cognitive-behavioral interventions (strategies used to change a person's problematic thinking and behavior, such as anger or anxiety) were the most effective, especially when offered in shorter intervals of one to four weeks (Barling & Cloutier, 2016). They also emphasize that low-dose, unobtrusive mindfulness interventions over short durations reduced emotional exhaustion and supported good sleep quality.

To be effective, these services and interventions should be offered by professionals who are trained to care for health and life crisis needs. This level of organizational support exceeds standard benefits programs and provides specialized support and care for its leaders and members.

Preparation for personal crisis: workshops and training

We asked participants, have you received any form of training or preparation that helped you deal with personal crises? The majority answered no (58%), about a third replied yes (33%), a few responded, I don't know (7%), and a small number of skeptics said they did not believe it was possible to prepare leaders for personal crisis (1%) (see Figure 6.4).

Most leaders in our survey actively endorsed the idea that organizations could create programs to help prepare current and aspiring leaders, though a few did not. The responses in Figure 6.5 detail advice on actions that may be taken in the workplace.

- Develop training programs on how to handle personal crises (54%);
- Develop training programs on stress management and self-understanding (54%);
- Provide organizational support for people in crisis such as counseling referrals or employee assistance programs (EAP) (42%);
- Handle personal crisis on your own (14%); and
- Preparation for personal crisis is not possible (8%).

The majority of our participants' responses suggest that organizations can prepare for, care for, and support their most valuable assets – their leaders and members – to handle inevitable life events. Additionally, we suggest developing social support

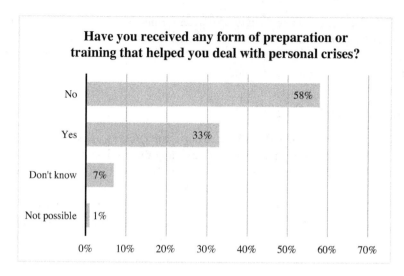

FIGURE 6.4 Preparation or Training for Personal Crisis

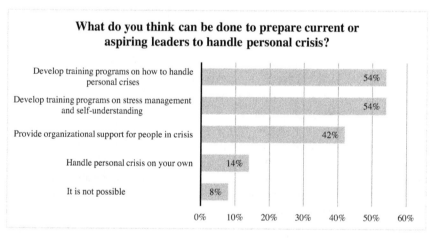

FIGURE 6.5 Recommendations for Preparing Leaders to Handle Personal Crisis

capabilities among members of the organization and stigma reduction workshops regarding mental illness. Researchers Logan, Thornton, and Breen (2018) stress that for social support to be effective, a need must be recognized, the potential supporter must be capable and willing, and the gesture must be perceived as helpful, as indicated in Chapter 1. These competencies may be developed through in-person or online seminars taught by experienced trainers with backgrounds in counseling, clinical psychology, or social work. Importantly, like other opportunities for social interaction, conducting trainings in groups of people from a variety of organizational units may also serve to strengthen social networks across team boundaries, which may enhance the availability of different kinds of social support and other resources (Hobfoll et al., 2018). Certainly, if organizations can prepare for unknown crises that may impact their businesses, nonprofits, universities or school systems, they can do the same for their people.

Return-to-work programs

The issue of return to work (RTW) is a unique problem for leaders who must cope with their own illness or injury while maintaining the profitability and functioning of their organizations. They are not always able to bury themselves in work to cope with their crisis; instead they struggle with how or when to return to work after a critical illness or injury. Gragnano, Negrini, Miglioretti, and Corbière (2018) conducted a review of research on return-to-work processes across varied diseases (cardiovascular diseases, common mental disorders, and cancers) to discover similarities in psychosocial factors. They found four common facilitators of RTW across different diseases – job control (i.e., the ability to influence one's work or a person's workplace autonomy); work ability (i.e., a self-measure of personal ability to work); perceived good health, and high socioeconomic status; as well as six barriers to RTW – level of job strain as perceived by the employee; anxiety; depression; comorbidity (meaning additional illnesses); older age; and lower educational levels (Gragnano et al., 2018). Among these facilitators and barriers, the researchers also discovered medical variables among the common RTW predictors. There were similar common predictors of RTW in other research on individuals with musculoskeletal disorders – job strain, job control, self-rated health, age, socioeconomic status, and comorbidity.

Many leaders have considerable job control and workplace autonomy inherent in their positions along with the ability to self-measure their capacity to work (especially with support from medical experts and family members), competence to perceive good health, and high socioeconomic status. Still, the ability to return to work, or the lack thereof, has even greater consequences for CEOs. Some CEOs (e.g., Jack Welch) chose to wait until after they recovered to report their condition to shareholders (Perryman, Butler, Martin, & Ferris, 2010), but often corporate and nonprofit boards must make critical decisions when leaders encounter long-term, debilitating health issues to appoint an interim person or replace the ailing CEO. Some leaders are determined to stay the course and remain at work, even when it is detrimental to them and their organizations. Other leaders in these circumstances choose to retire voluntarily, and still others face the risk of being removed by the organization (Perryman et al., 2010).

The researchers indicate that these findings provide a basis to build RTW intervention and training programs. Consistent with generating a culture of reciprocal care, they recommend that "all RTW interventions should be designed to increase the sense of workability of the workers and target the working conditions with the aim of increasing job control and decreasing job strain" (Gragnano et al., 2018, p. 228).

Work-life support

Work-family policies

Employees in today's workforce are seeking organizations that demonstrate a family-supportive environment. This kind of environment is especially important for leaders and team members who experience personal crises related to work-family support, such as the one in Jennifer's story at the beginning of the chapter. More employers are responding to the need for a family-supportive environment by providing work-family policies to employees, including family leave, flexible spending accounts for family dependent care, elder care resources and referral, childcare resources and referral, and on-site childcare. A meta-analysis conducted by Butts, Casper, and Yang (2013) found that family leave policies, in particular, are associated with a reduction in work-to-family conflict and that "both policy availability and use exhibited small positive relationships with job satisfaction, affective commitment, and intentions to stay" (p. 11). They indicated that "availability" of these policies was more strongly associated with positive work attitudes than actual use of these benefits. While work-family support policies may be a necessary condition for employees' positive perceptions, the researchers concluded that overall "organizational support for family may be more important in enhancing employee attitudes than formal policies" (Butts et al., 2013, p. 13).

Relatedly, providing work-family programs is certainly critical to helping people in the organization cope with day-to-day challenges as well as personal crises; research has also consistently shown that attitudes and norms about making use of those resources are also critical. People will be less likely to use a program if they believe that doing so would bring about professional and social costs such as negative judgments by others or higher expectations later because of having received the benefit. For example, an institution of higher education might have a university-wide policy that allows faculty on the tenure track to "stop the clock" during parental leave, providing an additional year of work that could be considered toward the tenure decision. In one university school, faculty commonly "stop the clock" during parental leave and are encouraged to do so by their senior colleagues. In another school at the same university, faculty considering stopping the clock are told by colleagues, "You can do that if you want to, but at tenure time you'll be expected to have accomplished that much more because of the 'extra' year." (And, not surprisingly, faculty in this school rarely take the benefit.) Informal norms, such as those in this example, therefore, have been shown to have a powerful impact on employee access to work-family resources. As Hobfoll and colleagues (2018) conclude:

> Overall, there is increasing evidence that merely providing employees with broad resources related to managing work and family roles simply isn't enough: The environment has to be supportive of utilizing those resources in ways that can help employees satisfy their goals across work and family domains.
>
> *(p. 116)*

Therefore, a culture of reciprocal care fosters positive attitudes toward the use of work-family resources and provides praise rather than punishment for using these benefits.

Work and informal caregiving

Increasingly, more working adults must provide informal care for ill partners, children, and aging parents. Among the leaders in our survey, 22% reported that their personal crisis involved the illness or injury of a family member. More than one in six adults working full-time and part-time provide informal caregiving in the U.S. – with 56% of employees working fulltime; 16% working between 30–39 hours; and 25% working fewer than 30 hours per week (Family Caregiver Alliance, 2016).

Workplaces with a culture of reciprocal care can play a vital role in supporting leaders and team members who are informal caregivers. Plaisier, van Groenou, and Keuzenkamp (2015) conducted a study of 1,991 employed informal caregivers in 50 organizations in Holland to determine how organizations facilitate the combination of work and informal care at individual and organizational levels. They found that the "care context," meaning a caregiver-supportive culture, was more likely to have a good balance between work and informal caregiving (WC-balance) and a lower need for job adaptation. Their results show that:

> Employed caregivers benefit from receiving social support at work from colleagues and from creative solutions negotiated with their supervisors that do not involve reducing their working hours or adapting work schedules. . . . Our study adds the finding that, in addition to working in an understanding team, working in an organization that was explicit about the issue of informal care contributed to positive outcomes of combining work and informal care.
> *(Plaisier et al., 2015, p. 277)*

Although formal leave arrangements were found to be important, especially to alleviate severe work-care conflicts, a supportive care context in the organization was associated with good work-care outcomes. The researchers further indicated that supportive management could provide help and advice for seeking solutions to the care situation.

Organizational support for caregiving during the career-life path

Fuller and Raman (2019) conducted a two-survey study of 301 human resources leaders and business owners and 1500 employees in the U.S. that identified a substantive disconnect between employers' knowledge (or lack thereof) about the care responsibilities of their employees and the impact of hidden costs to employees and the organization. They found that most employers (52%) did not measure their care demographics including:

- The extent of the employee population affected;
- The predictable timing of care milestones in employees' lives as they age;

- The changes in the demand for care solutions, due to factors like the changing age profile of their workforce or the increase of serious chronic illnesses among children and the elderly.

While few employers measure employees' caregiving responsibilities, 73% of employees in Fuller and Raman's (2019) survey reported having caregiving responsibilities for children, spouses or partners, elderly family members, and friends. These caregiving responsibilities directly contributed to employee turnover, weakened performance, and career progression; and caregiving responsibilities occurred regularly at different stages of the employee's career. Most importantly to our study of leaders during personal crisis, Fuller and Raman (2019) discovered that "workers in the upper reaches of an organization – those with the highest incomes and titles [i.e., those in senior leadership or executives roles] – were the most likely to leave a company because of irreconcilable tensions between the requirements of work and home" (p. 17).

The researchers suggested that organizations measure their care demographics (collect the facts about informal caregivers in the workplace), conduct cost-benefit analyses (to evaluate costs due to factors such as turnover, loss of institutional knowledge, productivity losses, overtime and replacements vs. providing relevant care benefits), redesign career paths that are compatible with employees' life paths, and determine what care benefits employees actually need. "Employees cited the most popular benefit for retention as referral services for caregivers; 78% of employees described that benefit as 'very important' to their decision to stay with their firm" while only 38% of employers thought that these services were an effective benefit (Fuller & Raman, 2019, p. 20).

Significantly, Fuller and Raman's (2019) research revealed that caregiving requirements for employees occurred throughout the life path, and they were different depending on age category.

- Workers between 18–25 years, needed support in flexible work hours (45%), on-site or near-site childcare (40%), caregiver referral services (40%), and the ability to telecommute (39%); and
- Workers between 26–35 years, expected they will need caregiver referral services in the near future (62%), some form of paid leave (50%), some form of on-site or near-site eldercare, and subsidies for those services (43%).

(Fuller & Raman, 2019, p. 25)

The researchers predict that employers who foster a culture of care emanating from the executive and board level will likely gain a competitive advantage for attracting and retaining top talent now and in the future.

Succession planning for illness and death

Leaders' personal crises have the potential to influence the health and profitability of their organizations. As discussed in Chapter 2, an intriguing pair of studies from Denmark suggests that when CEOs experience personal crises, the operating profitability of the firm is negatively impacted. Bennedsen, Pérez-González, and Wolfenzon (2010) found that operating returns on assets (ORA) declined 8% with the death of a CEO's spouse, 7% with the loss of a child, 6% with the loss of a parent, and 4% with the loss of a parent in-law during the two-year window after the event compared to two years before the event. In a second study (Bennedsen, Pérez-González, & Wolfenzon, 2012) found that firms whose CEOs were hospitalized for more than five days had significantly lower operating returns on assets (ORA), underperforming industry standards by 1.2 percentage points, and representing reductions in operating profitability of 14%. Such effects support the importance of succession planning to reduce the impact of CEO life events on the organization.

Perryman et al. (2010) compared succession planning in organizations to the U.S. Constitution's 20th and 25th amendments that detail requirements and procedures in the event that the U.S. president is temporarily or permanently disabled or that he or she dies. Organizations need to prepare in the same way as the chief of state for the illness or disability and potential death of the CEO. The author's note:

> Prompt disclosures of health concerns provide organizations more time to form unified plans, which aid in ensuring a path consistent with the desired strategic direction. Moreover, such plans can also help assuage concerns over organizational stability – from both internal and external constituents – by addressing who will lead the organization, and for how long.
>
> *(Perryman et al., 2010, p. 24)*

Perhaps the responsibility of developing a succession plan for the organization might be designated to individuals other than the CEO, such as a committee of board members or an outside consultant with input from the CEO and board. Many CEOs are often reluctant to develop succession plans that require them to prepare for the possibility of their own disability or death.

Shared leadership structures may also help ease the stress of a sustained leadership void when a CEO or president becomes disabled or dies. Some organizations in the U.S. and Europe have developed structures with co-presidents or co-CEOs, though the results have been mixed. These shared structures are increasingly popular among Gen-Xers and millennials (O'Donnell, 2017), who may be more comfortable or familiar with distributed power and decision-making than earlier generations.

Conclusion

The advice in this section, based on experiences, reflections, and insights of leaders in our survey and studies found in current literature, provide a more comprehensive understanding of the actions and responses that seem most effective for handling personal crisis and the care of both leaders and members of the organization. Combined insights from our participants and other research studies identify gaps in organizational responses to leaders and other members in crises.

A culture of reciprocal care that provides personal crisis support, personal crisis workshops and training, work-life support, return-to-work programs, and succession planning in a psychosocial safety climate enables people and organizations to thrive when personal crisis affects the leader or team members (Figure 6.1). These programs and policies can generate significant resources, but, as Zadow and Dollard (2015) contend, "the 'right' climate enables resources to do their job" (p. 427). These sources of support must be made accessible through relationships of mutual trust between individuals and climates of psychological safety within groups at all levels of the organization. Senior executives and board members must "walk their talk" by creating and fully endorsing a culture of reciprocal care; and senior executives must set the example by embracing and participating in the programs that support this dynamic culture.

References

Allen, K. E., Bordas, J., Hickman, G. R., Matusak, L. R., Sorenson, G. J., & Whitmire, K. J. (1998). Leadership in the 21st century. In G. R. Hickman (Ed.), *Leading organizations: Perspectives for a new era*. Thousand Oaks, CA: Sage Publications.

Barling, J., & Cloutier, A. (2016). Leaders' mental health at work: Empirical, methodological, and policy directions. *Journal of Occupational Health Psychology, 22*(3), 394. https://doi.org/10.1037/ocp0000055

Bennedsen, M., Pérez-González, F., & Wolfenzon, D. (2010). *Do CEOs matter?* Retrieved from www0.gsb.columbia.edu/mygsb/faculty/research/pubfiles/3177/valueceos.pdf

Bennedsen, M., Pérez-González, F., & Wolfenzon, D. (2012). *Evaluating the impact of the boss: Evidence from CEO hospitalization events.* Retrieved from http://conference.iza.org/conference_files/Leadership_2012/perez-gonzalez_f7878.pdf

Butts, M. M., Casper, W. J., & Yang, T. S. (2013). How important are work-family support policies? A meta-analytic investigation of their effects on employee outcomes. *The Journal of Applied Psychology, 98*(1), 1–25. https://doi.org/10.1037/a0030389

Byrne, A., Dionisi, A. M., Barling, J., Akers, A., Robertson, J., Lys, R., . . . Dupré, K. (2014). The depleted leader: The influence of leaders' diminished psychological resources on leadership behaviors. *The Leadership Quarterly, 25*(2), 344–357. https://doi.org/10.1016/j.leaqua.2013.09.003

Family Caregiver Alliance. (2016). Caregiver statistics: Work and caregiving. *Family Caregiver Alliance.* Retrieved August 12, 2019 from www.caregiver.org/caregiver-statistics-work-and-caregiving

Fuller, J. B., & Raman, M. (2019). The caring company. *Harvard Business School.* Retrieved from www.hbs.edu/managing-the-future-of-work/Documents/The_Caring_Company.pdf

Fuqua, D. R., & Newman, J. L. (2002). Creating caring organizations. *Consulting Psychology Journal: Practice and Research, 54*(2), 131–140. https://doi.org/10.1037/1061-4087.54.2.131

Gössling, T., & van Liedekerke, L. (2014). Editorial: The caring organisation. *Journal of Business Ethics, 120*(4), 437–440. https://doi.org/10.1007/s10551-014-2158-z

Gragnano, A., Negrini, A., Miglioretti, M., & Corbière, M. (2018). Common psychosocial factors predicting return to work after common mental disorders, cardiovascular diseases, and cancers: A review of reviews supporting a cross-disease approach. *Journal of Occupational Rehabilitation, 28*(2), 215–231. https://doi.org/10.1007/s10926-017-9714-1

Hobfoll, S. E., Halbesleben, J., Neveu, J.-P., & Westman, M. (2018). Conservation of resources in the organizational context: The reality of resources and their consequences.

Annual Review of Organizational Psychology and Organizational Behavior, 5(1), 103–128. https://doi.org/10.1146/annurev-orgpsych-032117-104640

Logan, E. L., Thornton, J. A., & Breen, L. J. (2018). What determines supportive behaviours following bereavement? A systematic review and call to action. *Death Studies, 42*(2), 104–114. https://doi.org/10.1080/07481187.2017.1329760

Newman, A., Donohue, R., & Eva, N. (2017). Psychological safety: A systematic review of the literature. *Human Resource Management Review, 27*(3), 521–535. https://doi.org/10.1016/j.hrmr.2017.01.001

O'Donnell, S. (2017). *Co-CEOs might be increasing, but do they mean twice the trouble?* Retrieved August 1, 2019 from www.forbes.com/sites/forbescoachescouncil/2017/11/09/co-ceos-might-be-increasing-but-do-they-mean-twice-the-trouble/#62a41f5d3c48

Perryman, A. A., Butler, F. C., Martin, J. A., & Ferris, G. R. (2010). When the CEO is ill: Keeping quiet or going public? *Business Horizons, 53*(1), 21–29. https://doi.org/10.1016/j.bushor.2009.08.006

Plaisier, I., Groenou, M. I. B. van, & Keuzenkamp, S. (2015). Combining work and informal care: the importance of caring organisations. *Human Resource Management Journal, 25*(2), 267–280. https://doi.org/10.1111/1748-8583.12048

Rynes, S. L., Bartunek, J. M., Dutton, J. E., & Margolis, J. D. (2012). Care and compassion through an organizational lens: Opening up new possibilities. *Academy of Management Review, 37*(4), 503–523. https://doi.org/10.5465/amr.2012.0124

Zadow, A., & Dollard, M. F. (2015). Psychosocial safety climate. In S. Clarke, T. M. Probst, F. Guldenmund, & J. Passmore (Eds.), *The Wiley Blackwell handbook of the psychology of occupational safety and workplace health* (pp. 414–436). Chichester, UK: John Wiley & Sons. https://doi.org/10.1002/9781118979013.ch18

7
LEADERS IN PERSONAL CRISIS

Proposals for practice and research

The goal of this chapter is to summarize the "lessons learned" from our research and to propose directions for practice and research in leadership studies and related disciplines. Because personal aspects of leadership is an under-researched and evolving field, we present our conclusions as proposals for practice and research. This chapter concludes with recommendations for future research on personal aspects of leadership and cultures of reciprocal care.

Recognize that leaders are people first

Our first proposal that we "recognize that leaders are people first" may seem overly simplistic, but it is one that even leaders may overlook or disregard. Leaders represent many things to many people – role models, heroes, visionaries, and symbols of hope, authority figures, or embodiments of power – but leaders are people who are vulnerable to human frailties, including personal crisis. During a personal crisis, leaders often become bereaved family members, patients, caregivers, or newly single individuals – people in crisis. These all-too-human situations are painful, disorienting, and difficult spaces for anyone, including leaders. We may know intuitively that leaders are people first, but neither our attitudes and expectations nor institutions and organizations are positioned to respond to what this realization may mean in theory or practice.

Adaptive leader responses to crisis are flexible, intentional, and self-compassionate

Personal crises trigger real and often painful losses of resources that leaders must spend time, energy, and other resources on to manage. The process of adaptation is rarely easy or straightforward and "cook book" approaches to responding to personal crisis run a high risk of being inaccurate and unhelpful. Each crisis, each leader, and each organizational context is unique and, as emphasized throughout this book, each layer of influence contributes to a leader's process of adaptation and adjustment. Yet, as explicated in Chapter 2, the scholarship of coping does point the way toward general principles that contribute to more successful adaptation to crisis events.

We recommend that leaders try to stay flexible in their approaches to coping with crisis because access to different resources is needed during different stages of adaptation. Leaders may even find themselves using strategies that are new to them and that take them outside of their comfort zone or push them beyond perceived boundaries. For example, decision-making around disclosure and help-seeking in the organization (Chapter 3) may require leaders to deviate from their typical way of working with others.

We also recommend that leaders, as much as possible given the situation, be intentional about the coping strategies they use. Although automatic, intuitive responses can certainly be adaptive, other aspects of coping with a crisis call for a more planful, intentional approach. For example, a leader might create a general plan to delegate work responsibilities in the event that the leader is less available during the crisis. Intentionality can also help the leader to engage more frequently in approach-oriented coping and less frequently in avoidance, as supported by research on successful coping.

Finally, we recommend that leaders practice self-compassion and self-care when managing a personal crisis. Engaging the problems and emotions inherent in coping with a crisis can often trigger other unpleasant thoughts and emotions that can leave the leader feeling depleted. Wise leaders will make plans to consider their own well-being and use respite, social support, and activities that allow for the experience of positive emotion, and other self-care activities that they know to be restorative for them personally. In addition, because leaders are accustomed to being in control, self-compassion may be needed in those moments where the leader feels distinctly out of control of the situation or her or his own emotions.

Practicing this type of adaptive coping is difficult. Leaders may need informal social support from friends, family, and religious leaders or formal support from a psychologist, social worker, or counselor to maintain effective coping. Savvy leaders rely on the resources afforded by these relationships.

Selective disclosure and help-seeking can minimize risks and maximize benefits

In order to manage the impact of the crisis on their role as a leader and on their own well-being, leaders may need to talk about the crisis and ask for assistance from others in the organization. Others in the organization are often in possession of substantial resources, such as information, social networks, and moral support, that could aid the leader in efforts to cope and sustain leadership activities. Leader disclosure can also help the organization anticipate and plan ahead for disruptions that may occur in leadership as a result of the crisis. Reasons for leader disclosure are diverse and depend on the nature of the relationship, the purpose of the disclosure, and the interpersonal culture of the organization; therefore, leaders are selective in their disclosure and help-seeking patterns.

When making decisions about disclosure and help-seeking, leaders seek to balance possible benefits and risks.[1] Risks may seem higher in organizations that espouse social norms of impersonal, non-emotional interactions with coworkers. Leaders may fear losing status or power, introducing instability into their organization, or having their needs rejected by others. While each of these outcomes is possible, leaders should also consider potential benefits that extend beyond the specific crisis-related support they receive. Disclosure has the potential to deepen trust and liking between leaders and their team members and enables leaders to actively manage uncertainty related to the situation. Leader help-seeking provides opportunities for enhanced trust and new ways of working between the leader and team members. While disclosure and help-seeking are likely to change the way that others see the leader, we propose that the consequences of change in perspective and leader identity have the potential to be beneficial to the leader's organizational relationships.

The organization's interpersonal context is powerful

The situations and social contexts in which people are embedded have a powerful influence on their behavior and, by extension, their coping responses. While leaders influence their organizational culture, they are also heavily influenced by it. Leaders embedded within cultures that are less trusting, less concerned with the well-being of individual members, and less tolerant of interpersonal risk-taking may find it more difficult to get the support they need to navigate a personal crisis and sustain their leadership role. Leaders in these contexts may feel more constrained in talking about the situation or seeking assistance or accommodations, and the organization surrounding the leader may become an additional source of stress rather than support. We propose that the psychological safety of the team and organization – the extent to which members mutually feel that they can take risks and bring their authentic selves to the organization – and interpersonal trust are resources that support successful coping for leaders in crisis and for all members. While conceptions of leadership excellence often focus on the personal qualities of the leader, we further propose that leadership success and thriving is a function of the interpersonal context surrounding the leader.

Leader relationships matter and may evolve in crisis

Leaders who have nurtured genuine relationships and enduring friendships throughout their time in the organization typically rely on these relationships in times of personal crisis. Leaders often count on valued team members, colleagues, and individuals to whom they report to share their personal crisis, help with job support, arrange accommodations, and provide emotional support.

---

1 In order to increase the likelihood of favorable disclosure and help-seeking outcomes, we have several more specific recommendations for what leaders should consider and how they should craft their messages (see Box 3.1).

Work friendships appear to play an important role in the lives of leaders during a personal crisis. We often hear in popular culture that leaders are isolated at the top. Yet, 43% of the leaders in our survey (among them more executive leaders [52%] than middle managers [37%]) reported disclosing their personal crisis to team members and peers "because they were friends"; and 21% disclosed to friends who were also individuals to whom they report.

We found that some leaders reported a positive impact on work relationships and friendships that we call "relationship growth benefit" (RGB). Greater RGB is associated with wider leader disclosure in their organization. And leaders who reported more positive impacts on work relationships also reported higher overall effectiveness in and satisfaction with handling the crisis.

Leaders need reciprocal care; wise organizations provide it

People frequently expect leaders to respond to their professional and personal needs in the organization. In the same way, can leaders expect people in the organization to respond to their conditions as human beings when they need support in their lives? Most organizations certainly provide compensation packages, health care and wellness benefits, and executive privileges to their leaders – in these realms, leaders are privileged. Yet, it is often difficult to admit that leaders may genuinely need support at certain points in their life path. Reciprocal care entails more than compensation, benefits, and privileges. It embodies an expectation that leaders and organizational members care for each other as people in an organizational context that provides a culture and infrastructure of supportive programs, policies, and people, beginning with board members and senior executives and permeating through the entire organization.

Some wise organizations have likely discovered that reciprocal care is not only a compassionate way to function, but it may also provide productive and cost-effective ways to attract and sustain high-quality leaders and members. Turnover, absences, illness, and disorientation are costly. What people are seeking, based on several research studies cited in Chapter 6, is a supportive context where managers and colleagues are considerate of their personal situations and are willing to help them devise creative solutions when crises or challenging situations enter their lives.

Personal aspects of leadership: a research agenda

In the preface to this volume, we described how leadership studies scholars have recently highlighted the puzzling lack of attention to personal aspects of leaders, including leader well-being, mental health, and stress. Our investigation of leadership in personal crisis falls under this broader umbrella of research on the personal aspects of leadership. And, while we learned much from the investigations reported in this book, our work highlighted the yawning gaps in what we know about leaders coping with crisis, how to help them, and about ways to promote the personal thriving of leaders more generally. Encouragingly, recent work by Kathleen

Brandert and Gina Matkin at the University of Nebraska–Lincoln on personal crisis as experienced by women in leadership represents the type of scholarship that we hope will become more prevalent in this field (see Brandert & Matkin, 2019). In this section, we outline specific questions, frameworks, and methods for research in what we hope will become an emerging and, eventually, thriving research area.

Investigate different types of leaders, organizations, and stressors

Although we did examine differences between middle managers and executive leaders in our Study 2 survey, future studies could examine whether leader responses to personal crises depend on other ways to distinguish leaders from one another, such as company size, position in the organizational structure, or tenure on the job. In particular, future studies can specifically target higher executive levels to determine whether the experience of these leaders differs. Because recruiting executive level leaders into survey studies is a recognized research challenge (Cycyota & Harrison, 2002, 2006), creative recruitment strategies may be helpful, including recruitment from organizations of retired leaders, support groups for leaders, or via networks of executive coaches. Leadership development seminars or training programs may be another fruitful recruitment source. Qualitative approaches to research may be particularly useful in this area because leaders may be more willing to be interviewed about personal matters vs. filling out a survey.

Future studies could also systematically investigate personal aspects of leadership in different types of organizations and cultures. The challenges of coping with a personal crisis may be very different based on organizational context; for example, the military, religious organizations and orders, political organizations, or family-owned businesses. Cross-cultural research on personal aspects of leadership might also illuminate how effective coping strategies vary based on culture or point the way toward effective practices that could be transferred from one culture to another. Finally, future research could investigate other types of personal and professional crises that we have not yet examined.

Move beyond self-report

Our research to this point has relied upon leader self-report and so future studies on personal aspects of leadership, and personal crisis in leaders, specifically, should investigate the experiences of team members when leaders are in crisis. Such investigations would validate (or challenge) leader views of what was effective and of what the effects of the crisis were on their relationships. Team members could provide valuable information about leader behaviors that they found beneficial or detrimental to their ability to function in the organization. The ideal method would be to obtain information from both leaders and team members regarding the same leader crisis event and ensuing adjustment period. As described earlier, such investigations could begin by using interview and qualitative methods and progress to larger samples using quantitative methods.

Future studies should also further investigate the relationship between leader personal well-being and the functioning, sustainability, and profitability of the organization. For example, the novel work of Bennedsen, Pérez-González, and Wolfenzon (2010, 2012) examines the relationship between CEO death, illness, and bereavement on firm performance using public records in Denmark (see Chapters 2 and 6). Studies that integrate review of records with interview or survey research might identify which personal and organizational circumstances – for example, wider availability of resources, certain organizational cultural factors, or particular policies – are associated with reduced negative impact of leader personal crisis on the organization.

Apply novel theoretical frameworks

As we reviewed the literature for this book, we encountered several theoretical frameworks that could be profitably applied to studying personal aspects of leadership and leaders in crisis. First, as introduced in Chapter 2, applying Conservation of Resources Theory (COR; Hobfoll, 2011) would generate a wealth of testable predictions that could guide the design of future studies. For example, future studies could use the Conservation of Resources Evaluation (COR-E; Hobfoll, 2007) to assess actual or threatened loss of resources as well as gains in the context of leader personal crisis. Second, job-demands-resources theory (Bakker & Demerouti, 2016), which is a theory more specifically applied to burnout but based upon the principles of COR theory, could be used to test whether resources (and which resources) buffer the effect of personal crisis on burnout for leaders and non-leaders. Such an application would be relatively novel because most studies using this theory focus on the impact of workplace demands on burnout but give limited attention to the effects of demands and crises in one's personal life.

Finally, theoretical frameworks on coping and emotion regulation from clinical psychology could be applied to better understand leadership in personal crisis. For example, studies could specifically examine the relationship between approach vs. avoidant coping responses and leader effectiveness. We are particularly intrigued by the possibility that focusing on one's work (Chapters 2 and 5) could serve different coping functions – that is, in some circumstances, focusing seemed to be a cognitive and emotional respite for participants while, in other cases, it could function as an unhealthy avoidance tactic. In future studies, examining the extent to which and under what circumstances focus on work contributes to engagement (feelings of dedication, absorption, and vigor regarding one's work; Leiter & Maslach, 2017) might clarify the dual nature of focusing on one's work as a coping strategy.

Investigate Relationship Growth Benefit (RGB)

Our results point to the intriguing possibility that a leader's personal crisis presents an opportunity for relationship growth with team members, colleagues, and those to whom they report. To our knowledge, this is a novel finding in the leadership studies literature. Future research should investigate how frequently this result occurs, under what circumstances, and what processes explain the relationship between personal crisis and relationship growth for leaders. Which types of organizational cultures, policies, and leader and team member characteristics are associated with RGB after personal crisis? What mechanisms and processes – for example, increases in trust, opportunities for team member role expansion, or increased team member perceptions of leader authenticity and decreases in perceived social distance – account for an RGB effect? Given our focus in Chapters 3 and 4, we are particularly interested in the extent to which RGB is predicted by leader disclosure and help-seeking during personal crisis and the extent to which it is associated with teams and organizations high in psychological safety and mutual trust.

Investigate the role of psychological safety and trust

Future studies could provide a much deeper exploration of the influence of organizational culture and climate on leader well-being and coping during crisis. In particular, interpersonal factors such as psychological safety (Edmondson & Lei, 2014) and mutual trust (Burke, Sims, Lazzara, & Salas, 2007) that seemed to be associated with better outcomes after personal crisis in our studies should be systematically investigated with respect to coping with crisis and other personal aspects of leadership. Because psychological safety in teams and organizations has been associated with a variety of positive outcomes (Frazier, Fainshmidt, Klinger, Pezeshkan, & Vracheva, 2017), additional research on leader behaviors that foster psychological safety would also be useful (see Newman, Donohue, & Eva, 2017 for a review of existing literature). For example, leader inclusiveness, including leader availability and proactive seeking of input from team members, is related to greater psychological safety as rated by individuals and teams (Hirak, Peng, Carmeli, & Schaubroeck, 2012; Nembhard & Edmondson, 2006). In future studies, psychological safety and trust could be conceptualized as a resource that leaders can build in their teams through supportive leadership behaviors and also draw on in times of professional and personal need.

Research cultures of reciprocal care

Researchers should study the most effective means to infuse a culture of reciprocal care into the organization. For example, Fuller and Raman (2019) found that most employers did not even measure their care demographics nor understand what employees actually need to combine work and caregiving. Further, the unspoken message in many organizational cultures conveys that it is unacceptable to use the care benefits that exist because executive leaders and managers do not use them. What do employees want and need from the organization to care for themselves, their families, and their leaders?

We have proposed that a culture of reciprocal care entails creating an infrastructure with policies and accompanying programs to support leaders and team members in the organization. We cited a study that found leaders in their prime years of leadership productivity were leaving the workforce due to irreconcilable tensions between the requirements of work and home (Fuller & Raman, 2019). Researchers should examine the costs and benefits of implementing a culture of reciprocal care where the benefits of programs (e.g., personal crisis support, personal crisis workshops and training, work-life support, succession planning, and return-to-work programs) are weighed against the costs of absenteeism, presenteeism, turnover, and retirement of employees who must leave the workforce due to caregiving responsibilities or accommodatable disabilities, and loss of operating returns on assets during personal crisis.

Future studies should investigate the most effective ways to operationalize reciprocal care for leaders. What organizational actors would be involved? What happens when leaders do not want reciprocal care or do not want to admit that they need care but organizational actors perceive that leaders do need it? Currently, some board members ask leaders to step down or leaders voluntarily retire or resign. What are the creative and productive alternatives to these courses of action? Which organizations currently provide the best approaches to care for their leaders (beyond compensation packages) and their team members? What are the most effective strategies for implementing reciprocal care in these organizations?

The scholarly literature revealed that friendships are valuable to the well-being of peers in the workplace (Sias & Cahill, 1998; Colbert, Bono, & Purvanova, 2015). Similarly, leaders in our survey endorsed disclosing to team members, colleagues, and people to whom they report in the workplace because they are friends. Future research could provide a deeper understanding of the role that workplace friendships play in the lives of leaders and how these friendships function to support the personal aspects of leadership.

Develop a theoretical framework

Finally, there are few theories that address personal aspects of leadership. The Conservation of Resources Theory serves as one exception to this void of theory in the field, but clearly this research focus is fertile ground for the development of future theories.

Conclusion

While the proposals in this chapter serve as an ending point for our book, we hope that scholars and practitioners will take up the mantle and continue the work in this vital area of study and practice. We hope that pairs and teams of interdisciplinary researchers and leaders will work and explore this topic together to enrich the understanding of the personal side of leadership. We plan to continue the work and we hope you will join us.

References

Bakker, A. B., & Demerouti, E. (2016). Job demands – Resources theory: Taking stock and looking forward. *Journal of Occupational Health Psychology, 22*(3), 273. https://doi.org/10.1037/ocp0000056

Bennedsen, M., Pérez-González, F., & Wolfenzon, D. (2010). *Do CEOs matter?* Retrieved from www0.gsb.columbia.edu/mygsb/faculty/research/pubfiles/3177/valueceos.pdf

Bennedsen, M., Pérez-González, F., & Wolfenzon, D. (2012). *Evaluating the impact of the boss: Evidence from CEO hospitalization events.* Retrieved from http://conference.iza.org/conference_files/Leadership_2012/perez-gonzalez_f7878.pdf

Brandert, K. T., & Matkin, G. S. (2019). When the crisis is personal: A phenomenological study of women in leadership. *Journal of Leadership Studies, 13*(3), 56–61. https://doi.org/0.1002/jls.21663

Burke, C. S., Sims, D. E., Lazzara, E. H., & Salas, E. (2007). Trust in leadership: A multilevel review and integration. *The Leadership Quarterly, 18*(6), 606–632. https://doi.org/10.1016/j.leaqua.2007.09.006

Colbert, A. E., Bono, J. E., & Purvanova, R. K. (2015). Flourishing via workplace relationships: Moving beyond instrumental support. *Academy of Management Journal, 59*(4), 1199–1223. https://doi.org/10.5465/amj.2014.0506

Cycyota, C. S., & Harrison, D. A. (2002). Enhancing survey response rates at the executive level: Are employee- or consumer-level techniques effective? *Journal of Management, 28*(2), 151–176. https://doi.org/10.1016/S0149-2063(01)00137-4

Cycyota, C. S., & Harrison, D. A. (2006). What (not) to expect when surveying executives: A meta-analysis of top manager response rates and techniques over time. *Organizational Research Methods, 9*(2), 133–160. https://doi.org/10.1177/1094428105280770

Edmondson, A. C., & Lei, Z. (2014). Psychological safety: The history, renaissance, and future of an interpersonal construct. *Annual Review of Organizational Psychology and Organizational Behavior, 1*(1), 23–43. https://doi.org/10.1146/annurev-orgpsych-031413-091305

Frazier, M. L., Fainshmidt, S., Klinger, R. L., Pezeshkan, A., & Vracheva, V. (2017). Psychological safety: A meta-analytic review and extension. *Personnel Psychology, 70*(1), 113–165. https://doi.org/10.1111/peps.12183

Fuller, J. B., & Raman, M. (2019). The caring company. *Harvard Business School.* Retrieved from www.hbs.edu/managing-the-future-of-work/Documents/The_Caring_Company.pdf

Hirak, R., Peng, A. C., Carmeli, A., & Schaubroeck, J. M. (2012). Linking leader inclusiveness to work unit performance: The importance of psychological safety and learning from failures. *The Leadership Quarterly, 23*(1), 107–117. https://doi.org/10.1016/j.leaqua.2011.11.009

Hobfoll, S. E. (2007). *Conservation of resources evaluation (COR-E) [self-report scale].* Retrieved from www.personal.kent.edu/~shobfoll/Pages/COR_E.html

Hobfoll, S. E. (2011). Conservation of resources theory: Its implication for stress, health, and resilience. In S. Folkman (Ed.), *The Oxford handbook of stress, health, and coping* (pp. 127–147). New York: Oxford University Press.

Leiter, M. P., & Maslach, C. (2017). Burnout and engagement: Contributions to a new vision. *Burnout Research, 5*, 55–57. https://doi.org/10.1016/j.burn.2017.04.003

Nembhard, I. M., & Edmondson, A. C. (2006). Making it safe: The effects of leader inclusiveness and professional status on psychological safety and improvement efforts in health care teams. *Journal of Organizational Behavior, 27*(7), 941–966. https://doi.org/10.1002/job.413

Newman, A., Donohue, R., & Eva, N. (2017). Psychological safety: A systematic review of the literature. *Human Resource Management Review, 27*(3), 521–535. https://doi.org/10.1016/j.hrmr.2017.01.001

Sias, P. M., & Cahill, D. J. (1998). From coworkers to friends: The development of peer friendships in the workplace. *Western Journal of Communication, 62*(3), 273–299. https://doi.org/10.1080/10570319809374611

APPENDIX A

Preliminary study

Objectives

The primary objective of this preliminary study was to gain greater understanding of a relatively unexplored area in the leadership field – leadership during personal crisis. Specifically, we wanted to understand how individuals in leadership roles handle personal crises. For the purpose of this study, a personal crisis is a disruptive event or emergency that affects the leader in a private or intimate area of his or her life.

The study focused on the following research questions:

1. How do individuals in leadership roles handle personal crisis?
2. Is there a relationship between leadership style and the leader's approach to handling personal crisis?
3. Do leaders handle personal and professional (i.e. role- or work-related) crisis the same or differently?
4. Does leadership style affect whether the leader handles personal and professional crises the same or differently?
5. How does the leader's approach to handling personal crises affect followers?

Participants

The initial interview sample consisted of 15 participants who were in leadership roles during their personal crises.

- 3 – CEOs (Business)
- 1 – Senior Executive (Non-CEO, Business)
- 1 – Division Manager (Business – Technology)
- 1 – Partner (Law Firm)

- 1 – Director (Public Agency)
- 1 – Assistant Director (Nonprofit)
- 3 – University Administrators
- 3 – Public School Principals (2) and Assistant Principal (1)
- 1 – Unavailable

Measures

A full interview protocol for the preliminary study is available on the Open Science Framework at https://osf.io/tdbzs/?view_only=2ebd6bb1faf14f9eb17b8defb368f 25b. The interview protocol consisted of several sections:

- Interview respondent and location codes (assigned to by the interviewer) to protect the identity of the respondent; date and time of the interview; and the interviewer's name;
- Preliminary information including a statement of confidentiality and option to discontinue the interview, background/demographic information, and Least Preferred Co-worker (LPC) instrument (the use of this instrument was discontinued and the completed LPCs were destroyed determining that the LPC was not a suitable match for the study and was not adding pertinent information about leadership during personal crisis);
- Leadership experience including the last three leadership positions held by the interview respondent, and a question about the interview respondents' predominate leadership style;
- Opened-ended, interview-guided questions about the nature of the respondent's personal crisis, how she or he handled it, and his or her advice for other leaders; and
- Nomination of another leader who had experienced a personal crisis (snowball sampling).

Procedure

Recruitment and screening

Procedures were approved by the Institutional Review Board at the University of Richmond. Participants were recruited using a qualitative research methodology. The study employed network sampling to identify potentially "information-rich" participants who had experienced a personal crisis while serving in a leadership role. In the beginning stages of the research, individuals who were highly knowledgeable about the background and experiences of leaders in specific contexts (i.e., business, political, nonprofit, education, and public sector) were asked to nominate potential participants. Once the interviews began, interview respondents were asked to nominate their peers for inclusion in the study.

Interview protocol

The researcher and research assistants conducted 45–60-minute interviews using an interview protocol with 32 open-ended questions including interview probes to elicit elaboration of details. Interview respondents were informed of the purpose of the study, the intended use of the research, and they were assured of confidentiality. We also mailed the interview protocol to five respondents due to their geographic locations and asked them to respond to the questions. In the mailed version, we explained the purpose and intended use of the research in a letter and included the statement of confidentiality and option to discontinue the process and background/ demographic information. The LPC was no longer in use for the mailed version.

Data analysis

We conducted two qualitative analyses. The purpose of the first was to identify the predominate patterns of responses to themes in the survey including: familial and nonfamilial crises; leadership style; initial responses to the crisis; effective coping mechanisms; ineffective coping mechanisms; sharing crisis with staff; organizational context; changes in behavior; sharing crisis with staff; sharing crisis with peers; physical problems accompanying crisis; resolution of crisis; ability to remain hopeful; turning point; advice about sharing crisis; advice to others for dealing with crisis; more or less inclined to share crisis; differences in handling personal vs. professional crisis; gender differences in how women and men handle crisis; and other advice and issues.

The second qualitative analysis was to identify and categorize findings that emerged from participant interviews and pair them with key concepts in the literature. The results of our second analysis are detailed in Table A.1 located on the Open Science Framework (https://osf.io/tdbzs/?view_only=2ebd6bb1faf14f9eb17b8defb368f25b).

APPENDIX B

Study 1 method and participant description

Participants

The survey sample consisted of 49 adults (20 women, 29 men) on Amazon's Mechanical Turk platform who met our inclusion criteria for having experienced a personal crisis while in a leadership role (see criteria next). Mechanical Turk is a crowd-sourced worker platform that has been used extensively in psychology research in the past decade (Mason & Suri, 2012), including in the field of leadership studies (e.g., Offermann & Coats, 2018). A majority of participants self-identified as white or Caucasian (82%) followed by black or African American (6%), Asian American, Native Hawaiian, or Pacific Islander (6%), Other (6%), and Native American (4%). Ten percent of the sample identified as Hispanic or Latino. The mean age of the sample at the time of the survey was 37.20 years ($SD = 10.22$) and the mean age at the time of the personal crisis was 32.25 years ($SD = 9.68$). For highest level of education at the time of the crisis, 43% of participants had a bachelor's degree, followed by 22% with some college, 20% with high school diploma, 12% with a master's degree, and 2% with an associate's degree. Leaders reported directly supervising, on average, 14 team members at the time of the crisis ($M = 14.14$, $SD = 16.82$; range of 2 to 100).

Measures

Screening

Participants completed a six-item screening questionnaire to determine eligibility for the study. First, they indicated whether they had worked in a paid or volunteer position in any of the following settings: Business, Nonprofit, Government, or Community Organization. Participants who indicated such a position were next asked whether they had ever held an appointed, upper management, or executive-level position in any of those settings and whether they had ever been an elected official. Participants who indicated such a leadership role were then asked whether they had experienced a personal crisis while in that leadership role defined for the participants as, "A disruptive event or emergency that affected you in a private or intimate area of your life." Participants also answered two questions about whether they had ever given or received a raise or promotion while in the leadership role. These two questions were included as distractor items to reduce the likelihood that participants would discern the purpose of the screening and show a positive response bias.

Survey

The full set of survey questions from Study 1 can be accessed on Open Science Framework (https://osf.io/tdbzs/?view_only=2ebd6bb1faf14f9eb17b8defb368f25b). Given the exploratory purpose of Study 1, the survey consisted of open-ended questions requiring text responses and single-item closed-ended items tapping a variety of domains, including description of the crisis, participant personal and leader-oriented responses to the crisis, patterns of disclosure to others in the organization, impact of the crisis on relationships within the organization, organizational environment, personal responses to the crisis, recommendations to other leaders, and demographic information.

Procedure

Recruitment and screening

Procedures were approved by the Institutional Review Board at the University of Richmond. An advertisement for the short screening questionnaire was posted on Amazon's Mechanical Turk. The posting indicated that participants would be paid $0.10 for completing a short screening survey and that eligible participants would be invited to participate in a longer study. Data were collected online through the Qualtrics survey platform. All participants received $0.10 for completing the screening. Participants who completed the screening and indicated experiencing a personal crisis while in a leadership role, as described earlier in the Measures section, were invited to participate in the full study. They received a message through Mechanical Turk inviting them to participate and granting them access to the posting for the full study through the platform. Interested participants consented and completed the online study.

Online survey procedure

Participants were instructed to complete the survey on a device with a keyboard (e.g., a laptop or desktop computer), since many of the survey items required typed text responses. Participants were first presented with the definitions of key terms used in the survey and then completed the remainder of the items, followed by a debriefing statement. Participants were paid $3.00 through the Mechanical Turk platform for completing any part of the survey.

Screening and recruitment results

Of 382 completed screenings, 28.5% of participants (109) reported being in a leadership role according to our definition. Of these, 73.4% (80) indicated that they had experienced a personal crisis, by our definition, while in that leadership role. Participation in the online survey was offered to these 80 participants, and 52 of these gave informed consent and completed it. We subsequently excluded data from three participants: one because of invalid and incomplete responding, another because the crisis they reported was not personal but rather experienced by the entire organization, and a third because their reported leadership role (an internship) did not meet our criteria. Thus, our final sample for analysis was $n = 49$.

Data analysis

Items with text responses were coded using a two-cycle coding process detailed in Saldaña (2016) to identify any group patterns in the data. We then developed a codebook to code and enter each response. The full codebook from Study 1 can be accessed on Open Science Framework (https://osf.io/tdbzs/?view_only=2ebd6bb1faf14f9eb17b8defb368f25b). The coded responses were then entered into QDA Miner, qualitative text analysis software, for analysis. Items with quantitative response scales were analyzed using descriptive statistics and exploratory bivariate correlation analyses.

References

Mason, W., & Suri, S. (2012). Conducting behavioral research on Amazon's Mechanical Turk. *Behavior Research Methods, 44*(1), 1–23. https://doi.org/10.3758/s13428-011-0124-6

Offermann, L. R., & Coats, M. R. (2018). Implicit theories of leadership: Stability and change over two decades. *The Leadership Quarterly, 29*(4), 513–522. https://doi.org/10.1016/j.leaqua.2017.12.003

Saldana, J. (2016). *The coding manual for qualitative researchers* (3rd ed.). Thousand Oaks, CA: Sage Publications.

APPENDIX C

Study 2 method, participant description, and supplementary tables

Participants

The survey sample consisted of 167 adults (85 women, 82 men) recruited via Qualtrics Panels who met our inclusion criteria for having experienced a personal crisis while in a leadership role (see criteria next). A majority of participants self-identified[1] as white or Caucasian (81%), followed by black or African American (14%), Asian American, Native Hawaiian, or Pacific Islander (3%), Other (3%), and Native American (2%). Sixteen percent of the sample identified as Hispanic or Latino. The mean age of the sample at the time of the survey was 37.95 years ($SD = 9.64$) with a range of 21 to 65 years. The mean age at the time of the personal crisis was 34.65 years ($SD = 8.92$). For highest level of education at the time of the crisis, 42% of participants had a bachelor's degree, followed by 27% with a master's degree, 15% with some college,[2] 6% with a high school diploma, 6% with an associate's degree, and 4% with a doctoral degree. Based on their descriptions of their positions at the time of the crisis, we classified 42.5% of participants as occupying executive leadership positions at the time of the crisis and 57.5% as occupying middle management positions. Participants reported an average of 9.47 ($SD = 6.70$) years of experience in their profession at the time of the crisis and that they were supervising a median of 25 employees (ranging from 1 to 5,000). Industries represented in the sample appear in Table C.1.

---

1 Participants could indicate more than one race.
2 Note that participants who indicated their highest level of education as "college" but did not indicate completion of a degree were classified as having completed "some college." Therefore, it is possible that these categories slightly underestimate the education level of the sample.

TABLE C.1 Industry Categories of Study 2 Participants at the Time of the Crisis

Industry category	n	Percent of sample
Computer Science/Technology	25	15.0
Banking and Financial Institutions	18	10.8
Health Care Industries	15	9.0
Education: K-12	14	8.4
Manufacturing	13	7.8
Retail/Wholesale Trade	11	6.6
Construction	9	5.4
Information Services	8	4.8
Transport: Rail, Air, and Shipping Companies	8	4.8
Hotels, Leisure, and Entertainment Industries	7	4.2
Property Services and Architecture	6	3.6
Education: Colleges and Universities	4	2.4
Insurance Services	3	1.8
Medical Professions	3	1.8
Nonprofit /Nongovernmental	3	1.8
Public Administration	3	1.8
Social Media	3	1.8
Legal Services	2	1.2
Elected Office	2	1.2
Warehousing	2	1.2
Marketing and Business Services	2	1.2
Agricultural Industries	1	0.6
Associations and Unions	1	0.6
Communication Industries	1	0.6
Military Service	1	0.6
Engineering	1	0.6
Industry Data Missing	1	0.6

Measures

The full survey for Study 2 is available on the Open Science Framework website at https://osf.io/tdbzs/?view_only=2ebd6bb1faf14f9eb17b8defb368f25b. Many descriptive items in Survey 2 consisted of questions in which participants could "check all that apply" to indicate which situations they had experienced in the context of the crisis or which strategies they had found most effective in managing it. The response choices for these items were derived from our qualitative work in Study 1 (see Appendix B).

With respect to more quantitative survey items, due to the exploratory nature of this study and our desire to measure a wide range of constructs while keeping the survey to a manageable overall length, we used short versions of measures with support in the literature for their reliability and validity. Where possible, we used short multi-item scales instead of single-item scales because of the superior psychometric properties of multi-item scales (e.g., the ability to estimate degree of measurement error).

"Big five" personality traits

Personality traits based on the Big Five model of personality were measured using the Ten Item Personality Inventory (TIPI; Gosling, Rentfrow, & Swann, 2003). The TIPI consists of ten items, two per trait, with adjectives that characterize the core features of the poles of each trait. Participants rate the extent to which the trait applies to them on a 7-point Likert scale. Although the TIPI's psychometric properties are not equivalent to longer personality scales, in prior research, the TIPI demonstrated convergence with longer and more established personality trait measures, adequate test-retest reliability, and expected patterns of correlations with other constructs (Gosling et al., 2003). Because each scale only consists of two items, low values of Cronbach's α are expected (e.g., .45–.73 in the scale development paper by Gosling et al., 2003). The authors of the scale describe how they emphasized content validity – that is, covering all aspects of the construct in their items – to offset the disadvantages of short scales. However, the Cronbach's α values in the current study for each two-item scale were particularly low: Extraversion $\alpha = .35$, Agreeableness $\alpha = .25$, Conscientiousness $\alpha = .33$, Neuroticism $\alpha = .53$, Openness $\alpha = .36$, with only Neuroticism meeting minimally acceptable standards. Given the exploratory nature of this research, we opted to report results using these scales but to indicate in the text where particular caution is warranted. We also report disattenuated correlation values in the notes so that the reader can gauge the possible impact of measurement error on the results (Onwuegbuzie & Daniel, 1999) using the formula described in the "Data Analysis" section that follows.

Trait trust/mistrust

Trait trust was measured using two items from the NEO Five Factor Inventory (Costa & McCrae, 1992) tapping the propensity to trust facet of agreeableness (as reported in Mooradian, Renzl, & Matzler, 2006). Internal consistency for this two-item scale was acceptable in this sample, Cronbach's $\alpha = .74$.

Psychological safety in the organization

Individual leader perception of "psychological safety" in their organization at the time of the crisis was measured using an adaptation of the 7-item scale developed by Edmondson (1999). We adapted the scale by replacing the term "team" with "organization," a strategy used in several prior studies (see Newman, Donohue, & Eva, 2017, p. 523). A sample item from the scale is, "No one in this organization would deliberately act in a way that undermines my efforts." We used a 7-point Likert scale with labels ranging from "Strongly Disagree" to "Strongly Agree" to be consistent with other scales in the survey. Internal consistency of the scale in our sample was just shy of the conventionally acceptable level of .70 ($\alpha = .67$). Given the exploratory nature of the work, we retained the scale and report disattenuated correlation values where appropriate so that readers can gauge the possible impact of measurement error on the associations with other scales.

Social constraints in personal life and organization

Participant perceptions of social constraints on discussing their crisis with others was measured using four items drawn from a study of social constraints in bereaved mothers (items 1–4 from Lepore, Silver, Wortman, & Wayment, 1996). We modified the wording of these items to indicate, generically, "the crisis" rather than bereavement. A sample item from the scale is, "When you talked about the crisis, how often did [family and friends/people at work] give you the idea that they didn't want to hear about it?" To assess perceived social constraints in participants' personal lives, they completed the scale once with items indicating "family and friends" and, later in the survey, with items indicating "people at work." Internal consistency of the scale in our sample fell below the conventionally acceptable level of .70 ($\alpha = .65$ for both scales). As described earlier, we retained the scale and report disattenuated correlation values where appropriate.

Trust in colleagues and the organization

We measured leaders' faith in the intentions of their colleagues and of the organization using two three-item scales adapted from Cook and Wall (1980) as reported in Mooradian et al. (2006). Sample items from the two scales include, "If I got into difficulties at work, I know my colleagues would try and help me out," for trust in colleagues and, "I feel quite confident that the organization will always try to treat me fairly," for trust in the organization. Internal consistency for the trust in colleagues scale was good ($\alpha = .85$), but the value for the trust in the organization scale fell below the conventionally acceptable level ($\alpha = .62$). As described earlier, we retained the scale and report disattenuated correlation values where appropriate.

Extent of disclosure

We asked participants to report on disclosure regarding the crisis to others in the organization at three different levels. Specifically, we asked, "Did you talk about the crisis with any STAFF/TEAM MEMBERS that you supervised?" With "any COLLEAGUES or PEERS at your same level in the organization?" With "the PEOPLE TO WHOM YOU REPORT (e.g., supervisors or board members)?" Participants answered on a 4-point Likert scale (None of them, A few of them, Most of them, All of them). For each type of relationship, if participants reported any disclosure, they were then asked to select from a list of reasons for disclosure and could choose all that applied to them. Participants then reported on the extent to which they were satisfied with their decisions about disclosure on a 7-point scale.

Relationship impact

Participants reported on how the personal crisis had impacted relationships with others in their organization on a 7-point Likert scale ranging from "Very Negative Impact" to "Very Positive Impact." Participants answered this question for each of the three relationship categories described earlier and also answered each question twice; once for work relationships and once for personal relationships or friendships with these individuals. If participants did not have personal relationships or friendships with individuals in a particular category, they were able to indicate this.

Perceived effectiveness and satisfaction in handling the crisis

Participants completed the single items, "All things considered, how effectively do you think you managed your personal crisis in the context of your leadership role?" and, "All things considered, how satisfied are you with how you managed the personal crisis in the context of your leadership role?" Responses were given on a 7-point Likert scale from Very Ineffectively/Very Dissatisfied to Very Effectively/Very Satisfied.

Procedure

Recruitment and screening

Procedures were approved by the Institutional Review Board at the University of Richmond. Participants were recruited through survey panels maintained by Qualtrics Online Samples, and the survey was created and deployed using the Qualtrics online survey platform. Participants provided informed consent and then completed a series of screening questions to determine eligibility for the survey. To screen into the study, participants had to meet the following criteria based on their responses to the screening questions: (1) served in a leadership position currently or at some time in the past, (2) have experienced a personal crisis while in a leadership position, and (3) the personal crisis occurred more than one year in the past. Participants who responded in a way that qualified them on all three criteria were permitted to proceed and complete the remainder of the survey. At the conclusion of the survey, participants read a debriefing statement. They received payment for survey completion from Qualtrics Online Samples.

Data analysis

We retained data from participants who completed the survey and then screened for valid responding. Participants who did not describe a valid personal crisis on the open-ended question for that information were removed from the dataset, as were any individuals who did not respond to the survey in English (since measures were presented in English and we could not ensure the validity of responses from non-English speakers). The screening questions regarding leadership position types did not result in adequate screening for this criterion, and so we screened participant responses post hoc regarding their leadership positions at the time of the crisis and retained responses judged to qualify as middle management ($n = 96$) or executive leadership positions ($n = 71$). These screening procedures resulted in a total final sample of 167 leaders for analysis.

Results of data analyses are presented throughout this volume. The primary purpose of our analyses was descriptive. For categorical variables, we generally examined percentages of participants endorsing those responses. For continuous variables, we examine descriptive statistics (means, standard deviations) and, in cases where scale points are relevant to describing the patterns of results, percentages of participants giving particular responses. We also present exploratory correlation analyses to begin to describe associations between variables, and we used two-tailed tests of statistical significance due to their exploratory nature. Readers are cautioned against over-interpreting these correlations because they reflect associations at a single time-point and therefore cannot be used to indicate causality. In addition, as described in the Measures section, because we often used very short multi-item scales to reduce the overall length of the survey, some of the scales have less than ideal internal consistency reliability, resulting in possible underestimation of the degree of association between variables (Onwuegbuzie & Daniel, 1999). To address this concern, we report disattenuated correlations in cases where variables show lower internal consistency using the formula presented next. In cases where the outcome variable was a single item scale, only the reliability (Cronbach's α) from the x variable was used in the calculation.

$$\rho_{xy} = \frac{r_{xy}}{\sqrt{r_{xx}r_{yy}}}$$

Finally, in order to take into consideration possible differences between leader levels (i.e., middle managers and executive leaders) in the sample, we tested for differences between these groups for all analyses (χ^2 analyses for categorical outcomes and independent samples t-tests for continuous outcomes) and report differences that were statistically significant at the level of $p < .05$. In general, we identified few between-groups differences based on leader level.

Supplementary tables

TABLE C.2 Correlations between Endorsement of "Private Person" Trait, Personality Traits, and Disclosure

	Pearson r	p	Disattenuated r
Openness	−0.29	0.001	−0.42
Extraversion	−0.42	<.001	−0.71
Agreeableness	−0.09	0.26	−0.18
Conscientiousness	−0.14	0.07	−0.24
Neuroticism	0.09	0.23	0.12
Mistrust	0.33	<.001	0.38

	Pearson r	p	Disattenuated r
Family social constraints on disclosure	**0.33**	**<.001**	0.41
Work social constraints on disclosure	**0.25**	**0.001**	0.31
Extent of crisis disclosure in organization	0.00	0.98	n/a

Note: p-values are for two-tailed tests. Disattenuated correlation coefficients are reported due to low internal consistency for some measures.

TABLE C.3 Disattenuated Correlation Coefficients for Table 4.1

	Psychological safety	Trust in colleagues	Trust in organization	Social constraints in organization
1. Organization hindered me in coping	−.34	−.03	−.44	.53
2. Organization supportive of those in crisis	.62	.62	.67	−.38
3. Perceived effectiveness of handling crisis in leadership role	.35	.28	.35	−.39
4. Satisfaction with handling crisis in leadership role	.30	.30	.33	−.40

References

Cook, J., & Wall, T. (1980). New work attitude measures of trust, organizational commitment and personal need non-fulfilment. *Journal of Occupational Psychology, 53*(1), 39–52. https://doi.org/10.1111/j.2044-8325.1980.tb00005.x

Costa, P. T., & McCrae, R. R. (1992). *Revised NEO Personality Inventory (NEO-PI-R) and NEO Five-Factor Inventory (NEO-FFI) professional manual.* Odessa, FL: Psychological Assessment Resources.

Edmondson, A. C. (1999). Psychological safety and learning behavior in work teams. *Administrative Science Quarterly, 44*(2), 350. https://doi.org/10.2307/2666999

Gosling, S. D., Rentfrow, P. J., & Swann, W. B. (2003). A very brief measure of the Big-Five personality domains. *Journal of Research in Personality, 37*(6), 504–528. https://doi.org/10.1016/S0092-6566(03)00046-1

Lepore, S. J., Silver, R. C., Wortman, C. B., & Wayment, H. A. (1996). Social constraints, intrusive thoughts, and depressive symptoms among bereaved mothers. *Journal of Personality and Social Psychology, 70*(2), 271–282. https://doi.org/10.1037/0022-3514.70.2.271

Mooradian, T., Renzl, B., & Matzler, K. (2006). Who trusts? Personality, trust and knowledge sharing. *Management Learning, 37*(4), 523–540. https://doi.org/10.1177/1350507606073424

Newman, A., Donohue, R., & Eva, N. (2017). Psychological safety: A systematic review of the literature. *Human Resource Management Review, 27*(3), 521–535. https://doi.org/10.1016/j.hrmr.2017.01.001

Onwuegbuzie, A. J., & Daniel, L. J. (1999). Uses and misuses of the correlation coefficient. Paper presented at *the Annual Meeting of the Mid-South Educational Research Association*, Point Clear, AL, November 17–19, 59. Retrieved from https://files.eric.ed.gov/fulltext/ED437399.pdf

INDEX

Note: Page numbers in *italic* indicate a figure on the corresponding page. Page numbers in **bold** indicate a table on the corresponding page. Page numbers with 'n' indicate a chapter endnote on the corresponding page.

CPSIA information can be obtained
at www.ICGtesting.com
Printed in the USA
BVHW091156190522
637468BV00006B/103